SHAKESPEAREAN

ROMANCE

Shakespearean

Romance

BY HOWARD FELPERIN

PRINCETON UNIVERSITY PRESS

PRINCETON, NEW JERSEY

This book has been set in Linotype Caslon Old Face

160524

Printed in the United States of America by

Princeton University Press,

Princeton, New Jersey

For my father
and the memory of my mother

The only *general* attribute of projected romance that I can see, the only one that fits all its cases, is the fact of the kind of experience with which it deals—experience liberated, so to speak; experience disengaged, disembroiled, disencumbered, exempt from the conditions that we usually know to attach to it and, if we wish so to put the matter, drag upon it, and operating in a medium which relieves it, in a particular interest, of the inconvenience of a *related*, a measurable state, a state subject to all our vulgar communities. The greatest intensity may so be arrived at evidently—when the sacrifice of community, of the "related" sides of situations, has not been too rash. It must to this end not flagrantly betray itself; we must even be kept if possible, for our illusion, from suspecting any sacrifice at all. The balloon of experience is in fact of course tied to the earth, and under that necessity we swing, thanks to a rope of remarkable length, in the more or less commodious car of the imagination; but it is by the rope we know where we are, and from the moment that cable is cut we are at large and unrelated: we only swing apart from the globe—though remaining as exhilarated, naturally, as we like, especially when all goes well. The art of the romancer is, "for the fun of it," insidiously to cut the cable, to cut it without our detecting him. What I have recognized then in "The American," much to my surprise and after long years, is that the experience here represented is the disconnected and uncontrolled experience—uncontrolled by our general sense of "the way things happen"—which romance alone more or less successfully palms off on us.

—Henry James, Preface to *The American*

As its title suggests, this book has a double commitment. It attempts to explicate a group of plays written at the end of Shakespeare's career and to explore a set of problems arising from their romance mode. Although my first and last interest is in the plays, I discovered (after several frontal and fumbling assaults on them) that I could not fulfill my first obligation without incurring the second; that is, I could not arrive at readings of the romances worth having without venturing into the poetics and problematics of romance. My personal difficulties with these plays also mirror, I suspect, the difficulties of modern criticism with them. They have received less than justice in this century, not so much because they have lacked sensitive readers as because those readers have lacked a working theory of romance. While most criticism of Shakespeare is doggedly pragmatic, enough has been thought and said on tragedy and comedy to give the critic something to fall back on, however un-self-consciously, in his dealings with *Macbeth* or *Twelfth Night*. When the same critic approaches *The Winter's Tale*, he has little or nothing to fall back on, and his pragmatism results, paradoxically, in mystification. Either he mistakes features common to much romance—rebirth, resurrection, reconciliation—for qualities peculiar to Shakespeare's, or he resorts to nonliterary sanctities—their "lastness" or their Christianity—to account for their felt power.

The issue is larger than the interpretation of the romances. Do we really understand even tragedy and comedy deeply or fully enough to continue on our pragmatic and picaresque course without fundamental rethinking of all our categories? How much more positivist scholarship and formalist scrutiny will our present theoretical substructure sustain? Short of a moratorium on further publication—and who would be willing to strike that Canute-like posture?—our alternative is to follow the example of those areas of literary study where new perspectives are beginning to open up. I am thinking of recent works concerned with the psychology of expectation and response in readers and audiences, with the self-reflective and self-critical dimension of literature, with relations between literature and historiography, with new and speculative models for constructing literary history and influence, with paraliterary and subliterary structures—all of which entail a basic reconsideration of fiction-making itself. Precisely because he occupies the still center of our total literary experience, Shakespeare could shed considerable light on these movements and these movements reflect considerable light back on Shakespeare. Of course there is no salvation in methodology alone. A change of matrix or perspective, while it may refresh our vision and preclude old distortions, cannot save us from new errors of perception. Yet the worst of the errors I have no doubt committed in this reconsideration of romance result, I now think, not from my having been too speculative but from my not having been speculative enough.

Those who wish to know more about the special problems the romances have historically raised, or who want evidence that they have raised problems, are advised to turn first to the Appendix, where I survey their critical and sometimes theatrical history from the viewpoint of developing romance theory. Otherwise the argument is straightforward and, I hope, cumulative. Part I sets out to define and delimit romance and to situate the romances, synchronically and diachronically, within that continuum, with particular stress on native and dramatic influences and analogues. I try to relate the romances to the rest of Shakespeare's work in Part II, to bring into clearer focus the romantic dimension of all Shakespearean art while distinguishing Shakespearean romance from Shakespearean comedy and tragedy. This groundwork having been laid, I proceed to the final and longest part devoted to readings of the romances as romances, each of which I hope can also stand on its own.

A word on certain technical matters is required. I have avoided as much as possible the longstanding debate over divided authorship in *Pericles* and *Henry VIII*, because it does not substantially affect interpretation of those plays and because I have nothing new to contribute to it. There is no external evidence that Fletcher or anyone other than Shakespeare had a hand in either play, and for practical purposes I have regarded them, with many (though not all) Shakespeareans as entirely by Shakespeare. Similarly, I have excluded *The Two Noble Kinsmen* from discussion, because there is external evidence that Fletcher was primarily responsible for it and because there is no reliable way of ascertaining the extent or location of Shakespeare's share in it, if indeed he had one. All quotations of Shakespeare are from the appropriate volume of the New Arden edition, except in the case of *Hamlet*, where I have used the Pelican text, ed. Willard Farnham (Baltimore, 1957).

References to *Paradise Lost* and *The Faerie Queene* within my text are to *Paradise Lost*, ed. Merritt Y. Hughes (New York, 1935) and *The Poetical Works of Spenser*, eds. J. C. Smith and E. DeSelincourt (Oxford Standard Authors, London, 1963).

With a work that has passed through more than the conventional career of shipwrecks and metamorphoses before deliverance, it is particularly sweet to look back and acknowledge those who have helped it on its way, and I beg the reader's indulgence. In what now seems the dark backward and abysm of time, Herschel Baker and Alfred Harbage of Harvard assisted at its premature and rough-hewn birth in the corridors of Warren House. Although they would scarcely recognize and probably deny the product of their midwifery now, I thank them for not drowning it then. In its growth and travels it met with two learned counselors, A. Bartlett Giamatti and Mark Rose of Yale, faithful to the book and its author even in extremes of madness and adversity. Only the decorum of the prefatory form, already under strain, prevents me from enumerating all I owe them. Had I known the gentle mind of that *genius loci*, Geoffrey H. Hartman of Yale, as well when I first wrote as when I last revised, my work would have fewer false themes. His tutelage has helped it to think about, if not finally to know, itself. I look back on my students in many Yale seminars as Odysseus must have on his crew: though they are all gone now, I could not have reached my goal without them. My wife Marilyn had an inexpressibly large share in every stage of the work except the typing. That painful labor was generously and efficiently performed by Doris Pfuderer. Finally, I must change these romantic notes to tragic and record the passing of Andrew J. Chiappe of Columbia, with whom I first studied Shakespeare and whose eloquence on that poet, particularly on the romances, approached most closely that of the poet himself.

H.F.

New Haven, Connecticut
October 23, 1971

CONTENTS

PART I

BACKGROUND AND

THEORY

CHAPTER 1

Golden-Tongued Romance

> O golden-tongued Romance with serene lute!
> Fair plumed Syren! Queen of far away!
> Leave melodizing on this wintry day,
> Shut up thine olden pages, and be mute.
>
> —Keats

JUPITER's words in the last act of *Cymbeline*—"Whom best I love I cross; to make my gift, / The more delay'd, delighted"—sum up not only the fortunes of the principals within Shakespeare's final romances but the fortunes of the plays themselves. Critical and theatrical recognition of *Pericles, Cymbeline, The Winter's Tale, The Tempest,* and *Henry VIII* as a distinguished and wholly Shakespearean group, though long delayed, has not been denied. More has been written on them in the past three and a half decades than over the previous three and a half centuries. This rebirth of interest has been aided by the reaction of modern textual criticism against the nineteenth-century custom of dividing Shakespeare's plays on little more than instinct among other playwrights—each of the last plays has at some time been denied in part to Shakespeare. Meanwhile stage revivals have multiplied. What Bernard Shaw wrote of *Cymbeline* in 1896, that it "is absolutely unactable and unutterable in the modern theatre, where a direct illusion of reality is aimed at,"[1] no longer holds true.

[1] *Shaw on Shakespeare*, ed. Edwin Wilson (New York, 1961), p. 56.

3

Now that the naturalism of Ibsen and Stanislavsky has faded from the scene, the contemporary theater can approximate more closely than ever before the condition of the unlocalized stage within which the romances were first successfully mounted. Their revival may owe something as well to the congeniality with the spirit of romance and capacity for magic and spectacle of our own visual media—television and the movies. But whatever has conditioned or caused it, the fact is that the fortunes of Shakespearean romance are rapidly coming full circle.

Yet even though studies of the romances are beginning to catch up with the output of the rest of the Shakespeare industry, nothing like general agreement yet exists over their nature and significance. Many of the problems that have beset modern reinterpretation and revaluation of these plays remain to be solved:

Cymbeline, The Winter's Tale, The Tempest, with (sometimes) *Pericles* and (sometimes) *Henry VIII* as outriders, form a group with similar characteristics, incidents, and endings. They seem more closely related than any other group of Shakespeare's plays. What they have in common makes them startlingly different from the plays which go before them. They are, moreover, written at the close of the author's writing career. So there is something of a mystery to be solved. The mystery is all the more interesting because the change in character appears to be a change away from the control and concentration which Shakespeare had achieved in the great tragedies. Construction and characterization seem to show not greater artistic maturity, but less . . . . The question, "Why should Shakespeare turn to writing these plays?'" is inextricably entwined with the question, "What is the significance of these plays?" For some, the first question has been much more absorbing than the second, and, indeed, the second has only troubled them as a means of answering the first.[2]

There are still other unanswered questions. What is the relation between the romances and the preceding tragedies? Is there really a sharp break between them, as was once thought, or are the romances in some sense continuous with the tragedies, as is now generally believed? If the latter, in what sense? What is the relation between the early romantic comedies and the final romances to which they seem so near and yet so far? What has each of these groups to do with the "dark" or "problem" comedies, written in between and based on similar materials? What do the last plays have in common with the other great romances and romantic epics of the English Renaissance, the *Arcadia*, *The Faerie Queene*, and even *Paradise Lost*? And not the least mysterious of mysteries that surround the last plays although it is an historical one: Why have they been held in relative disfavor ever since the early seventeenth century when they were among the more popular of Shakespeare's works?

All of these problems are aspects of a more fundamental and abiding problem, one that confronts not only students of Shakespeare but students of literature: what are we to make of romance as a literary genre? How seriously is it to be taken in the first place, and on what terms are we to take

[2] Philip Edwards, "Shakespeare's Romances: 1900-1957," *Shakespeare Survey 11*, ed. Allardyce Nicoll (Cambridge, 1958), p. 1.

it seriously? For romance, though it is as ancient and enduring an offspring of the human imagination as tragedy, comedy, or satire, has traditionally been eyed askance by critics, suspected of being somehow illegitimate—owing perhaps to its very popularity in every age and culture— and has received less than its share of sympathetic and thoughtful regard. The history of criticism of Shakespeare's last plays is in effect a record of response (most often of unexamined and antipathetic response) to their peculiarly romantic character, to the features that distinguish them as a group and link them with romance tradition. Until very recently indeed, the prevailing modern approach has been to seek the significance of the romances not in their manifest genre and their relation to it but in something latent or reflected in them: ancient mystery-rites (mainly *The Tempest*); the myths and rituals of comparative anthropology (mainly *The Winter's Tale*); the doctrines of Christianity (all the last plays); and the spiritual biography of their author.[3] While attempting to establish the seriousness of the romances, such approaches actually call it in question by locating it in something other than the plays themselves and outside their authentic critical context—in something remote, in something universal, in something lofty, in something mysterious, but always in

---

[3] See Edwards' illuminating retrospect of modern criticism of the romances. The headnotes to the articles in *Stratford-upon-Avon Studies 8: Later Shakespeare*, edd. John Russell Brown and Bernard Harris (London, 1966), provide a useful account of past work. A brief and sanguine summary appears in D.R.C. Marsh, *The Recurring Miracle* (Pietermaritzburg, 1962), pp. 1-12. My own Bibliographical Appendix attempts to survey critical response to the romances from their first days to the present from the viewpoint of developing romance theory.

something *else*. In the deathless words (slightly rephrased) of a modern subspecies of romance, a soap opera about the quest of a girl from a small mining town in the west for happiness in the big city, can a tale of long-lost children and star-crossed lovers, of shipwreck and reunion, be taken seriously in and for itself? "To criticize the last plays in terms of the formal requirements of romance, and the emotional response of the audience," writes Philip Edwards, "seems to me a very strenuous task considering the temptations we are exposed to of taking short cuts to Shakespeare's vision. But it is probably the only way of not falsifying those moments in these fantastic plays when Shakespeare's verse rarefies the air and we know perfectly well that something important is being said."[4] Just so. Any attempt to come to grips with the romances, to pluck out the heart of their mystery, must sooner or later come to terms with romance.

Coming to terms with romance is a difficult task, precisely because romance, of all imaginative modes, is the most fundamental, universal, and heterogeneous. For whatever reasons poets write, the act of *poesis* is the making of a world by its very nature different from the one the poet inhabits, just as the act of reading, for whatever reasons we do it, transports us out of ourselves, out of the here and now of our existence and into a world elsewhere. To the extent that all literary experience involves a journey into another world inherently removed from present time and place, all literature is fundamentally romantic. As Don Quixote pointed out to the Canon, the *Iliad* must be deemed a lie if *Amadis of Gaul* is. In romance proper, with

---

[4] "Shakespeare's Romances: 1900-1957," p. 18.

its cultivation of faraway places and legendary times, the process by which all literature works is given its head, allowed its fullest and freest operation. But because romance is least inhibited or guarded about doing what other modes do, it is also most open to charges of escapism from philosophical quarters that think they know where "reality" lies. Such systems of thought as the Platonic, the Puritan, the Baconian, the Freudian, and the Marxist share a built-in mistrust of *poesis*; yet each has nonetheless generated its own "ur-fantasies" and official myths—the utopia, the pilgrim's progress, science fiction, the family romance, socialist realism—romances all. Defenses of poetry like Sidney's or Shelley's are at base defenses of romance against parochial demands for "relevance" and tendentious definitions of the "real," of the autonomy of the imagination against the special interest groups within culture who would bind it to their own service.

Not only does the action of romance, with its tendency to sprawl across continents and take years to accomplish, transcend considerations of time and place, but so does the mode itself. There are fallow periods and fallow cultures for tragedy, comedy, and satire, but romance seems to flourish in all ages and societies. When romance was dislodged from the playhouse during the seventeenth century by the comedy of manners, it did not freeze to death but found new auspices in narrative prose and verse, opera and musical comedy, homes it had known from the beginning. Although we associate classical Greece with epic, tragedy, and comedy, it is actually the birthplace of romance in all its subsequent forms. The *Odyssey* is not only an epic but the first romance. Euripides is known mainly for his tragedies, but his *Ion, Helen,* and *Iphigenia in Tauris* are really the first romantic comedies. Longus's *Daphnis and Chloe* inaugurates a tradition of erotic idylls in prose extending through the popular *Paul et Virginie* (one of the romances read by Emma Bovary) to the sensationally popular *Love Story,* in which (for the few who have not read it) a young aristocrat makes love and plays hockey in the pastoral groves of Harvard away from parental tyranny and social pressures until he discovers, like many a previous swain, that *et in Arcadia, ego.*

Segal's *Love Story,* the latest romance, like Homer's *Odyssey,* the first, suggests by its title a characteristic feature of the entire mode. But even though all romance is in some sense or on some level a love story and an odyssey, the varieties of loving and questing it can accommodate are wide indeed, everything from the passionate *Liebestod* of Wagner's *Tristan* to the exalted communion of his *Parsifal,* from the tireless geographical wandering of Ibsen's *Peer Gynt* to the short climb toward rebirth of his *When We Dead Awaken.* (The temporal and physical limitations of the theatre have always held a special challenge for romance.) Perhaps the common denominator of romance in all its manifestations, however, is that it is a "success story." Although that term is associated with the *ethos* of primitive American capitalism celebrated in the novels of Horatio Alger—such titles as *Adrift in New York* and *The World Before Him* proclaim their generic affiliation—it also describes the careers of countless earlier heroes of romance: Moses, King Arthur, King Horn, Havelock the Dane, George a Greene, the Fair Maid of the West, to name but a few. In their rise from "rags to riches," from obscurity to preeminence within their societies, all are variations on the myth of the birth of the hero familiar in folk tale, fairy tale, and the "tall story," as the parallel careers of St. George, Cinderella, and Paul Bunyan illustrate. The last instance suggests that romance is always in some sense a tall story in that its plots are often hard to believe and its characters tend to be larger than life, qualifications that help distinguish it from comedy. Whatever else it may be, then, romance is a success story in which difficulties of any number of kinds are overcome, and a tall story in which they are overcome against impossible odds or by miraculous means.

But given these common denominators, it is apparent even from these few examples that the romance mode consists of a number of related yet distinct historical developments, at least three of which converge in Shakespearean romance, the goal of our quest. One is classical romance, a group of third-century prose narratives that includes Longus's *Daphnis and Chloe*, Heliodorus' *Aethiopica*, Achilles Tatius' *Clitophon and Leucippe*, and Xenophon's *Ephesiaca*. Although Orsino in *Twelfth Night* seems to have read the *Aethiopica*, it is impossible to say which or how many of the Greek romances Shakespeare knew at firsthand, but all of them (except the *Ephesiaca*, which was known in Italy but not in England) were translated into English in the late sixteenth century, and related stories, such as *Apollonius of Tyre*, were known and retold throughout the Middle Ages. They certainly left their mark, however, on the Elizabethan prose romances of Sidney, Lyly, Greene, and Lodge, which provide Shakespeare with several of his romantic plots. *Daphnis and Chloe*, with its contrast of court and country, urbanity and innocence, and nurture and nature, is the *locus classicus* of the characteristic features of pastoral romance, and to that extent lies behind Shakespeare's *As You Like It* as well as Sidney's *Arcadia*. Greek romance deals with the hardships of separated lovers, is replete with storms, shipwrecks, pirates, and savage beasts, covers many countries and many years, and concludes with virtue preserved, nobility discovered, and lovers reunited in improbable recognition scenes. Their recognitions usually come about through the chance working of fortune, but sometimes, as in the *Ephesiaca*, through the revealed providence of a benevolent deity. Obviously Greek romance forms part of the background of "old tales" to which Paulina compares the action of *The Winter's Tale*, and against which all the final romances take shape.[5] But its influence remains, I for one believe, vague and elusive, even in his recognition scenes a matter of general similarities of incident and situation.

The same can be said of another strain of romance available to Shakespeare, the chivalric romance of the Middle Ages. Again it is impossible to say precisely which or how many English and continental romances Shakespeare knew, but it is certain that he alludes in *Henry VIII* (not without skepticism) to the heroic glorifications of *Bevis of Hampton* and *Sir Guy of Warwick*; that he consulted Chaucer and Gower on occasion; and that Malory's

[5] See Samuel Lee Wolff, *The Greek Romances in Elizabethan Prose Fiction* (New York, 1912), and Carol Gesner, *Shakespeare and the Greek Romance* (Lexington, 1970).

Morte Darthur was among the most popular books of sixteenth-century England. Because medieval romance is heterogeneous even by romantic standards, it is difficult to extrapolate from it a typical plot structure inclusive enough to satisfy all its students and exclusive enough to be of some use. It seems fair to say, however, that the most common plot structure of chivalric romance is the one adopted for parody by Chaucer in *Sir Thopas*, Cervantes in *Don Quixote*, and Beaumont in *The Knight of the Burning Pestle*: that of the *roman d'aventure*. A young knight launches out into a fabulous landscape and performs a series of heroic exploits, often undertaken in the name of an idealized mistress and often of an increasingly demanding nature. Frequently the hero is on a specific quest, the successful completion of which depends upon his ability to measure up to an ideal of conduct—in Chrétien's *Lancelot*, if we read that work without a sense of irony, the ideal is the self-abasement of courtly love; in several of the Grail romances, it is the Christian ideal of *contemptus mundi*. Chivalric romance was clearly of more direct use to Spenser than to Shakespeare, but its values and ideals are expounded and sometimes embodied by many of the latter's romantic lovers, notably by that perfect, gentle knight Sir Eglamour in *The Two Gentlemen of Verona*, and the plots of all his comedies and romances at some level illustrate the ennobling power of romantic love.

There is, however, another tradition of romance available to Shakespeare, one that is related to the classical and chivalric strains, but whose influence on his work seems to me more powerful and immediate. That is the religious drama of the later Middle Ages, particularly the miracle and morality play. The miracle play actually derives on one side from Greek romance, since the stories of the trials and tribulations of the Christian martyrs and saints that it dramatizes were assimilated very early in the Middle Ages to the plot structure and Mediterranean setting of Greek romance, the accidents of fortune yielding to the providence of God. Though few plays of this type survive in English, there is evidence that they were popularly performed late into the sixteenth century above and beyond the Biblical mystery cycles. The second part of the Digby *Mary Magdalene* (1480-90) illustrates the kind of play we are dealing with. It traverses the Mediterranean from the Holy Land to "Marcylle" and back, presents the birth in a storm of the Queen of Marcylle's child, and eventually, her resurrection from death at the hands of Mary and reunion with her husband at sea. Whereas classical and chivalric romance, and the Elizabethan prose romances that derive from them, are narrative, the miracle tradition is dramatic. Whereas the former could furnish or suggest a wealth of incident and situation, the latter could supply the conventions for shaping and presenting that material on the popular stage. Whereas the former was, in sum, an influence or source for Shakespeare and his fellow dramatists, the latter was a living presence to them and their audience.

The obvious affinities of the miracle play with Greek romance make it easy to recognize as a version of romance. The morality play also has from its beginning many of its motifs in common with chivalric romance. One of the two oldest moralities, *The Castle of Perseverance* (1400-25), exploits the metaphor of man's life as a castle under siege by the vices of the world and defended by the Christian virtues. The other, the fragmentary *Pride of Life* (1400-25), has its hero Rex Vivus send a challenge to Death, who overthrows him and his knights, Strength and Health, in the lost second part of the play. The motifs of a castle under siege and trial by combat are the common property of homiletic and romantic tradition in the Middle Ages; in the former they are employed allegorically and in the latter literally. The purest example of what might be termed morality-romance is the humanist *Wit and Science* (c. 1531-47), explicitly cast as a quest romance full of the language if not the actuality of physical journeying. The young hero Wit (who swears by St. George) battles and slays a monster named Tediousness (who swears "by Mahownd's nose"), climbs Mount Parnassus, and marries the object of his quest, Lady Science—but not before Wit has himself been slain by the monster and magically resurrected, like the saint he swears by, through the offices of Honest Recreation. Like *The Faerie Queene* to which it looks forward, the plot structure of *Wit and Science* is that of chivalric romance; only the names have been changed to protect the allegory.

Among morality plays, *Wit and Science* may be more transparently romantic in structure than most, but it is by no means uniquely so. The typical action of the morality, no less than that of medieval or classical romance, is a quest for self-realization through love, a journey ending in homecoming and reunion in spite of all the obstacles and detours thrown up by the world. A few early moralities present that spiritual progress in its entirety. *Mundus et Infans* (1508-22), for example, divides its protagonist's lifetime into four ages through which he grows during the one hour's traffic of the play: the infant Wanton, the youth Lust-and-Liking, Manhood-Mighty, and old Repentance. The names carry the weight of the Christian allegory, but the structure, arching as it does from cradle to grave, is the romantic one that, as we shall see, so displeased Sidney, among others. It is worth pointing out that the late point of attack employed in *Everyman* (1480-1500), now the best known of the moralities, is in effect if not in intention a classicizing device that never really took hold in native English morality tradition.[6]

Still more central to the romantic structure of the morality play than its handling of time, however, is its handling of the reclamation of its errant hero. More often than not his reformation is completely unmotivated and his salvation effected by some form of divine machinery—*Everyman* is again atypical in its dramatic concentration on the psychology of the hero's conversion. Usually the protagonist is simply preached into remorse by one of the virtues, frightened into it by an agent of God's nemesis, or saved by the intervention of the Virgin or the Four Daughters of God.[7] The conversion scene thus occupies a place within

---

[6] Even in the relatively late *Nice Wanton* (1560), for example, where the theme has narrowed to child-rearing and allegorical names have given place to Greek and Hebrew ones, time is sharply telescoped in the middle to underscore the degradation of the coddled children, suddenly grown up. Compare Shakespeare's similar handling of time in *Macbeth* and *The Winter's Tale*.

[7] The fates, respectively, of Juventus in *Lusty Juventus*, Rex Humanitas in *A Satire of the Three Estates*, Rex Vivus in *The Pride of Life*, and Humanum Genus in *The Castle of Perseverance*, to offer only a few of many possible examples. It is in the exemplary nature of the morality drama to emphasize the fact of conversion more than the

morality-romance similar to that of the recognition scene, with its strategically placed moles and birthmarks (variants of Odysseus' famous scar) in classical romance. The laws of causality and probability, which govern the processes of life as we know it and make the conversion of real sinners anything but inevitable, become as flexible to the needs and wishes of the morality playwright as the passage of time, and the difficulties that have impeded the protagonist in his progress toward salvation are miraculously overcome.

Shakespeare's debt to morality tradition, as is now beginning to be discovered, is almost unfathomably deep. Near or at the center of most of his comedies and romances we find one or more characters whose careers resemble that of the morality hero. Proteus, Oliver, Duke Frederick, Bertram, Angelo, Pericles, Leontes, Alonso (to offer only a partial list) are all fallen or misguided worldlings who undergo reformations of a more or less miraculous nature and win through to a kind of secular salvation in the end. Like the morality drama, their plays may be seen as comedies of amendment or atonement,[8] with which elements from other traditions of romance are combined. The reformations of *As You Like It* occur within a forest named

---

process. *Wisdom, Who Is Christ* (1461-85) initiates the convention, repeated in many later moralities, of having its newly converted protagonist, Anima, appear in fresh garments, the change of costume dramatizing her change of heart. Compare Shakespeare's use of costume changes in *Hamlet, Lear*, and *The Tempest*.

[8] I prefer these terms to that used by R. G. Hunter in his *Shakespeare and the Comedy of Forgiveness* (New York, 1965) because they focus on the romantic rather than the Christian dimension of the plays in question. I am deeply indebted, however, to Hunter's excellent study of the comedies against their medieval background.

Arden that reflects many of the wonderful properties of classical Arcadia and Christian Eden. Iachimo's morality-style conversion at the end of *Cymbeline* follows hard upon a welter of family reunions and recognitions by birthmark in pastoral Wales. Pericles' adventures are based partly on chivalric romance, as in the scene of his wooing of Thaisa, and partly on the miracle play, as in his reunions with his daughter and wife. In each case, such combination of various strains of romance is facilitated because all share the same basic structure of difficulties miraculously overcome. It is the central place that Shakespearean comedy and romance accords to the extraordinary in experience which distinguishes it from the other tradition of comedy that presents, in Sidney's phrase, "the common errors of our life,"[9] and which enables it to add the effect of "wonder" to the "delight" of most comedy. For despite its own debt to Greek romance, particularly in its recognition scenes, Roman new comedy and the great tradition of English comedy beginning with Jonson that derives from it, stops at the seashore; it does not venture out, literally or figuratively, onto the high seas.

Although there are examples of new comedy on the pre-Shakespearean stage, most of the comedies that held the boards during the 1570's, 1580's, and early 1590's are dominated by one or more of the traditions of romance we have seen converging.[10] Robert Greene, for example,

[9] *An Apology for Poetry*, ed. Geoffrey Shepherd (London, 1965), p. 117.
[10] Such plays as *Tom Tyler and His Wife* (c. 1560), *Ralph Roister Doister* (1553), *Supposes* (1566), and *Gammer Gurton's Needle* (1560-75) are all cast in the mold of new comedy, yet all of them (except *Supposes*, Gascoigne's translation of Ariosto's *I Suppositi*) are rich in

is sometimes credited with inventing the genre of romantic comedy (which is a bit like crediting Robert Fulton with the invention of steam), but his real contribution to the history of the mode was to blend one part morality-romance with one part native pastoral—the Fressingfield of *Friar Bacon*, the fairy world of James IV's Scotland, the forest near Wakefield in *George a Greene*—a formula he repeated several times and Shakespeare took over from him. In his best known play, *Friar Bacon and Friar Bungay* (1589), the anomalies that Bacon is hardly responsible for the emblematic deaths that prompt him to break his glass and repudiate his magic, and that several characters express their bewilderment at his sudden repentance, are the by-products of the play's adoption of morality design. (The behavior of Bacon's successors on the Elizabethan stage, Faustus and Prospero, will cause bewilderment as well unless it is understood in terms of the same convention.) The morality structure also shapes the play's pastoral action, where Prince Edward's unmotivated renunciation of his lustful designs on Margaret and reconciliation with Lacy precipitate the happy ending. Similarly in Greene's pseudo-historical *James IV* (1590), the onset of James's lust for the virtuous Ida in the opening scene is as sudden as his repentance of it is in the closing scene, a scene of mock resurrection and marital reconciliation that prefigures those of *Much Ado*, *All's Well*, and *The Winter's Tale*.

---

native elements, from the allegorical frame of *Tom Tyler* to the Vice Diccon of *Gammer Gurton* and the Virtue Dame Custance of *Roister Doister*. The assimilation of Roman and Italian comedy into Elizabethan drama is discussed by Madeleine Doran, *Endeavors of Art* (Madison, 1954).

The affinities of structure and tone sometimes pointed out between the romantic plays of Greene and Shakespeare result, I would suggest, not so much from direct influence as from their common recourse to the same repertory of dramatic models; what each playwright makes of them is of course another matter.

In those Elizabethan romances and romantic comedies dominated, like Greene's and Shakespeare's, by the conventions of morality-romance, we usually find not only the older dramatic structure persisting in a more or less prominent form but the older ethical system as well. But there are other early Elizabethan dramatic romances, less overtly moralistic and explicitly Christian, in which the values of other romance traditions predominate, in which the conflict is not between virtue and vice but between peace and war, for example, or love and hate. Yet these more secular romances tend to remain for some time on the Elizabethan stage, like the morality, a larger-than-life conflict for the human life that is its subject. The action of Peele's *Arraignment of Paris* (c. 1581) is a pastoral idyll framed by a prologue, in which the goddess Atè threatens that there will be hell to pay for Paris's amatory adventures in the form of the Trojan War, and an epilogue, in which her threat is neutralized by the awarding of the golden apple to Elizabeth, ruler of the New Troy or Britain. The play becomes, in retrospect, a power struggle between Atè, whose nature it is to bring golden worlds to grief, and Elizabeth, whose nature it is to establish and maintain them, with Elizabeth winning out in the end at the expense of historical and mimetic considerations. *Mucedorus*

(1590) opens with a quarrel between personifications of
Envy and Comedy over which of them will prevail in the
action about to begin. Comedy has the last word:

> Then, uglie monster, doe thy woorst,
> I will defend them in despite of thee:
> And though thou thinkst with tragic fumes
> To brave my play unto my deepe disgrace,
> I force it not, I scorne what thou canst doe;
> Ile grace it so, thy selfe shall it confesse
> From tragick stuffe to be a pleasant comedie.[11]

The opening scene of *Love and Fortune* (1582) similarly
resolves into a debate beween the classical fury Tisiphone
and the medieval goddess Fortune on the one side, and
Venus on the other, over who will control the course of
mortal affairs. Every time Fortune manages to sunder the
lovers, Venus succeeds in reuniting them, until Jupiter sees
fit to reconcile the warring goddesses and deliver the
lovers.

These early dramatic romances take few pains to moti-
vate or otherwise rationalize their actions. Their oscil-
lations between adversity and prosperity are presented
simply as the fallout of a divine altercation, which, from
the *Odyssey* through Chaucer's *Knight's Tale* and Spenser's
"Mutability Cantos" to *A Midsummer Night's Dream*,
is what traditionally frames and shapes the action of romance. The figures of Atè, Tisiphone, and Envy still lurk
behind the scenes of Shakespearean romance to stir up the
unmotivated jealousy of Leontes and the disastrous in-

---

[11] Induction, lines 64-70. *The Shakespeare Apocrypha*, ed. C. F.
Tucker Brooke (Oxford, 1908), p. 106.

transigence of Cymbeline. Whatever it is in human nature or society that works to roughen the course of true love is simply ascribed in those early plays to the machinations of a cranky god. By the neoclassical standards of unity and decorum adopted by later playwrights like Jonson and even Beaumont and Fletcher, they are crude, that is, they are not illusionistic. But the very absence of illusion allows us to glimpse the inward structure of Elizabethan romance in all its clarity, a clarity already partially obscured in the better made plays of Shakespeare.

The genius presiding over Elizabethan dramatic romance is ultimately Eros, or an Eros figure, who embodies the principle of love in either its narrower sense of sexual union or in its wider ones of family solidarity and social harmony or in its widest Christian one of "the love that moves the sun and the other stars," as Dante puts it at the end of *The Divine Comedy*. Chaucer represents the love between man and woman, the amity between allied nations, and the geophysical concord of nature itself as links in an embracing "faire cheyne of love," which Theseus expounds at the end of *The Knight's Tale*, and which is omitted from *The Two Noble Kinsmen*, perhaps because its action focuses exclusively upon sexual love. In the actions of Shakespeare's final romances sexual union is always complemented by family reunion and international alliance. The Eros figure who eventually conquers all opponents in Elizabethan romance may take various shapes within a given play—the personified abstraction Comedy in *Mucedorus*, the goddess Venus in *Love and Fortune*, the spirit Ariel in *The Tempest*, even the all too human and ambiguously named Firk in Dekker's *The Shoemaker's Holi-*

day—but he always works toward the goal and mood of celebration and is usually lighthearted himself. The celebration toward which romance moves is not lawless or abandoned; it is the disciplined vitality of resolved form, which the Elizabethans saw reflected in the dance of the stars and the music of the spheres. Music and dance depend on the internal order suggested by the word "measure," which they applied to both with singular precision.

Our Eros figure sometimes takes the form of Orpheus, whose music had cohesive powers analogous to those of love, and Mucedorus, with uncharacteristic acumen, credits him with the formation of society itself:

> In time of yore, when men like brutish beasts
> Did lead their lives in loathsom celles and woodes,
> And wholy gave themselves to witlesse will,
> A rude, unruly rout, then man to man
> Became a present praie, then might prevailed,
> The weakest went to walles:
> Right was unknowen; for wrong was all in all.
> As men thus lived in this great outrage,
> Behould, one *Orpheus* came, as poets tell,
> And them from rudenes unto reason brought:
> Who led by reason soone forsooke the woods;
> Insteade of caves they built them castles strong;
> Citties and townes were founded by them then:
> Glad were they they found such ease,
> And in the end they grew to perfect amitie;
> Waying their former wickednesse,
> They tearmd the time wherein they lived then
> A golden age, a goodly golden age.[12]

[12] *Mucedorus*, IV.iii.72-89. *The Shakespeare Apocrypha*, p. 120.

Orpheus is also the archetypal poet, and his founding of the golden age is emulated by the romancer in creating his own golden world. Music thus becomes not only an activity within romance but an analogy for romance. Shakespeare's final romances contain many legitimate Orpheus figures—Marina in *Pericles*, Philharmonus in *Cymbeline*, Apollo in *The Winter's Tale*, Prospero and Ariel in *The Tempest*—and many illegitimate ones as well—the Cloten who sings an *aubade* to Imogen and whose death parodies that of Orpheus, the balladmonger Autolycus, the cacophonous Caliban, and even Gonzalo, whose word is described as "more than the miraculous harp" of Amphion. Milton's Comus, who preaches free love and leads a band of drunken revellers in song and dance, and whose name suggests *komos* or merrymaking, would seem to be related to Eros and Orpheus. But Comus is not really an Eros figure at all; he merely masquerades as one. Actually he is one incarnation of the figure whom romance opposes to Eros.

That opponent figure, as *The Arraignment of Paris* makes clear, is Atè, the goddess of discord. Envy, Tisiphone, and Fortune are versions of the same figure. The Vice Ateukin in Greene's *James IV*, who does his best to encourage the king's lust and tyranny, bears the name as well as the function of Atè, for the role of the Vice in morality and morality-derived drama is also to raise hell, literally and figuratively. The figure of Rumor who enters "painted full of tongues" to introduce *2 Henry IV* discloses in vicelike fashion her intention of bringing the comic action of the *Henriad* to confusion, but she may also derive from her namesake in the *Aeneid*, who comes very close to subverting the romantic action of the founding of Rome. Like their opposites, the Atè figures who stalk the boards of Elizabethan romance embody the full range of stylization, from the allegorical and mythological to the all too human. Witches and magicians like Dipsas in Lyly's *Endymion* (1588), Sacrapant in Peele's *Old Wives' Tale* (1590), and Maudlin in Jonson's final and fragmentary *The Sad Shepherd* (1637) occupy the middle of that range and are especially congenial to pastoral romance, since their mischief consists in tampering with the harmony of nature.

Perhaps one reason Fletcher's *Faithful Shepherdess* (1608) was a flop on the popular stage is that he abandons the supernatural dimension of native English pastoral in favor of the more naturalistic conventions of Tasso and Guarini and makes his chief troublemaker, Amarilla, wily but not really "witchy." Daniel's *The Queen's Arcadia* (1605), where Colax, "a corrupted traveller," and Techne, "a subtle wench of Corinth," discombobulate by their arts idyllic Arcadia until they are finally expelled, is also modeled on Italian pastoral drama but had the benefit of a courtly audience. Shakespeare's pastorals are firmly rooted in the "green" world of native folk tradition and are full of elemental figures, some of whom, like Sycorax and even Titania, bear a strong resemblance to the shrill Atè. Most of the Atè figures in Shakespeare's comedies and romances, in fact, retain a larger-than-life or other-than-life quality. Although Don John, Oliver, Duke Frederick, Dionyza, Cymbeline's nameless Queen, the jealous Leontes, among others, are human, they do not act out of consistently human motives, and some of them even express bewilderment, like their ancestor the medieval Vice, over why they act as they do. The massive figure of Shylock, though he insists on his common humanity with the rest of Christian Venice, can come up with no better explanation for his antisocial, almost cannibalistic, actions than that it is his "humour." Such figures, in their compulsive attempts to block their plays' realization of romantic values, have been called "killjoys," but in Shakespeare's case, there is still warrant for terming them "Kill-Joys." Shylock, incidentally, states in no uncertain terms his antipathy to music and revelry.

The conflict between Eros and Atè in the typical action of Elizabethan romance is analogous up to a point to that discerned by Nietzsche between Apollo and Dionysus behind the action of Greek tragedy, but of course the outcome is just the opposite. The recognition toward which romance moves is more than a matter of stripping away a few disguises and sorting out a few cases of mistaken identity; it is an epiphany of Apollonian order, clarity, and harmony in the universe. Just at the point when confusion seems to have made her masterpiece, when the truth of the principals' birth, sex, and identity seems disguised beyond recognition—a phase that might be technically termed the *confusio* in contrast to the ensuing *cognitio*—a god steps in and wrenches the crazy universe of the play into significant form. "Hye time it is that now we did appeare," announces Venus in *Love and Fortune*, "If we desire to end their misery." Venus does exactly that, reveals the noble birth of the hero Hermione, unites him with his love Fidelia, reveals his father's unjust banishment from court ten years earlier, and effects forgiveness on all sides. The hero had already expressed his faith in the ultimate justice of things—"A joy deferr'd is sweeter to the minde"—and cited in evidence the romantic precedent of Ulysses' homecoming after years of enforced exile. His father feels himself similarly vindicated—"Thrice happy now for all my misery"—after Venus's timely appearance.[13] The gods who appear in several of these plays are not merely *dei ex machina*, who bring resolution to a hopelessly complex and otherwise insoluble plot, but *dei absconditi*, who precipitate recognition of the meaning of the principals' experience and who are themselves embodiments of that meaning, of the order and justice that have been hidden all along behind the appearance of change and chance.

The theophany of Venus may come as no surprise in a play that has shifted between the human and suprahuman levels throughout. But even those romances not set within a mythological or allegorical superstructure press toward theophany when the moment of recognition nears. Shortly before the multiple reunions of *Clyomon and Clamydes* (1570-83), for example, the heroine Neronis, disguised as a shepherd's boy, despairs when she comes upon her beloved Clyomon's abandoned shield and is about to commit suicide. "Let desparation die in thee," announces a descending Providence in creaking fourteeners, "But be assured, that thou shalt ere long thy knight attaine."[14] Though hardly a naturalistic play (its action roams from ancient Macedonia to medieval Norway, and its settings include a Forest of Marvels and an Isle of Strange

[13] *The Rare Triumphs of Love and Fortune*, ed. W. W. Greg (Malone Society Reprints, Oxford, 1930), lines 1741-2, 1472, 1824, sigs. G3^r, F3^r, G4^v.

[14] *Clyomon and Clamydes*, ed. W. W. Greg (Malone Society Reprints, Oxford, 1913), lines 1563-4, sig. F4^v.

Marshes) *Clyomon and Clamydes* reveals its origins in morality-romance in only two features: a Vice by the name of Subtle Shift, who is a walking contradiction of faith and honor, and a theophany of Providence, through which those romantic virtues are vindicated. All romance moves toward poetic justice; some earlier examples of romance, classical and Christian, move toward theodicy as well; and some of these examples move toward outright theophany.[15] They present, that is, not only a world in which all's right, but the god in his heaven who keeps it that way. If they "would but apprehend some joy," in Theseus's words, they "comprehend some bringer of that joy."

The theophanies of those pre-Shakespearean plays bring us tantalizingly close to the much wondered and much worried theophanies of Shakespeare's final romances, the source of wonder and worry alike being not only dramaturgic but theological.[16] Actually it is only in *Pericles* and *Cymbeline* that the recognitions are accompanied or pre-

---

[15] The Book of Job, for all its somber tonality and divided authorship, is technically a perfect example of romantic form. Like *Mucedorus* or *Love and Fortune*, it is an *agon* between an Atè and an Eros figure, which takes the form of a wager between Satan and God. We know from the start that for all the mischief with which Satan plagues Job, he cannot take his life, and for all the material and human loss he suffers, his wealth is doubled and his children restored. God finally appears in a theophany which is also a recognition, dispelling the clouds of spiritual confusion spread by Job's comforters, clarifying the meaning of his trial, and blessing the latter end of Job more than his beginning.

[16] For wonder, see G. Wilson Knight, *The Crown of Life* (London, 1947); for worry, D. G. James, *Skepticism and Poetry* (London, 1937), pp. 205-41. Although their conclusions are antithetical, both proceed on the assumption that Shakespeare's theophanies attempt to present what James calls "myths of immortality."

ceded by onstage theophanies, and even there Shakespeare goes half-way with illusionism by having his deities appear in dreams. But even in *The Winter's Tale*, with its oracle of Apollo and chorus of Time, and *The Tempest*, with its masque of Juno and Ceres, the principals' recognition of the meaning of their trials would seem to be dramatized and authorized in terms of a higher order than the merely human. Such moments as Pericles' outcry upon his reunion with Thaisa—"No more, you gods! your present kindness / Makes my past miseries sports"—or Leontes' comment during the statue scene—"This affliction has a taste as sweet / As any cordial comfort"—or Gonzalo's summing up of everyone's fortunate misfortune—"Was Milan thrust from Milan that his issue / Should become kings of Naples?"—cannot help but recall that moment in the Christian story when sorrow is turned to joy through the intervention of another love god. The Christian epic moves from paradise lost to paradise regained, and is formally a romantic tragi-comedy set in the order of grace. It too is an *agon* between an Eros and an Atè figure for control of the lower mortal world, that is, between God and Satan; it too brings its human protagonists, Adam and Eve and all their children and grandchildren, through spiritual death to deliverance; and it too employs a theophany in the form of the Incarnation and Atonement to bring off its happy ending. The bursting of Christ into human history at once clarifies the meaning of the Fall and redeems all the woe wrought by Satan. As Michael makes clear to Adam at the very end of *Paradise Lost*, it must be a happy fault that will earn mankind so great and so good a Redeemer. Christ as peacemaker will replace war and rancor

with peace on earth and goodwill toward men. As the Good
Shepherd he will restore the spiritual and social integrity
of the flock. That restored society is the counterpart of the
classical and pastoral Golden Age, which we have seen
ascribed to Orpheus, and the social harmony brought by
Christ is also expressed in a musical and poetic figure. Christ
is the word made flesh, the creative principle incarnate. Like
Eros, he is a love god, but the bridegroom of the Songs of
Songs and author of the Sermon on the Mount is also an
Orpheus figure, whose voice has the power to redeem dead
souls from the underworld and transform a society divided
by rancor and legalism into one united by forgiveness and
charity. That all Shakespearean comedy and romance (not
merely the last plays) repeat this latter movement has
as much to do with the fact that the Christian epic is a
romance as that Shakespeare's plays ultimately derive from
the medieval religious drama.

The further fact that the Christian epic is the canonical
romance of medieval and Renaissance culture means that
it exerts a strong pull on most of the romances of those
periods (not merely Shakespeare's) to adopt its ethical and
eschatological system, above and beyond the poetic structure it shares with them anyway. Dante's *Divine Comedy*,
with its encyclopedic form and invitation to fourfold allegorization, embraces both within its romantic structure,
but many secular romances of the Middle Ages eventually
seek them out as well. With the palinode to *Troilus and
Criseyde*, Chaucer at once turns his action from tragedy
into romance and sets it within a Christian context. Sometimes, as with Chrétien's Perceval, or Malory's Lancelot,
or Guy of Warwick, the hero's more or less secular adven-

tures issue in his withdrawal from the world into an eremitical or monastic life. Among Renaissance romancers, Milton corresponds to Dante, in that his two epics wholly adopt the ethical and eschatological systems of their Biblical source, and Spenser to Chaucer, in that he is capable of employing the same romantic structure in the service of Christian or natural virtue, as the first and second books of *The Faerie Queene* illustrate. Yet the fact that *The Faerie Queene* as a whole begins and breaks off in Christian vision may help explain Milton's unqualified admiration for it as against his qualified disapproval of Sidney's *Arcadia*, set in a classical world and illustrating Stoic fortitude, though Charles I's quoting from it while awaiting execution would not in any case have recommended it to Milton. Charles is not the only student of romance, incidentally, to fail to see that the structure it shares with Christianity does not make it Christian in everything else.

All of these English humanist romancers were Protestants, however, and their Protestantism not only lends a distinctive moral tone to their work but affects its romantic structure as well. Spenser sends his knight of holiness into something resembling a monastery, but only to fortify his spirit before sending him out to engage the dragon. Red Crosse can only contemplate the New Jerusalem from afar; he cannot remain there gazing at it. And even after killing the dragon, he is required to report back to the Faerie court for further duty while his marriage to Una is indefinitely postponed. For "the true warfaring Christian," as Milton terms him, life is continuous trial and tribulation. Because the ethics of Protestantism are this-worldly and utilitarian, even an "amatorious" romance like the *Arcadia* is "a book in that kind full of worth and wit" in so far as its ethical orientation, if not its ethical system, accords with Milton's.[17] Sidney would no more think of removing his heroes from their proper sphere of ethical action than of becoming a monk himself. In the *Arcadia*, as his first biographer puts it,

> his purpose was to limn out such exact pictures, of every posture in the minde, that any man being forced, in the straines of this life, to pass through any straights, or latitudes of good, or ill fortune, might (as in a glasse) see how to set a good countenance upon all the discountenances of adversitie, and a stay upon the exorbitant smilings of chance.[18]

Sidney's purpose as much as Spenser's is to fashion the model of a gentleman by feigning notable images of virtue under combat conditions.

Although trial and testing have always had a central place in romance, in the humanist romances of Sidney, Spenser, and Milton they assume a special prominence and are presented with a new self-consciousness. Each book of *The Faerie Queene* is constructed as a series of tests designed to try and to strengthen (to strengthen *through* trial) its hero's particular virtue. Duessa, Archimago, Acrasia, and the other Spenserian Atè figures are the agents of that testing, but like Milton's Satan they unwittingly effect long-range good by performing short-term evil. Cecropia in the *Arcadia* similarly afflicts Pamela, Philoclea,

[17] *Eikonoklastes*, Ch. 1, *The Student's Milton*, ed. Frank Allen Patterson (New York, 1933), p. 783.

[18] Fulke Greville, *Life of Sir Philip Sidney*, ed. Nowell Smith (Oxford, 1907), p. 16.

Musidorus, and Pyrocles; but each by a different course of thought and action withstands the test and emerges the stronger for it. At certain points in the *Arcadia*, Sidney is quite explicit about the moral principle that shapes his work:

> The sweete minded *Philoclea* was in their degree of well doing, to whom the not knowing of evill serveth for a ground of vertue, and hold their inward powers in better forme with an unspotted simplicitie, then many, who rather cunningly seeke to know what goodnes is, then willingly take into themselves the following of it. But as that sweet & simple breath of heavenly goodnesse, is the easier to be altered, because it hath not passed through the worldlie wickednesse, nor feelingly found the evill, that evill caries with it; so now the Ladie *Philoclea* (whose eyes and senses had receaved nothing, but according as the natural course of each thing required; which from the tender youth had obediently lived under her parents behests, without framing out of her own wil the fore-chosing of anything) when now she came to appoint wherein her judgement was to be practized, in knowing faultines by his first tokens, she was like a yong faune, who comming in the wind of the hunters, doth not know whether it be a thing or no to be eschewed; whereof at this time she began to get a costly experience.[19]

The conventional motifs of classical and medieval romance —mysterious oracles, storms and shipwrecks, malevolent

[19] *The Countesse of Pembrokes Arcadia* (1590), Bk. II, Ch. 4, *The Prose Works of Sir Philip Sidney*, ed. Albert Feuillerat (Cambridge, 1923), II, 169.

enchanters, and so on—compose for the humanist poet well read in romance tradition the elements of a world specially constructed to test the mettle of the friends, lovers, princes, and families thrust into it. The *Arcadia* presupposes an ethical orientation remarkably close to that expounded in a famous passage of Milton's *Areopagitica*:

> I cannot praise a fugitive and cloistered virtue, un-exercised and unbreathed, that never sallies out and sees her adversary, but slinks out of the race where that immortal garland is to be run for, not without dust and heat. Assuredly we bring not innocence into the world, we bring impurity much rather; that which purifies us is trial, and trial is by what is contrary. That virtue therefore which is but a youngling in the contemplation of evil, and knows not the utmost that vice promises to her followers, and rejects it, is but a blank virtue, not a pure; her whiteness is but an excremental whiteness. Which was the reason why our sage and serious poet Spenser, whom I dare be known to think a better teacher than Scotus or Aquinas, describing true temperance un-der the person of Guion, brings him in with his palmer through the cave of Mammon, and the bower of earthly bliss, that he might see and know, and yet abstain.[20]

The golden world of humanist romance thus contains ex-tremes of virtue and vice, prosperity and adversity, which our brazen world does not, while its kaleidoscopic shiftings from one extreme to another are concomitantly more rapid

[20] *The Student's Milton*, p. 738. Milton seems to have forgotten that Guyon enters the Cave of Mammon on his own, without benefit of Palmer.

and less predictable, since "trial is by what is contrary." Philoclea's virtue would have remained fugitive and cloistered, if Sidney had not prepared a costly experience for her. The ethics of Protestantism, in which inward trial replaces outward ritual as the chief means of self-purification and self-realization, condition the poetics of humanist romance.

We are used to talking about Spenser's *Faerie Queene* as a romantic epic, but the epics of his greatest poetic disciple also fit comfortably into that tradition. The Milton who at various points in his career and for a variety of reasons could dismiss out of hand "the polluted orts and refuse of *Arcadia's* and *Romances*" and an Arthur "more renown'd in Songs and Romances, than in true stories,"[21] was in effect clearing his desk for a new kind of romantic epic:

> Since first this Subject for Heroic Song
> Pleas'd me long choosing, and beginning late;
> Not sedulous by Nature to indite
> Wars, hitherto the only Argument
> Heroic deem'd, chief maistry to dissect
> With long and tedious havoc fabl'd Knights
> In Battles feign'd; the better fortitude
> Of Patience and Heroic Martyrdom
> Unsung.   (*PL*,ix.25-33)

The "better fortitude" is what the penitent Wolsey in *Henry VIII* calls "fortitude of soul"—the kind exemplified by Job and Christ as against that of Odysseus or Sid-

---

[21] *Ibid.*, p. 784, and *The History of Britain*, in *The Works of John Milton*, ed. F. A. Patterson, et al. (New York, 1932), X, 128.

ney's heroes—and forms the argument of both his Christian epics, which deal with the trials and temptations of the first and second Adams. "It was from out the rind of one apple tasted," writes Milton in *Areopagitica*, "that the knowledge of good and evil, as two twins cleaving together, leaped forth into the world . . . . As therefore the state of man now is; what wisdom can there be to choose, what continence to forbear without the knowledge of evil?" In the course of *Paradise Lost*, Eden changes from a paradise into a proving-ground, as certain key words like "taste" and "tempt" realize their undertones of "test." As a result of their temptation and fall, Adam and Eve gain access to a higher spiritual status than the fugitive and cloistered virtue of their untried innocence: a paradise within, happier far than Eden.

This romantic aspect of the poem seems to have been totally lost on Thomas Ellwood, who claims to have told Milton: "Thou hast said much here of Paradise Lost, but what hast thou to say of Paradise Found?"[22] *Paradise Lost* may contain a tragedy—the archetypal tragedy of human history—but the poem as a whole is a romance. Much of

[22] *The History of the Life of Thomas Ellwood, Written by His Own Hand* (1714), excerpted in *The Student's Milton*, p. xlviii. For some time critics have been reading *Paradise Lost* as a romance without realizing it. See for example, Geoffrey Hartman, "Milton's Counterplot," *ELH*, xxv (1958), 1-12. A scholarly account of Milton's lover's quarrel with romance is provided by Barbara K. Lewalski, "Milton: Revaluations of Romance," in *Four Essays on Romance*, ed. Herschel Baker (Cambridge, Mass., 1971), pp. 57-70. She ends her essay on this unintended paradox: "Like *Paradise Lost, Paradise Regained* is conceived as a heroic poem grounded upon a true event; it is not a romance. In the brief epic, however, the romance allusions do not revalue the romance ethos so much as exalt it to the order of perfection."

the power of Miltonic romance in fact derives from its inclusion or accommodation of tragedy, from the formidableness of its Atè figures. Yet even though Milton's tempters invariably dominate the works in which they appear, they also underestimate the inner resources of their victims. The Christ of *Paradise Regained* grows from awareness of his humanity to awareness of his divinity in humanity as a direct result of his temptation at Satan's hands. *Samson Agonistes*, like its chief classical model *Oedipus Coloneus*, moves well beyond tragedy, as the efforts of Manoa, Dalila, and Harapha to "comfort" or taunt Samson work cumulatively to restore his heroic resolve. *Samson* begins where tragedy would normally end, with its hero blinded and fallen, but the greater glory he goes on to achieve is earned through his painful reenactment of the tragic past with each of his successive antagonists. From *Comus*, where "Heav'n hath timely tri'd their youth, / Their faith, their patience, and their truth" (970-71), or even "Lycidas," where the temptation to abandon poetry for sensual pleasure is successfully withstood, through *Samson*, Milton's romantic vision may grow darker and more threatened, but this shadowing works only to deepen it. The moral urgency many of us still find in Milton results not from his Christian humanism, as some of his commentators seem to believe, nor from the "historical truth" of his epics, as he himself seemed to believe, but from his masterful manipulation of the romance mode he never really outgrows. This raises once again the problem of romantic seriousness, and it is to this problem, inherent in all versions of romance, that I want to turn next.

THE poetics of romance are eloquently formulated in Sidney's *Apology for Poetry*, where in a famous passage he defends the right of the poet to depart from imitating nature:

> Only the poet, disdaining to be tied to any such subjection, lifted up with the vigour of his own invention, doth grow in effect into another nature, in making things either better than Nature bringeth forth, or quite anew, forms such as never were in Nature, as the Heroes, Demigods, Cyclops, Chimeras, Furies, and such like: so as he goeth hand in hand with Nature, not enclosed within the narrow warrant of her gifts, but freely ranging only within the zodiac of his own wit.
>
> Nature never set forth the earth in so rich tapestry as divers poets have done; neither with pleasant rivers, fruitful trees, sweet-smelling flowers, nor whatsoever else may make the too much loved earth more lovely. Her world is brazen, the poets only deliver a golden.
>
> But let those things alone, and go to man—for whom as the other things are, so it seemeth in him her uttermost cunning is employed—and know whether she have brought forth so true a lover as Theagenes, so constant a friend as Pylades, so valiant a man as Orlando, so right a prince as Xenophon's Cyrus, so excellent a man every way as Virgil's Aeneas.[23]

Given this view of the poem as heterocosm, as "another nature" related but superior to this one, it becomes the legitimate prerogative of art, which Renaissance critics frequently liken to the creative activity of God, to body

---

[23] *An Apology for Poetry*, p. 100.

forth the forms of things unknown. Sidney thus furnishes the license necessary not only for his own Arcadia, but for Spenser's Fairyland, for the "other" worlds of Shakespeare's comedies and romances—Arden, Illyria, Bohemia, and the like—and even for Milton's Heaven, Eden, and Hell. "The mind of man being gotten by God," writes Sir John Harrington following Sidney, "and so the childe of God killing and vanquishing the earthliness of this Gorgonicall nature, ascendeth up to the understanding of heavenly things, of eternall things, in which contemplacion consisteth the perfection of man."[24] The argument does not depend on Christianity or Neoplatonism as such, though in its Renaissance form it usually enlists their support. But even neoclassicists like Dryden and Addison would later exalt "the fairy way of writing" above historiography or mere *mimesis*.[25]

[24] "*A Preface, or rather a Brief Apologie of Poetrie* prefixed to the translation of *Orlando Furioso*" (1591), in *Elizabethan Critical Essays*, ed. G. Gregory Smith (Oxford, 1904), II, 201-02. For the Platonic and Neoplatonic basis of Sidney's and Harrington's golden poetics, see Joel E. Spingarn, *Literary Criticism in the Renaissance* (New York, 1963), pp. 166-78; C. S. Lewis, *English Literature in the Sixteenth Century* (New York, 1954), pp. 318-22; M. H. Abrams, *The Mirror and the Lamp* (New York, 1953), pp. 272-85; and E. N. Tigerstedt, "The Poet as Creator: Origins of a Metaphor," *Comp. Lit. Studies*, V, 4 (1968), 455-88.

[25] Addison goes so far as to say "it shows a greater genius in Shakespear to have drawn his Caliban, than his Hotspur or Julius Caesar: the one was to be supplied out of his own imagination, whereas the other might have been formed upon tradition, history, and observation." *Spectator*, No. 279, in *Works of Joseph Addison*, ed. George W. Greene (Philadelphia, 1876), VI, 45. In the phrase, "the fairy way of writing," Addison is paraphrasing Dryden, who speaks in his dedication to *King Arthur: Or, The British Worthy, A Dramatick Opera* of "that Fairy kind of writing, which depends only upon the Force of Imagination."

In the nineteenth century, however, relations between
the golden world of romance and the brazen world of
reality begin to break down, and Keats is a case in point.
The sonnet from which I have taken the title of this chapter restates in the widest terms the familiar idea of the
truancy of romance, especially when compared with tragedy. Whether Keats has in mind his beloved *Faerie
Queene*, his own recently published *Endymion*, or romance
in general, he clearly thinks of it as seductive ("Fair
plumed Syren"), unperturbed and tranquillizing ("with
serene lute!"), and physically and temporally remote
("Queen of far away," "thine olden pages") from the
grave and compelling realities represented by *King Lear*;
in sum, as a distraction, however delightful, from the real
business of the poet. Many of Keats's early poems are, in
fact, romantic bromides, something of which he himself
was often aware. Toward the end of *Sleep and Poetry*,
whose very title suggests escape from the burdens of consciousness, he imagines himself leaving behind the realm
"Of Flora, and Old Pan" for that of "the agonies, the
strife / Of Human hearts," passing, that is, from romantic
reverie to tragic awareness. From the beginning of his
poetic career, Keats thought of himself as seeing the better but following the worse. From "Calidore: a Fragment"
through *Endymion: A Poetic Romance* to *The Eve of
Saint Agnes*, Keatsian romance explores the remote, the
mysterious, and the marvellous out of a strong escapist
impulse, which is only checked at the end of each of the
two great odes. We should recall that Keats found in
Spenser an enchanting otherworld where Milton had found
a sage and serious import for this one. A sentimental view

of romance as "the name for the sort of imagination that possesses the mystery and the spell of everything remote and unattainable"[26] describes the efforts of the early Keats as well as those of Leigh Hunt, his first poetic master and Romantic escape-artist par excellence. Throughout Keats's poetic career there was a frustrated medical student struggling to get out.

Keats's ambivalence toward romance, toward the romantic element in his own work, is in part a problem of the age and culture in which he wrote and in part a problem inherent in the form itself. It is a central and ineluctable paradox, not only of romance, but of all imaginative endeavor that to represent the world a writer must create a rival world in an important sense unreal by its very nature. The poet who would be a healer or teacher or benefactor of society may come to regard his literary efforts with guilt or mistrust, as a flight from the society he wishes to help, especially if he is a poet with a strong romantic bent. "Players and painted stage," reflects Yeats in the middle of his career, "took all my love, / And not those things that they were emblems of." As the imaginative mode which allows itself the freest license with respect to reality, romance raises the problem of literary escapism in its starkest form. But there is a sense in which this problem is particularly acute for the Romantic and post-Romantic poet. In a culture that regards the forms of civilization as man-made rather than God-made, the poet must appear either a heroic exemplar of human and social activity, in so far as he is by definition a maker, or else a haunted outcast from the life of society, in so far as the worlds he

[26] W. P. Ker, *Epic and Romance* (London, 1906), p. 321.

creates are not real.[27] Modern poets tend to think of themselves alternately under both figures: as Shelley's "unacknowledged legislator of the world" and as William Morris's "singer of an empty day." In recreating the Middle Ages as the setting for so many of their romances, Romantic and Victorian writers reveal their uneasiness within their own culture. The elements of medieval life that they prize—tournaments, guild craftsmanship, stained-glass, etcetera—more truly reflect their own sense of a lost nobility and grace than the actual life of the Middle Ages. Remoteness in the dark abysm of time is the first requirement of any golden age, and the Middle Ages perfectly fulfill that condition for the Jacobite nostalgia of Scott and the anti-industrialism of the pre-Raphaelites:

> Dreamer of dreams, born out of my due time,
> Why should I strive to set the crooked straight?
> Let it suffice me that my murmuring rhyme
> Beats with light wing against the ivory gate,
> Telling a tale not too importunate
> To those who in the sleepy region stay,
> Lulled by the singer of an empty day.[28]

We still tend to think of romance as escapist, and of the romancer as the idle singer of an empty day, largely be-

---

[27] See Northrop Frye's discussion of the exaltation of the poet in the Romantic period, *A Study of English Romanticism* (New York, 1968), pp. 3-49. His view needs to be qualified, however, by recognition of the Romantic poet's new alienation. It should be remembered that Shelley's hieratic *Defense of Poetry* was evoked by his friend Peacock's irreverent *Four Ages of Poetry*.

[28] William Morris, "An Apology" prefixed to *The Earthly Paradise*, *Selected Writings*, ed. G.D.H. Cole (New York, 1934), p. 437.

41

cause for a long time now writers have been tempted to think of themselves and their function in that way. They did not always do so.

In recreating classical antiquity as a setting for their own romances, medieval poets are certainly no more historically scrupulous than nineteenth-century writers are toward the Middle Ages, but they are unscrupulous in a different way. Whereas the nineteenth-century writer makes the Middle Ages as remote as possible, the medieval poet makes classical antiquity as familiar as possible. Orpheus becomes Sir Orfeo and Aeneas a Scots laird. Medieval romance exploits the mysterious and the marvelous but rarely for purposes of escape. More important, for a discussion of romantic truancy than the fabulous content of romance is the author's way of presenting and the audience's way of regarding that content.[29] The miraculous in fiction must mean something very different to a culture that accepted miracles as literal fact than it does to one that does not. The Middle Ages did not divide as sharply as we do the credible from the incredible and this world from an otherworld, nor was the compartmentalization of literature and life as distinct modes of experience so absolute then as it is now. Although the author of *Sir Gawain and the Green Knight* claims to be recounting an episode from the distant past, his poem is wholly contemporary in detail; although its hero ventures into a strange otherworld in the course of the poem, Bercilak's castle turns out to be not the place of rest and recreation before trials that Gawain thinks it is, but their real battleground. The

[29] See Dorothy Everett, *Essays on Middle English Literature* (Oxford, 1959), pp. 1-22.

ubiquitous didacticism of the Middle Ages works generally to keep the fabulous and the familiar on speaking terms and romance more than just diverting.

This is not to suggest that there are no bad medieval romances, only that there were no amoral or unserious ones. Dante, for example, had harsh words for the romance of Lancelot's suffering in love which purchased his Paolo and Francesca an eternity of their own: *"Galeotto fu il libro e chi lo scrisse."*[30] Because literature instructs by example, even an immoral romance was a serious matter. It was the hedonist potential Roger Ascham saw in Arthurian romance that moved him to moralize for page after page against its imagined dangers: "What toyes the dayly reading of such a book [the *Morte Darthur*] may work in the will of a yong jentlman, or a yong mayde, that liveth welthelie and idelie, wise men can judge, and honest men do pitie."[31] Ascham's animadversions on romance proceed in part from his Protestant abhorrence of anything medieval and therefore "Papist" but even more from his humanist belief in the didactic function of literature. Since literature delights by teaching and teaches by delighting, it is impossible for him to conceive of romance as simply amoral, a harmless diversion; rather, it must be positively immoral, an incitement to vicious conduct, in the case of the *Morte Darthur*, to "open mans slaughter and bold bawdrye." In this respect, Ascham has much in common with the Dante whose works he would no doubt have condemned, for their views of the nature and function of literature are not essentially different. The romancer of

[30] *Inferno*, v.137. "A pander was the book, and he who wrote it."
[31] *The Scholemaster*, ed. Edward Arber (Boston, 1898), pp. 164-5.

earlier periods could always fall back on the "moralite" enunciated by Chaucer's Nun's Priest, "Taketh the fruyt, and lat the chaf be stille," the assumption being that any tale could be made to illustrate prevailing Christian doctrine, be it positively or negatively, from within or without. Hence the ease with which classical authors were moralized and thereby updated.

The romancer of later periods, by contrast, having cut his moorings in a shared ethical system may find himself aboard a drunken boat heading not toward engagement or epiphany but escapism or solipsism. Because the experience of the Ancient Mariner transcends and transvalues Christian categories, he cannot authoritatively sum up its meaning in the Christian moral, "He prayeth best, who loveth best / All things . . . ," so that both Mrs. Barbauld and Coleridge are right, the former in claiming that the poem has no moral and the latter that its moral is pushed too vigorously upon the reader.[32] Meanwhile the Mariner is doomed to collar every unsuspecting wedding guest in sight and obsessively retell his tale in the quest for an epiphany that never comes and a communion with mankind he can never have. Paradoxically it is only when literature realizes its full autonomy in creating a world apart,

---

[32] "Mrs. Barbauld once told me that she admired *The Ancient Mariner* very much, but that there were two faults in it,—it was improbable, and had no moral. As for the probability, I owned that that might admit some question; but as to the want of a moral, I told her that in my own judgment the poem had too much; and that the only, or chief fault, if I might say so, was the obtrusion of the moral sentiment so openly on the reader as a principle or cause of action in a work of such pure imagination." *Table Talk*, May 31, 1830, in *The Poetical Works of Samuel Taylor Coleridge*, ed. James Dykes Campbell (London, 1925), p. 597.

and the poet claims his full authority as a creator in his own right, that the value of his quest becomes wholly problematic. In the opening lines of *The Fall of Hyperion*, Keats distinguishes among the sectarian dreams of "fanatics," the inarticulate dreams of "the savage," and the dreams of true "Poesy," which are both articulate and communal. The prophetess Moneta later reduces these three to the basic two of escapist and humanitarian:

> The poet and the dreamer are distinct,
> Diverse, sheer opposite, antipodes,
> The one pours out a balm upon the World,
> The other vexes it.   (1. 199-202)

But which is which? And which is Keats? It is no longer easy for him or us to be sure. The full range of these new and alarming possibilities is projected in such haunted questers as Keats's palely loitering knight-at-arms, Coleridge's Mariner, Mary Shelley's Frankenstein, Browning's Childe Roland, Melville's Ahab, and Conrad's Kurtz, Jim, and Marlow. This is not to imply that the works in which they appear are inferior to their medieval and Renaissance prototypes, only the problems of escapism and solipsism under which their creators labor have intensified. In fact, these latter-day romancers solve their problems in much the same way their predecessors solved theirs: by making them part of their subject. As the old Irish song quoted by Yeats puts it, "In dreams begin responsibilities."

For even though Renaissance poets were spared the cultural anxieties of their Romantic and post-Romantic successors with respect to poetry, they nevertheless had their own reservations about romance. Ben Jonson's reiterated objection to the dramatic romances of the day, including Shakespeare's, that they "runne away from Nature," is as much an ethical as it is an aesthetic one.[33] To run away from nature is to abdicate the poet's proper function of holding a mirror up to it, a social and moral function as Hamlet's speech on the subject reminds us. Shakespeare is not a very good witness in his own defense, not only because of the playful titles he gives many of his comedies and romances, but because he frequently suggests that his own dramas are not essentially different from the silly old tales and musty old plays he mentions or includes in them: "The best in this kind are but shadows, and the worst are no worse if imagination amend them." (Of course one could argue conversely that his inclusion of or allusion to old tales and plays works to bring home the seriousness and insure the acceptance of his own by contrast.) Sidney too had harsh words for the romantic drama of his day— which must have included some of those plays discussed above—mainly for the strain it places on our credulity by violating all the rules of verisimilitude. "Now ye shall have three ladies walk to gather flowers," writes Sidney, "and then we must believe the stage to be a garden. By and by we hear news of shipwreck in the same place, and then we are to blame if we accept it not for a rock. Upon the back of that comes out a hideous monster, with fire and smoke, and then the miserable beholders are bound to take it for a cave." In the same neoclassical vein he censures the old playwrights' violation of the unity of time: "ordinary it is that two young princes fall in love. After many tra-

---

[33] "Preface to *The Alchemist*," *Critical Essays of the Seventeenth Century*, ed. Joel E. Spingarn (Oxford, 1908), I, 16.

verses, she is got with child, delivered of a fair boy; he is lost, groweth a man, falls in love, and is ready to get another child; and all this in two hours' space: which, how absurd it is in sense, even sense may imagine, and art hath taught, and all ancient examples justified."[34]

The *ne plus ultra* of the spatial and temporal anarchy Sidney describes occurs in *Common Conditions* (1576), where after a scattering of misadventures by land and sea, a Chorus appears not so much to end the play as to stop it:

Time is pictured foorth to vew all bare and bauld
behinde,
With sickel in his hand to cut when it doth please
his minde.
With that his sickell all are cut, and all thing brought
to ende.
As wee are now by Time cut off from farther time
to spende.
So time saith to us seace now here, your audience
much ye wrong
If farther now to weary them the time ye do
prolonge.[35]

[34] *An Apology for Poetry*, p. 134. One of the few points on which Sidney and Stephen Gosson were agreed was that this sort of sprawling play was to be condemned: "Sometime you shall see nothing but the adventures of an amorous knight, passing from countrie to countrie for the love of his lady, encountering many a terible monster made of broune paper, & at his retorne, is so wonderfully changed, that he can not be knowne but by some posie in his tablet, or by a broken ring, or a handkircher, or a piece of a cockle shell. What learne you by that?" *Playes Confuted in Five Actions*, in *The English Drama and Stage*, ed. W. C. Hazlitt (London, 1869), p. 181.

[35] *Common Conditions*, ed. Tucker Brooke (New Haven, 1915), lines 1889-94.

The play stops short of the recognition that might have justified, at least in its own romantic terms, the confusion it presents, and illustrates how easily the freedom of the imagination to go its own way (defended by Sidney) can defeat its own purpose in going that way. The Chorus of *Common Conditions* cannot help but recall the Chorus of Time in *The Winter's Tale*, and disjunctures of setting, time-scheme, and action abound in Shakespeare's romances (*The Tempest* excepted) with a frequency which would set the teeth of any good neoclassicist on edge. Shakespeare, though never exactly captivated by the unities, at the end of his career plays faster and looser with them than ever before. And it is not just the unities that the romances violate, but the whole notion of drama that underlies and generates them in the first place. The unities, as Sidney was well aware, are simply the working principles of dramatic illusionism; they exist to make what appears on stage a credible imitation of life. When Sidney rebukes playwrights of the 1570's for the unruliness of their plays, and Jonson chides Shakespeare for the untidiness of his, they are in effect pointing out how dramatic romance handicaps itself in producing and sustaining such an illusion. To break the rules of neoclassical unity—what Pope would call "nature methodized"—is for Jonson, who confined his furthest flights of fancy to the court-masque, nothing less than to run away from nature itself.

On the other hand, Sidney would be the first to argue that it is the abuse of romance and not romance itself that deserves censure, and the last to sacrifice its peculiar freedom to body forth the ideal and exemplary—witness his own long efforts to conform his *Arcadia* to the classical and heroic standards upheld in the *Defense*. "Truly, I have known men," he writes, "that even with reading *Amadis de Gaule* (which God knoweth wanteth much of a perfect poesy) have found their hearts moved to the exercise of courtesy, liberality, and especially courage."[36] Don Quixote is the obvious example. His dedication to the lost or non-existent ideals embodied in Amadis and Palmerin becomes, as many commentators have observed, not merely a futile and ridiculous exercise in self-delusion but the means of bringing out the best in his world. But how can the romancer fulfill his ethical and social responsibilities if his fictions are not credible in the first place, and his aesthetic responsibilities if his ethical and social commitments are not fundamentally sound? This dilemma, one that confronts all Renaissance romancers, has been cogently formulated by Harry Berger:

Both [Neoplatonic idealism and Sidney's golden poetics] seem to presuppose a desire to move beyond the imperfections and unresolved tensions of actual life. "To move beyond," however, is an ambiguous phrase; does it mean, in any particular case, "to cope with and master," or "to escape from"? Is resolution achieved by true reconciliation, or by avoidance? Is the goal an ethical ideal (what *should* be) or a hedonist idyll (what *could* be)? It is tempting to construe a vision of the ideal or idyllic as a vision of the real. In the quest for God it may not always be easy to distinguish the urge to transcend oneself from the urge to get rid of oneself. The mind may visualize the condition to which it aspires as a perfect

---

[36] *An Apology for Poetry*, p. 114.

place—heaven, paradise, utopia, fairyland, arcadia—but this *locus amoenus* may be designed primarily as a mental hideout from one or another set of earthly imperfections.[37]

Northrop Frye formulates the problem more generally in Freudian terms: "the quest-romance is the search of the libido or desiring self for a fulfillment that will deliver it from the anxieties of reality but will still contain that reality."[38] How does the serious romancer represent the ideal or idyllic and accommodate at the same time the nagging claims of the real?

The answer lies not in the authority of a given system of ethics, Christian or otherwise, but in the techniques of fiction itself. An open-ended tale of the successful adventures of an idealized hero—the simplest form that romance can take, and the one in fact taken by so many examples of the mode from Amadis to James Bond—by its very nature runs the risk of being either or both aesthetically tedious and morally unenlightening. What the best romancers have done with a mode that opens the door to infinite possibility is to fasten a chain on it, to impose strict limits on the capabilities of their heroes and on the success they enjoy, in Freudian terms, to establish a reality principle firmly within their work that holds the pleasure principle in check. In this way the best romances invariably contain a strong anti-romantic dimension. They are aware of the limits of their validity, of the fine line that divides daydream and vision. Under such conditions an Amadis may

[37] "The Renaissance Imagination: Second World and Green World," *Centennial Review*, IX, No. 1 (Winter, 1965), 40.

[38] *Anatomy of Criticism* (Princeton, 1957), p. 193.

turn into a Gawain. One of the central concerns of *Sir Gawain and the Green Knight* is precisely the impossibility of escape from personal anxieties and public duties. The Gawain poet repeatedly folds back the mantle of courtly lover and heroic knight with which French and native romance tradition had invested Gawain to reveal the vulnerable man beneath, to catch him in the act of being human:

So mony mervayl bi mount ther the mon findes,
Hit were to tore for to telle of the tenthe dole.
Sumwhile with wormes he werres and with wolves als,
Sumwhile with wodwos, that woned in the knarres,
Bothe with bulles and beres, and bores otherwhile,
And etaines, that him anelede of the heghe felle;
Nade he ben dughty and drighe, and Drighten had
    served,
Douteless he hade ben ded and dreped ful ofte.
For werre wrathed him not so much, that winter
    was wors,
When the colde cler water fro the cloudes shadde,
And fres er hit falle might to the fale erthe.[39]

The knight may dispose easily enough of the "wormes," "wolves," "bulles," "beres," "bores," and marvelous "wodwos" he encounters on his journey, but the man is sorely afflicted by the mundane cold and frost. We are pleased when Red Crosse, like many a previous knight, slays the dragon at the end of the first book of *The Faerie*

[39] Lines 718-28. To facilitate comprehension I quote from the normalized text prepared by Francis Berry for *The Pelican Guide to English Literature 1: The Age of Chaucer*, ed. Boris Ford (Baltimore, 1966), p. 372.

Queene; but we are edified when the old dragon, unlike previous dragons, does not die so easily. Since "the raskall many" (*FQ*,ɪ.xii.9) who draws near to inspect it on the ground have not gone through what Red Crosse has to kill it, as far as they are concerned it is still alive and twitching. Near the end of the *Odyssey*, after Odysseus has dispatched the suitors, cleansed his house, and proven his identity to Penelope, Homer describes their reunion with a truly remarkable simile:

> Now from his breast into his eyes the ache
> of longing mounted, and he wept at last,
> his dear wife, clear and faithful, in his arms,
> longed for
> as the sunwarmed earth is longed for by a swimmer
> spent in rough water where his ship went down
> under Poseidon's blows, gale winds and tons of sea.
> Few men can keep alive through a big surf
> to crawl, clotted with brine, on kindly beaches
> in joy, in joy, knowing the abyss behind.[40]

Not only does Homer recall the prolonged pain of Odysseus' experience at the moment of climactic joy, but he presents all that joy in terms of all that pain, remembers it when the temptation to forget it is greatest. In so doing, he sets an example for all good romancers since. It is through this technique of shadowing or qualifying or problematizing the triumphs it presents that the best romance manages to pass itself off as an image of the real.

There will be ample opportunity later to show how Shakespeare's romances, particularly the last two, tran-

[40] *The Odyssey*, trans. Robert Fitzgerald (London, 1962), p. 392.

scend reality while recognizing its claims. Two examples will serve for now. Looking on Hermione's "statue" in the last scene of *The Winter's Tale*, Leontes remarks that his wife "was not so much wrinkled, nothing / So aged as this seems." To which Paulina replies: "So much the more our carver's excellence, / Which lets go by some sixteen years and makes her / As she lived now." Devouring time is transcended even as its power is acknowledged, and it becomes clear that the excellent carver at work here is not Julio Romano. A lesser romancer than Shakespeare would have produced an unwrinkled Hermione, as Lyly had produced an unwrinkled Endymion more than two decades earlier. In that old play, the presiding figure of Cynthia is numinous enough to revive the hero from his forty-year sleep, restore his lost youth with a kiss, transform another from a tree back into a maid, and even reform her antagonist, all without even breathing hard. This is such stuff as wish-dreams are made on, and Paulina and Prospero himself might well envy her success. For not even in *The Tempest* does Shakespeare allow his romancer within the romance such easy or total victory. Although Prospero stages a betrothal masque that recalls the mythological plays of Lyly, Peele, or *Love and Fortune*, and although Prospero's masque is a higher and stronger vision than any other in a play full of visions, it too turns out to be too fragile for this world, or for that matter, for the world of *The Tempest*, and falls apart at the thought of a Caliban. What Shakespeare does, here and elsewhere in the romances, is to take an older romance model and show its inadequacy to contain and comprehend the experience of his play, to expose the dangers inherent in the mode he uses by testing it against a reality it cannot cope with, to avoid escapism by making his plays about escapism. Shakespeare's romances, like Milton's, are on one level a stern reprimand of romance (while remaining romance) and test to the breaking point not only the characters they contain but the mode they employ. The moral and mimetic dimension of Shakespearean romance comes into being through its stubborn refusal to accept and repeat the conventions of romance without revaluating them. Not to do so would be to avoid the very trial and testing to which the romancer subjects his characters, and that would be a fugitive and cloistered virtue indeed.

PART II

TOWARD SHAKESPEAREAN

ROMANCE

CHAPTER 2

From Comedy to Romance

> My happiness has its tears in it; but there is more
> sweetness here than pain.
> —Euripides

ONE OF THE aims of this study is to demonstrate the pervasive presence of romance within Shakespeare's entire work, even within the major tragedies. But the focal points of Shakespearean romance are, of course, the two groups of plays that stand at the beginning and end of his career: the romantic comedies and the romances proper. From *The Comedy of Errors*, with its framing action of old Aegeon's travails by sea and land, to *Twelfth Night*, with its separation of Viola and Sebastian by shipwreck, Shakespearean comedy draws freely upon most of the traditions of romance described in the previous chapter and employs their familiar motifs for purposes of moral trial and testing in ways that remind us of the humanist romances of Sidney and Spenser. The tyranny of error the fairies exert over the lovers of *A Midsummer Night's Dream* works ultimately to sift out the elements of fancy and fantasy, of sentiment and sentimentality in their love. The trial of the three caskets in *The Merchant of Venice* is well designed by Portia's father to discriminate between the false love of Morocco and Aragon and the true love of Bassanio. Our sense of the unity of Shakespeare's total work, from his early comedies to his last romances, is reinforced by the frequency with which romantic motifs of the earlier plays reappear in the later ones. The scene of the three caskets, for example, anticipates the scene of the riddle in *Pericles*. The Sicilian setting of Hero's slander in *Much Ado* prefigures the Sicilian setting of Hermione's slander in *The Winter's Tale*. Oberon's control over the wood outside Athens in *A Midsummer Night's Dream* anticipates Prospero's over the island of *The Tempest*. Yet it does not take a very sophisticated reader or theatergoer to recognize that the experience and effect of reading or seeing *The Tempest* is utterly different from that of *A Midsummer Night's Dream*—despite the obvious similarities of the two plays. It is this strong sense of difference between the romantic comedies and the romances, given their generic resemblance, that has not been adequately accounted for and that I want to turn to next. For it strikes me that Shakespeare's romances are actually closer in tone and mood and effect to the epics of Spenser and Milton than to his own romantic comedies, and that the qualitative change one feels in moving from the earlier to the later plays reflects changes in his handling of the romance form.

If both the romantic comedies and the romances issue in the formation of a renewed and raised society, the path the characters of the latter plays must follow to get there is, in the words of Edgar to Gloucester, "horrible steep," and how they must labor to climb it—again, especially when compared with the route traveled in the earlier plays. The cloistered academic virtue of the King and courtiers of Navarre in *Love's Labour's Lost*, of which their linguistic excess is the symptom, must be tested against the realities of love and desire before they are fit for marriage. But even though that quadruple wedding is deferred for the further trial period of a year, and even though that year will be spent jesting in a hospital for the witty Berowne, the inner resources of these characters are not very seriously taxed. If *Love's Labour's Lost* is felt to be in some ways atypical of the comedies, consider *As You Like It*. All that Duke Senior need do to regain his dukedom is wait for his wicked brother to follow him into the forest, where he undergoes a religious conversion. Orlando, it is true, regains his birthright after saving his brother from a hungry lioness, an act of physical strength and courage recalling that he had earlier shown against Charles the wrestler. But few, if any, of the protagonists of the comedies are called upon to exert a comparable moral effort. Which of them performs, like Pericles or Leontes, "a saint-like sorrow," or exerts himself, like Camillo, Paulina, and Prospero, not merely for his own benefit but for the benefit of the rest of the cast? The labors of Petruchio or Bassanio are self-interested as well as slight by comparison. Even Portia's legal gymnastics on Antonio's behalf form the exception that proves the rule, in so far as Shylock's well-being never really enters her sphere of concern. (Compare Prospero's treatment of Antonio.) If Ferdinand's task of log-bearing seems trivial, it is not only more than most of the lovers of the comedies have to perform but is specifically designed by Prospero as a moral labor of self-qualification, "lest too light winning make the prize light." The abundant good that flows to the youthful lovers at the end of the comedies is not similarly hard-earned. Prospero's caveat also bears directly on Shakespeare's own romantic artifice. For just as the characters of the romances earn their prosperity through the severity of their trials, so the romances themselves earn their right to end happily by refusing to mitigate the severities they also present—another instance of how the ethics of Protestantism condition the poetics of romance. It is no wonder that Samuel Johnson's belief that Shakespeare's comedies are the product of "instinct" rather than "skill" made him ever so slightly uneasy with them.[1]

It has been pointed out that the chief obstacle to the movement of the comedies toward their festive conclusions often takes the form of a rigid or unreasonable law—the laws governing the disposition of marriageable daughters in *A Midsummer Night's Dream* and *The Taming of the Shrew*, the law which upholds Shylock's bond, the law of primogeniture in *As You Like It*, the King of Navarre's silly edict, and so forth.[2] In several of the plays the obstacle is a blocking or "killjoy" figure who is repressive, antisocial, and generally unmusical—the heavy father of *A Midsummer Night's Dream*, Shylock, Malvolio, and so forth. Although the wishes of the lovers, their sense of identity, and finally the social vision of the plays themselves gain in value and integrity as a result of their being

[1] In for example, his general observation on *Twelfth Night*: "This play is in the graver part elegant and easy, and in some of the lighter scenes exquisitely humorous. . . . The marriage of Olivia and the succeeding perplexity, though well enough contrived to divert on the stage, wants credibility and fails to produce the proper instruction required in the drama, as it exhibits no just picture of life." *Samuel Johnson on Shakespeare*, ed. W. K. Wimsatt, Jr. (New York, 1960), pp. 80-81.

[2] See Northrop Frye, *A Natural Perspective* (New York, 1965), pp. 73-4; and C. L. Barber, *Shakespeare's Festive Comedy* (Princeton, 1959), pp. 8-9.

tested by these counter-romantic laws and figures, the threat they pose to the romantic vision of the play is not very grave. Shylock is easily outwitted, first by Jessica and later by the disguised Portia. The bumbling constables of *Much Ado* can apprehend Don John, only because he is an even more inept villain than they are policemen. Meanness—for evil does not really exist in the world of the comedies—is presented in them as more or less an accident and is usually overcome by accident. The natural and social orders are seen as essentially good, given that the creatures who compose them are always fallible and sometimes perverse. Their festive conclusions proclaim with Miranda: "O brave new world, / That hath such people in't." In some of the comedies, notably *Love's Labour's Lost* and *Twelfth Night*, the note of festivity is muted by a reminder of "the wind and the rain" that have for the time being been forgotten. But in the romances this qualifying note of anti-romance is more fully and harshly realized throughout and culminates in Prospero's almost sinister rejoinder to Miranda's innocent exclamation of joy: " 'Tis new to thee." The natural and social orders are seen not as essentially good in the romances, but at best as not good enough.

For in these plays it is not the irrational law of one society or another nor a single cranky figure that blocks the movement toward a braver and newer world, but a recalcitrance to human desire built into the universe itself— the humiliation, loss, and brutality that Pericles and Marina meet at every turn in their wanderings. The visions of the romances are tested against what amounts to a universal law of frustration:

Be not with mortal accidents opprest,
  No care of yours it is; you know 'tis ours,
Whom best I love I cross; to make my gift
  The more delayed, delighted. Be content.

Jupiter discloses himself and his design very late in *Cymbeline*, so late in fact that our final impression of the play may well give greater weight to the mortal accidents which oppress "mortal flies" than to the virtuoso deliverance from them in the last scene. Similarly in *Pericles* it is the sense of the world as "a lasting storm, / Whirring me from my friends" that stays with us, for even in the joy of reunion that storm is recalled: "thank the holy gods as loud / As thunder threatens us." And at the end of *The Winter's Tale* and *The Tempest* Shakespeare does not allow us to forget that restitution of loss is never perfect and complete, that rebirth is not the same as birth (no more than they are in life) which may help to account for the bitter-sweetness of the romances, as opposed to the sweetness of the comedies. For the anti-romantic movements in each of the last plays (while a necessary structural component of all good romance) gain their peculiar force, as the phrase "mortal flies" reminds us, from drawing upon the greatest anti-romantic structures ever created: Shakespeare's own tragedies.

There is a sense then in which the romances would not have been possible without the preceding tragedies—I do not mean psychologically impossible, but *structurally* impossible. For like *Paradise Lost* and *Samson Agonistes*, Shakespeare's final romances subsume tragedy in the process of transcending it—not only *The Winter's Tale*, where the first three acts form a tragedy unto themselves, but the other romances as well. The adversity (if that term is not altogether too bookish to describe what a character like Leontes undergoes) presented in these plays does not resemble that of the comedies so much as that of the tragedies. There is nothing in the comedies to compare with the loss and isolation of Pericles, though there is much in *Lear*; nothing to match the rage and desperation of Leontes except in *Othello*; no counterpart to the humiliation of Hermione and Imogen other than that of Desdemona and Cordelia. Side by side with the magical speech-music of each of the last plays exist the harshest cacophanies of the tortured soul familiar from the great tragedies. If it is true that many of his tragic heroes try in vain to romanticize or redeem themselves to the bitter end (more on this in the next chapters) and that this effort is an essential part of their tragedy, the suffering principals of the romances—Pericles, Posthumus, Leontes, Alonso—are stripped of all hope or illusion of redeeming themselves, are rendered "absolute for death" (in a way that Claudio, to whom these words are addressed in *Measure for Measure*, never really is), and this is essential to their redemption. The tragic heroes, and we along with them, persist in expecting romance and get tragedy; the romantic protagonists are disabused of all romantic expectations and get romance.

At the outset of *Pericles*, the young hero thinks he is in the world of *The Merchant of Venice*, where to choose the right casket is to win the holy, fair, and wise Portia and to choose the wrong one is to go on one's not so merry way. But he soon discovers that to fail to solve Antiochus' riddle is to die and to solve it is also to die—and even though he manages to escape, he is still haunted by death in the form of Antiochus' assassin. The play immediately establishes a world in which all choice has tragic consequences, and the riddle Pericles solves is ultimately more like that of the Sphinx than that of Portia's father. Similarly, Duke Senior can say with some justice of his banishment in Arden that "Sweet are the uses of adversity," but no one in *The Tempest*—least of all Prospero—can rationalize his castaway status into sweetness. When Gonzalo tries to do so in order to cheer up Alonso, he is effectively discredited by the cynical wisecracks of Antonio and Sebastian. (When old Belarius in *Cymbeline* tries to persuade the princes of the moral superiority of the Welsh hills to the court, he too is shouted down.) The anti-pastoral figures of Jaques and Touchstone pose nothing like the threat to Duke Senior's benign vision that the comparable figures of Antonio and Caliban do to Gonzalo's, and even to Prospero's. Prospero's island is an imaginative setting prodigiously more trying to the characters thrust into it than is the Forest of Arden. To Alonso, who is not allowed to think of the island as anything other than the wasteland of his hopes, it is as trying in its way as the heath is to Lear. Although *The Tempest*, as well as the other romances, draws heavily on the conventions of pastoral romance, it is for most of its action more like what one critic has called *Lear*: "the greatest anti-pastoral ever penned."[3]

Because their protagonists expect the worst, the endings of the romances come to them, and I venture to say to us as well, as nothing less than a "miracle" in a way that the endings of the comedies do not. What had seemed all but

[3] Maynard Mack, *King Lear in Our Time* (Berkeley, 1965), p. 65.

impossible has come to pass. When the reformed Kate does her husband's bidding at the end of *The Taming of the Shrew*, Lucentio remarks, "Here is a wonder, if you talk of a wonder." When Paulina calls upon the reviving "statue" of Hermione to approach her husband and "Strike all that look upon with marvel," her words are no mere figure of speech. In the recognition scene of *The Comedy of Errors*, the Merchant says to Antipholus of Ephesus, "you fled into this abbey here, / From whence, I think, you are come by miracle." Although magic, witchcraft, and miracles are often invoked by the confused protagonists of that play to account for their confusion and hover, as it were, on the fringes of the action, Antipholus is absolutely right, as the scene soon makes clear, in denying that miracles had any part at all in his presence there. If the comedies frequently liken the experience they present to the workings of magic or miracles, the romances present "the thing itself." Pericles, for example, calls his reunion with his wife at Diana's temple after fifteen years of separation "this great miracle," referring at once to the special providence which, as has been revealed to him and us, actually has shaped his end and to the mode of the play itself, as we shall see in a later chapter. In Portia's moonlit garden at Belmont, Lorenzo says he could hear the angelic choirs but for "this muddy vesture of decay." Reunited with Marina, Pericles does hear the music of the spheres and falls asleep to the sound. The appearance of Hymen at the wedding festivities that conclude *As You Like It*, though unanticipated and unexplained, perfectly embodies and expresses the holiday humor which pervades the closing scene. The theophanies that occur in *Pericles* and *Cym-*

beline, however, give a local habitation and a name not simply to the spirit of nuptial festivity, but to all the forces that have shaped the life of man in those plays for better and worse. In *The Winter's Tale*, the Chorus of Time— "I that please some, try all, both joy and terror / Of good and bad, that makes and unfolds error"—takes over this role.

The replacement of the marriage-god by the greater presiding deities of Neptune, Diana, and Jupiter begins to suggest the expansion of scope and concern that has occurred from the comedies to the romances in their respective dramatic universes. I do not mean simply that the romances deal with two generations and span more than a decade, for the action of *The Comedy of Errors* does both these things. I mean that the actions of the romances include a dimension of existence, which is ultimately made flesh in their theophanies, that the actions of the comedies generally do not. Although both groups of plays turn upon an axis that stretches between the poles of mistaken identity and recognition, the universe of the romances contains that of the comedies and something more. The comedies end, after much division and confusion, with the recovery of the personal, familial, and social identity of their characters: lovers are paired off in marriage with their proper mates; friends are reconciled; families are reunited; and all take their places within a society that has been rejuvenated and will be perpetuated. The romances contain these actions within a larger one. When Gonzalo proclaims toward the end of *The Tempest* that "all of us [found] ourselves / When no man was his own," he is talking about the recovery of spiritual integrity as well as personal and social identity. It is not necessary to view the romances as "religious allegories" to see that they deal with aspects of human experience—guilt and contrition, the problem of evil, death and rebirth—the mystery and the tears of things that may (not inappropriately) be called religious.[4]

When a playwright introduces a deity into his play (whether he does so reverently like the author of *Everyman* or ironically like Euripides) he also introduces a new and suprahuman perspective into the play. A chief difference between *Much Ado* and *Cymbeline* (and by extension between the comedies and romances generally) is that the

---

[4] Reacting against the once fashionable practice of theologizing the final romances, John F. Danby writes: "To theologize the last plays . . . is to distort them. . . . St. Paul is taken for granted but not allegorized in every Whitsun pastoral. Shakespeare's last plays are not conceived at the same level of seriousness as Dante's *Paradiso*." *Elizabethan and Jacobean Poets* (London, 1964), pp. 97-8. Though the thrust of Danby's remarks is right-headed, his last statement surely confuses religious sincerity or sublimity with literary seriousness, which has nothing to do with religion. Northrop Frye talks more rigorously to the point: "The difference between *Cymbeline* and the problem comedies is not that *Cymbeline* is adding a religious allegory to the dramatic action. What it is adding . . . is the primitive mythical dimension which is only implicit in the problem comedies. *Cymbeline* is not a more religious play than *Much Ado*: it is a more academic play, with a greater technical interest in dramatic structure." *A Natural Perspective*, pp. 69-70. The confusion arises in the first place because the "primitive mythical dimension" and "technical interest" that Frye finds in the last plays reflect those aspects of the mystery, morality, and miracle plays which are Shakespeare's primary dramatic models, and which also happen to be Christian. To write more primitive plays meant for Shakespeare to write more overtly Christian plays. The needed corrective to naive allegorization now having been provided, we can all relax a bit and feel free to discuss their Christian elements as they arise—which is neither all the time nor not at all.

complications of the former are seen entirely from within by its characters, whereas the complications of the latter eventually come to be seen from above. Such an overview of human error and perversity is fitfully attained in some of the comedies by way of analogy to Christian myth and mystery, as in Valentine's forgiveness of Proteus at the end of *Two Gentlemen* or Portia's appeal to divine mercy in the trial scene of *The Merchant of Venice*, but in the romances it is fully developed. Even in those romances which contain no theophany as such, the Chorus of Time, Apollo's oracle, and the prescience of Prospero's magic provide what amounts to a god's-eye view of the action. Human experience must look very different from above than it does from within: the social patterns of everyday life, though they do not disappear, do diminish in prominence, and the spiritual contours of a lifetime become unmistakably visible—to the characters and audience alike.

To the extent that the vision of the final romances is at once secular and religious, many of the themes and much of the vocabulary of the comedies are endowed with new and wider meaning. No one would question the central importance of faith in the comedies, the faith in love demanded of the characters and the poetic faith required of the audience; but when Paulina tells Leontes before the unveiling of Hermione's "statue" that "It is required you do awake your faith," she means more than his faith in love and our faith in incredible comic plots. She means "faith" in the sense of her possible namesake, St. Paul: a creative, almost magical, power which, in the terms of this scene, positively brings Hermione back to life. Similarly, the word and concept of "grace" is not confined to the last romances, but its insistent repetition in the opening scene of *The Winter's Tale* amid recollections of lost innocence and intimations of immortality lend it more than the social and aristocratic value it has in the comedies. *As You Like It* might well be termed a comedy of "atonement" in so far as it issues in a society at one with itself, but the implications of inward struggle and reformation contained in Hymen's term are not fully realized until the last plays, which, as I hope to show, represent a return to the poetics of the medieval comedy of atonement from which both groups of plays ultimately derive.

Finally and most importantly, if the avowed purpose of Shakespearean comedy and romance is recreation (and Shakespeare himself tells us often enough that it is) we should be prepared to see that recreation may have, and in the last plays has, as much to do with St. Paul as it does with Hollywood. When the penitent Leontes says at the lowest point in the action of *The Winter's Tale* that tears only "Shall be my recreation," he unwittingly plays on the Pauline meaning of the word, the kind of recreation he in fact experiences and the play as a whole illustrates. The old man dies that the new may be born. Without being unduly hard on the early comedies (which I no doubt have been throughout this extended comparison), I would submit that it is not until the romances that this kind of recreation becomes part of Shakespeare's designs upon his audience. In the epilogue to *As You Like It*, Rosalind comes forward to flirt with the audience, to involve them in the holiday humor of the play to the extent of applauding it. In the epilogue to *The Tempest*, Prospero humbles himself before the audience and petitions them to exercise that charity toward him by applauding which he has exercised toward others in the play. In *The Tempest* not only does Prospero regain his dukedom as Duke Senior does in *As You Like It* (this could have been accomplished in the first act) but he does so by healing the soul of his antagonist—the "rarer action" of the play. Among the reconciliations that take place in the closing scenes of the romances is the reconciliation of the orders of nature and grace, of the claims of the world and the spirit, which in the problem comedies had been wrenched apart with so much damage to the social fabric and which Helena and Duke Vincentio had not had the power to repair. Paulina and Prospero do have the power, and that power consists largely in art. Their art, like that of the romances in which they appear, is controlled by a moral earnestness that turns the "undream'd shores" of those Mediterranean islands into the "vale of soulmaking" that Keats, with the true vision of the good romancer, termed this world.

CHAPTER 3

The Problem Plays

Our erected wit maketh us know what perfection is, and
yet our infected will keepeth us from reaching unto it.

—Sidney

BETWEEN THE romantic comedies and the romances proper
stand the so-called problem plays—*Troilus and Cressida,
Measure for Measure*, and *All's Well That Ends Well*—
and any attempt to trace the development of Shakespearean romance must come to terms with them. No group of
Shakespeare's plays, with the possible exception of the
romances themselves, has generated such divided response
and diverse speculation, so much (in Guildenstern's
phrase) "throwing about of brains." They have been
grouped on the basis of a widely felt, though variously
conceived, community of theme or mood or effect. Other
plays have from time to time been added to their number,
and their status as a discrete and coherent group has not
gone unchallenged.[1] To those who doubt that they present any special or intrinsic problems and trace our uneasi-

[1] The term "problem plays" has been recently redefined by Ernest
Schanzer, *The Problem Plays of Shakespeare* (New York, 1963), pp.
1-10, 187-91, for whom it properly applies only to *Julius Caesar,
Measure for Measure*, and *Antony and Cleopatra*. A more convincing
case, to my mind, for the by now traditional application of the term
to *Troilus, All's Well*, and *Measure for Measure* is made by A. P.
Rossiter, *Angel with Horns* (London, 1961), pp. 108-28.

ness with them to the Victorian spiritual biography of Shakespeare, the first attempts to classify *Troilus* should be cautionary.[2] The titlepage of its first quarto called it a "history"; the self-styled Never Writer of the euphuistic epistle prefixed to it was magisterially confident he was introducing a "comedy"; while Hemminge and Condell placed it among the tragedies in the first folio. I hope to show not only that these three plays share certain formal features which justify their being discussed together, but that these common denominators arise from the unique relation of these plays to romance convention.

That relation is fundamentally a new ambivalence toward the romance mode itself, particularly the naive romanticism that informs Shakespeare's early work, an ambivalence already adumbrated in the plays immediately preceding the problem comedies. In *Hamlet*, often discussed in conjunction with the problem plays, the will to woo and wed to which even the most reluctant lovers of the comedies are finally subject is seriously problematized. Hamlet's bitter interdictions to the girl he once loved and Gertrude hoped he would marry—"Get thee to a nunnery: why wouldst thou be a breeder of sinners?"—at once divorces his world from that of the comedies and allies it

---

[2] Nor are the difficulties most of us feel with *All's Well* and *Measure for Measure* of recent origin. Johnson's uneasiness with both plays and Coleridge's with *Measure for Measure* directly prefigure our own. See *Samuel Johnson on Shakespeare*, ed. W. K. Wimsatt, Jr. (New York, 1960), pp. 76 and 84; and Coleridge's *Shakespearean Criticism*, ed. Thomas Middleton Raysor (Everyman's Library, London, 1960), I, 102. Bernard Shaw repeatedly singled out these three plays from the rest of Shakespeare's comedies for praise, on the grounds that plays as unpleasant and unpopular as they are cannot be all bad. See *Shaw on Shakespeare*, ed. Edwin Wilson (New York, 1961), pp. 25 and 259.

with that of *All's Well* and *Measure for Measure.* Honor fares little better than love. How "divine" is that ambition which moves Fortinbras (he recalls both Hotspur and Henry V) to risk twenty-thousand lives for "a fantasy and trick of fame"? The chivalric world of ritual single combats had already seemed slightly outmoded when Hotspur had appropriated its terms, and with the murder of the elder Hamlet, it has faded into a lost golden age. When Troilus champions a similar code of honor in a world even less hospitable to chivalric modes, he becomes not only a bit ridiculous, as Fortinbras had been, but finally pathetic.

Similarly, the noble Romans and Roman nobility of *Julius Caesar* are so seriously undercut, it is not surprising to find that play too recently classified and discussed as a problem play. No one has yet considered, to my knowledge, the *Henriad* as a problem tetralogy, but there is warrant for doing so, particularly in the case of its latter two plays. Like *Measure for Measure* and *All's Well, Henry V* has a romance ending despite the fact that the strong counter-romantic forces which have been raised have not been altogether charmed to rest. The various public voices of that play (the Chorus, the Archbishop of Canterbury, and Henry himself) use all the rhetoric at their command to erect the romantic myth of a sun-king purged of "the offending Adam," winning the angelic Katherine, and regaining "this best garden of the world, / Our fertile France." But the hard facts of the play jar against the myth and threaten to shatter it: the quibbling legal pretext on which Henry invades France in the first place, as well as his motives for doing so; his inability to rationalize away Williams' legitimate doubts on the eve of battle; his habit of making deals with God before major encounters; and his cruel and gratuitous slaughter of French prisoners. Then too, the triumphant note of the final Chorus is muted by the reminder that Henry's achievements will prove short-lived. As for the common sort, we learn that Falstaff is dead and all but forgotten, that Doll Tearsheet "is dead i'th'spital / Of malady of France," that Bardolph and Nym have been hanged for stealing, and that Pistol means to turn pimp and thief and make for England. As at the end of the problem comedies, even though its unhealthy elements have been put down with a vengeance unprecedented in the earlier comedies— perhaps *because* they have been so ruthlessly put down— we may question whether all is any more "well" in Henry's England than it is in Vincentio's Vienna or in Helena's France. *Henry V* could well be regarded, as Polonius might say, as "problem-comedy history."[3]

The historical mode of *Henry V*, *Julius Caesar*, and *Hamlet* allows wide scope for problematic elements without jeopardizing their generic status or upsetting our concomitant expectations. Of course romance and romantic comedy also deal in problems, or more precisely, in the overcoming of problems, and the best romances work to some degree against the genre by making their problematic forces as recalcitrant as possible to solution. Even in the early comedies, Shakespeare takes pains to ballast the buoyancy of a Duke Senior and an Orlando with the melancholy and skepticism of a Jaques and a Touchstone. When the lovers of the comedies cast about for romantic

---

[3] I owe the phrase to a letter from Northrop Frye. See also his *Anatomy of Criticism* (Princeton, 1957), p. 284.

prototypes, and come up with the example of Troilus and Cressida, it does not go unqualified. Troilus is "one of the patterns of love" for Rosalind, even if he "had his brains dashed out with a Grecian club." Lorenzo opens his catalogue of romantic exemplars in the moonlit garden of Belmont with Troilus, sighing "his soul toward the Grecian tents, / Where Cressid lay that night," though Jessica's replies point up the fact that each of those legends of love ends in disaster. There, in any case, is the equipoise between romantic and anti-romantic sentiment characteristic of Shakespearean comedy, the fulcrum of which is usually centered in his witty heroines. Their romantic genre is established, mildly threatened, and reestablished stronger for the testing.

Such is not the case with *Troilus* and the problem comedies. As the foregoing examples from the comedies suggest, the matter of Troy had been, along with Arthurian legend, the great repository of romantic and heroic materials in medieval and Tudor England, of "fierce warres and faithfull loves," as Spenser announces the subject-matter of his romantic epic. When Byron wittily misquoted, "Fierce loves and faithless wars," to describe the twin subject of his satiric epic, he might have been describing *Troilus*. "All the argument is a cuckold and a whore," barks Thersites, "and war and lechery confound all!" (II.iii.73-7). Heroic warriors and romantic lovers are reduced by the end of the play to "traitors and bawds" (v.x.38), a phrase spoken by Pandarus in what amounts to an epilogue. Someone has said that there is not a single characterization of the Greek "heroes" in *Troilus* that is not embryonic in Homer. The Thersites of the first book of the *Iliad*, for example, who takes at face value Agamemnon's suggestion that they abandon the war and go home, is hardly more attractive than the scurrilous rogue of Shakespeare's play. But anti-heroic sentiments in Homer usually serve as safety-valves for the audience's own skepticism, are quickly squelched, and work ultimately to validate the heroic norms of the poem. In Shakespeare, however, Thersites' cynical rant threatens to drown out the voices of order and idealism altogether and to sum up the status of love and honor at the end. The apparent triumph of the ignoble would seem to suggest the poetics of satire or burlesque, where from *Don Quixote* through *Candide* and *Gulliver's Travels* to *Don Juan* and *Brave New World* a romantic myth is consistently invoked or implied in order to be systematically subverted. *Troilus* and the problem comedies have been discussed under this rubric, and there are no doubt moments when they do work on satiric principles. One thinks of Helena's invocation of Marlowe's mighty line on another Helen to underscore the indignity of her own situation in *All's Well*, or Aeneas's glorification in *Troilus* of "the high and mighty Agamemnon" (i.iii.232) and subsequent failure to recognize him in the flesh, or Achilles' sordid butchery of Hector against all the rules of chivalry and his own reputation. For not only do the heroes of antiquity fall short of their legendary status (even for Hamlet they are types of heroic action, the bywords of a humanist education) but they fail to live up to their own ideals of themselves within the play. In the problem plays generally, and *Troilus* in particular, the romantic imagination—be it Homer's, Chapman's,

Troilus's, or Shakespeare's own—is subjected on all sides to unprecedented stresses and strains.

But for all its ironic moments, *Troilus and Cressida* is not finally a satire of the vanity of honor and the folly of love, nor its relation to the romantic legend of Troy simply parodic. The play is ambivalent toward romance, not scornful of it. At times its romantic ideals are allowed to shine forth in so pure a form that their after image persists in the mind's eye, whatever their fate within the play. This persistence of vision beyond its apparent demise is suggested by the fact that the best-remembered utterances in the play are Ulysses' monologue on order and degree and Troilus's impassioned advocacy of assigned over intrinsic value, of faith over expediency. Neither ideal is set up solely to be knocked down, as they would be in a purely ironic work. Ulysses' exhortation is not invalidated because Achilles and Ajax fail to follow it; if anything, it is negatively borne out. Troilus's insistence that "the life of our design" consists in "glory" rather than "the performance of our heaving spleens," though it is betrayed by the brutality of Achilles and Ajax, by his brother Paris's dalliance, and by his own eventual rage for revenge, is nonetheless upheld by Hector, in action if not in principle. Ulysses is no Pangloss, and Troilus, though he is related to the *naïf* of satire, is no Candide. In everything but his end Troilus has more in common with Don Quixote, who also tries to impose the "high designs" of romance on a world too late, and who also has the power of temporarily drawing others into his vision of grace and nobility.

For Troilus, like Quixote, has been reading too many

chivalric romances and repeatedly tries to cast his experience of war and love into that mold. He insists on seeing Helen as the conventional exalted lady of quest romance, with whose metaphors he invests her:

> Why, she is a pearl,
> Whose price hath launch'd above a thousand ships,
> And turn'd crown'd kings to merchants.
>
> (ii.ii.82-4)

> A spur to valiant and magnanimous deeds,
> Whose present courage may beat down our foes,
> And fame in time to come canonize us.
>
> (ii.ii.199-201)

That Helen seems closer to the "flashy bauble" described by Yeats than the "pearl" described by Troilus may not disturb him—"What is aught but as 'tis valued?"—but it bodes ill for his love affair with Cressida, whom he invests with the same imagery:

> I cannot come to Cressid but by Pandar;
> And he's as tetchy to be wooed to woo
> As she is stubborn, chaste, against all suit.
> Tell me Apollo, for thy Daphne's love,
> What Cressid is, what Pandar, and what we.
> Her bed is India; there she lies, a pearl.
> Between our Ilium and where she resides
> Let it be called the wild and wand'ring flood,
> Ourself the merchant, and this sailing Pandar
> Our doubtful hope, our convoy, and our bark.
>
> (i.i.99-108)

Troilus romanticizes his situation into a risky and arduous quest for a rare object guided by an expert merchant-adventurer, in the course of which the best in everyone will be brought out. But the speech, like so many of Troilus's utterances, is bedeviled by a curious *double entendre* of which he himself is unaware. He superimposes the exotic image of a pearl lying in India upon the erotic image of a flesh-and-blood woman lying in bed. When he later complains to Cressida of "the monstruosity in love . . . that the will is infinite and the execution confined; that the desire is boundless and the act a slave to limit" (III.ii.82-5), we again recognize two possible constructions. Though Troilus speaks out of his adopted role of the servant of love faced with the impositions of a cruel but ennobling mistress, Cressida takes his references to "will," "execution," and "act" in their unabashed sexual sense, the sense that informs her frequent exchanges of puns with Pandarus. Troilus's speeches are chronically and unwittingly subverted from below, and the action proceeds to fulfill, not the high designs and roles they project, but their low undertones. Pandarus is revealed, not as a highminded merchant-adventurer, but as a prurient "broker" and "trader." And Cressida, far from "stubborn, chaste, against all suit," proves in the end to be only too pliable to the nearest male will.

There is, however, another romantic model and matrix embedded in *Troilus* besides that of chivalric romance, one which seems for a time adequate to contain the experience of the principals, and that is the morality play. During the scene of their union, Cressida falls back on its terms out

of her uneasiness with the high romantic role in which
Troilus has cast her: "I have a kind of self resides with
you; / But an unkind self, that itself will leave / To be
another's fool." (III.ii.149-51) Cressida, that is, recasts
herself in the role of the morality protagonist wavering
between the best and worst in her nature and her world,
a role better suited to what we see of her than that of exalted mistress. For it is a mistake to view Cressida simply
as a slut, as many interpretations and productions have.
To do so is to play Thersites' game (Troilus's in reverse)
and coarsen the play's special quality of anti-romance.
Shakespeare's Cressida fluctuates throughout between the
dignity of Chaucer's heroine on the one hand and the indignity and degradation of Boccaccio's and Henryson's on
the other. During their love scenes, Cressida reveals a heart
warm enough to make romantic protestations and a head
cool enough to realize she protests too much. In her combination of romantic and anti-romantic attitudes, her ability to speak the language of both Troilus and Pandarus,
she recalls the witty heroines of the early comedies. But
whereas Rosalind or Portia have no difficulty reconciling
contrary attitudes, Cressida is divided by them; hence her
recourse to the imagery of the moralities. In the scene of
their separation, Troilus adopts her terms:

Troilus. But I can tell that in each grace of these [Greeks]
   There lurks a still and dumb-discoursive devil
   That tempts most cunningly. But be not tempted.
Cressida. Do you think I will?
Troilus. No!
   But something may be done that we will not;

And sometimes we are devils to ourselves
When we will tempt the frailty of our powers,
Presuming on their changeful potency.

(iv.iv.89-97)

When the temptation scene he imagines is realized outside Calchas's tent, Cressida proves to be neither the personification of faith-in-love Troilus would have her nor the personification of lechery he believes he beholds, but the fallible figure in between. In the world of the morality play proper, Cressida's infidelity and Troilus's desperation would eventually be repaired. But in the world of this play, the model of morality-romance, like that of chivalric-romance, turns out to be misapplied.

The ability to see "Helen's beauty in a brow of Egypt" is in Shakespeare's early comedies always harmless and usually vindicated. The lovers of those plays may exert their romantic imaginations on the wrong object, as Orsino does on Olivia and Romeo does on Rosalind, but sooner or later their worlds yield up the right one. The dual setting characteristic of Shakespearean comedy insures an objective correlative for the imagination's highest flights, a local habitation where the greeting of the spirit with its object can take place. However muddled Bottom's description of his dream, its content was real and the passage in St. Paul on which it is based not ill-chosen. But the not-impossible-she Troilus describes is in fact impossible within the world of his play, unseconded as it is by any superior reality:

O that I thought it could be in a woman—
As, if it can, I will presume in you—

To feed for aye her lamp and flames of love;
To keep her constancy in plight and youth,
Outliving beauty's outward, with a mind
That doth renew swifter than blood decays.

(III.ii.159-64)

Attainable as this ideal will again become in Cleopatra's Egypt, it is doomed to destruction, along with everything else, in Cressida's Troy. It is a critical, if often overlooked, feature of *Troilus* and the problem comedies that they contain no fully realized second world where the romantic imagination has room to maneuver, is free to create constructs that rival and rehabilitate the first.

Shakespearean comedy and romance typically moves from a world in which no one is really or fully himself (dukes are usurpers, brothers are unkind, lovers are in love with love or with the wrong person, fathers are not fatherly) to a world in which everyone, or almost everyone, regains his lost integrity and society its pristine structure. In Renaissance Christian terms, this movement is often portrayed as an emergence from a lower or fallen order of nature, human and external, into a higher order of nature and is often accomplished through the exertions of a figure both powerful and virtuous. Prospero is the best example, but most of the comedies and romances contain a "stage-manager" or *architectus* figure.[4] Troilus projected just

---

[4] Northrop Frye coins the term *architectus* (with some help from Plautus) and discusses his role in the action of comedy in *Anatomy of Criticism*, pp. 173-74. In the less naturalized and well-built action of romance, usually resolved by marvellous means, a term such as *magus* might be more appropriate. The chief Virtue performs such a role in morality-romance.

such a movement at the outset of his play and entrusted its management to Pandarus. It is hard to imagine a less promising piece of casting, a more "doubtful hope," than Pandarus, who lacks all the virtue and authority the role demands. (Ulysses, the would-be *architectus* of the war-plot, is similarly ineffective.) The dramatic movement of *Troilus* diverges from that of a romance like *The Tempest*, where the stage-manager Prospero can transmute flesh and blood into "something rich and strange," where Ferdinand can say convincingly that "the strong'st suggestion / Our worser genius can, shall never melt / Mine honour into lust," and Gonzalo can claim that "all of us [found] ourselves / When no man was his own" and not be far wrong. But Prospero's island lies a long way from Troy, where men and women prove devils to themselves, love collapses into lust, honor into "spleen," and in the portentous words of Ulysses, "will into appetite."

The movement from a lower to a higher nature, achieved in *The Tempest* and abortive in *Troilus*, is even more clearly presented in the allegories of Spenser's *Faerie Queene* and Milton's *Comus*. Comus bases his appeal, like the Renaissance lyrists of seduction who lie behind him, on nature as a fallen order, while the Lady rebuts from nature as a "superior power." His version of humanity would most naturally express itself in sensual and sensuous abandonment; hers through spiritual discipline, so that what seems negation to him—"the lean and sallow Abstinence"—is affirmation to her—"the Sun-clad power of Chastity." Like its chief models, *The Faerie Queene* and *The Tempest*, *Comus* proceeds by pitting images of higher nature against their degraded counterparts: the barbarous dissonance of Comus's drunken crew gives way before the "Divine enchanting ravishment" of the Lady's and Sabrina's songs; the charms of Comus's black magic yield to the charms of "divine philosophy" and the white magic of the Attendant Spirit and Sabrina. When Sir Guyon, in the second book of *The Faerie Queene* breaks the staff of the bad Genius in the Bower of Bliss, and the Palmer (who serves as Guyon's good Genius throughout) waves his more potent staff, the men Acrasia has transformed into beasts regain their proper shapes. All are pleased to be human again except for one Grille, who "Repined greatly, and did him miscall, / That had from hoggish forme him brought to naturall." (*FQ*,ii.xii.86) Grille corresponds to those characters in Shakespeare's comedies and romances who resist change when the logic of romance demands it and who remain outside the magic circle of raised humanity at the end—Shylock, Malvolio, Antonio, among others. For humanist romance is not so naive as to presume everyone redeemable or even educable: "Let Grille be Grille and have his hoggish minde," as Spenser puts it. If we imagine somewhat different versions of Spenser's allegory of temperance and Milton's masque, versions in which several Grilles resent and resist the reformation imposed on them and the protagonist himself is more like Grille, or the charms of the Palmer and Sabrina fail to work, we would have the Spenserian and Miltonic equivalents of Shakespeare's problem comedies.

All's Well and *Measure for Measure* open onto degenerate worlds, societies fallen on evil days. When Duke Vincentio looks around his Vienna after years of loose law enforcement, he finds "that there is so great a fever on goodness that the dissolution of it must cure it." (III.ii.217) To legislate lechery out of existence now it would be necessary, according to no less an authority than Pompey, "to geld and splay all the youth of the city" (II.i.227), and Lucio corroborates that "it is well allied . . . and impossible to extirp . . . till eating and drinking be put down." (III.ii.97-9) In the delinquent duchy of Vienna, lust is the great leveller; it afflicts low and high, libertine and puritan alike. When the "precise" and repressive Angelo discovers he is no different from the Claudio he condemns, he too must give his "sensual race the rein" and resort to the argument of Comus:

> Be that you are,
> That is, a woman; if you be more, you're none.
> If you be one—as you are well express'd
> By all external warrants—show it now.
>
> (II.iv.133-5)

It is precisely because Isabella knows of the "natural guiltiness" Angelo has just discovered that she asks for an even "more strict restraint" on the already restrictive sisterhood of nuns she is about to enter. Although the claims of lower nature are more peremptory in *Measure for Measure* than *All's Well*, the status of sexual desire is in the worlds of both plays the index of moral and social degradation.

When Parolles expostulates with Helena in the opening scene, it is almost as if the palace of Rossillion were Ludlow castle and we were listening to a prosy and down-at-heels Comus:

It is not politic in the commonwealth of nature to preserve virginity. Loss of virginity is rational increase,
and there was never virgin got till virginity was first
lost. . . . 'Tis against the rule of nature.

(1.i.123-34)

Were it only Parolles, "a very tainted fellow," who expressed and followed this program, all would indeed be
well once he is discredited; but Bertram arrives at Comus's
position independently:

> In your fine frame hath love no quality?
> If the quick fire of youth light not your mind
> You are no maiden, but a monument. . . .
> > Stand no more off,
> But give thyself unto my sick desires,
> Who then recover.   (iv.ii.4-36)

Throughout his attempted seduction of Diana, Bertram
casts himself in the role of courtly lover pining away for
love, much as Troilus had done before him. But Bertram's
terms, even more than Troilus's, conspire against him to
betray desires not romantic but diseased. The arrogant Bertram and the braggart Parolles are poor replacements for
an older aristocracy of honor and virtue, whose passing is
lamented by the ailing King of France. The "commonwealth of nature," in both *Measure for Measure* and *All's
Well*, has deteriorated beyond the power of law or medicine to rehabilitate.

The degraded worlds of the problem comedies, whatever they may say about Shakespeare's state of mind or
the spirit of the age, are primarily a function of their ro-

mantic form, which traditionally begins in adversity. Adversity so extreme and deep-seated, however, does make the task facing the *architecti* of these plays an unusually formidable one. Yet the art Helena employs to cure the King of France seems equal to the challenge—"There's something in't / More than my father's skill" (i.iii.237-8) —and its success is described in the language of Christian miracle:

Lafew. A showing of a heavenly effect in an earthly
    actor. . . . [The] very hand of heaven.
Parolles. Ay; so I say.
Lafew. In a most weak—
Parolles. And debile minister; great power, great
    transcendence. (ii.iii.18-36)

In the medieval religious drama such an act would indeed have been the very hand of heaven, for it would have been performed on stage by Mary or Christ, something of whose nature and function are resurrected here in Helena.[5] But Helena is preeminently human, and the choric commentary that surrounds her miraculous act stresses her human frailty as much as her superhuman power, her womanly appeal— in bringing her to the King, Lafew likens himself, after a series of bawdy puns, to Pandarus—as much as the sun-

---

[5] See R. G. Hunter, *Shakespeare and the Comedy of Forgiveness* (New York, 1965), pp. 106-31, 204-26, for excellent readings of *All's Well* and *Measure* against the background of the morality play. My treatment of these plays owes much to his, but he generally ignores the deliberate irony with which Shakespeare employs his medieval models in them. The problem comedies, in my view, are not so much about forgiveness as about the inadequacy of forgiveness.

clad power of chastity that she, like the Lady of *Comus*, embodies. By staging a scene right out of the miracle play, Helena (and the audience as well) expects her design to end like that of the miracle play, that is, in the eternal bliss of union with her lord, or at least happily ever after. But even though she brings off her miracle, cures the King, and secures Bertram for her husband, her plan fails of its intent. For human nature being what it is in this play, Bertram may see the better—the "blessed spirit" that "doth speak / His powerful sound within an organ weak" (ii.i.174-5)—but he follows the worse and wants no part of the wife he should by all rights embrace.

Similarly in *Measure for Measure*, Isabella is entreated to plead for her brother's life, for as Lucio puts it, "All hope is gone / Unless you have the grace by your fair prayer / To soften Angelo" (i.iv.68-70). She proceeds to do so, using all the "prosperous art" (i.ii.174) at her command (just as Helena employs her "inspired merit" to recover the King), and her arguments mount to this climax:

> Why, all the souls that were, were forfeit once,
> And He that might the vantage best have took
> Found out the remedy. How would you be
> If He, which is the top of judgement, should
> But judge you as you are? O, think on that,
> And mercy then will breathe within your lips,
> Like man new made.   (ii.ii.73-9)

Now it is Isabella who takes on a recognizably medieval role, that of Mercy, who pleads to save the figure of Hu-

manum Genus in the morality play, after Justice has argued for his eternal damnation—a role the Countess of
Rossillion also assigns to Helena:

> He [Bertram] cannot thrive,
> Unless her prayers, whom heaven delights to hear
> And loves to grant, reprieve him from the wrath
> Of greatest justice.   (III.iv.26-9)

In *Measure for Measure*, Escalus further reminds us of
this dimension of the play when he says "I have found
[Angelo] so severe, that he hath forced me to tell him he
is indeed Justice." (III.ii.246-8) Mercy wins her case in
the moralities by appealing, like Isabella, to the compelling
precedent of Christ's atonement. But Isabella, unlike her
predecessor, succeeds in "softening" Angelo by her "fair
prayer" only in the sense of arousing his lust, his "sensual
race" and not in the expected sense of awakening his
mercy. Shakespeare recreates these scenes from the drama
of Christian redemption only to have them misfire within
All's Well and *Measure for Measure*.

To the extent that these scenes conjure up an older (one
is tempted to say, simpler and more innocent) dramatic
world, they hold no solutions for the more problematic
worlds in which they now occur. By virtue of their roles
at this point in their plays, both heroines cannot help but
appear what Lucio terms "a thing enskied and sainted"
(I.iv.34) occupying a pedestal far above common humanity—the last place either really wants to be. Lafew expressly disclaims such a role when Parolles attempts to
cast him into it:

Parolles. It lies in you, my lord, to bring me in some
grace, for you did bring me out.

Lafew. Out upon thee, knave! dost thou put upon me at
once both the office of God and the devil? One brings
thee in Grace and the others brings thee out.

(v.ii.43-7)

When the recovered King begins to play God to Bertram's
Humanum Genus one cannot help but feel, with Helena
herself, some sympathy for Bertram, for who wants to be
morally pressured into marrying someone, particularly
a saint? Ironically, the medieval roles performed by Helena and Isabella work to widen rather than heal the divi-
sions between body and spirit, nature and grace that make
the worlds of these plays so unhealthy. Isabella's speeches
to Angelo, her *ars rhetorica*, serve to polarize humanity
into saints and sinners, sheep and goats—a tendency inherent in the medieval religious drama. The *contemptus
mundi* she so passionately expounds, while appropriate to
the morality play, is inappropriate to the secular drama
she appears in now:

> No ceremony that to great ones longs,
> Not the king's crown nor the deputed sword,
> The marshal's truncheon, nor the judge's robe,
> Become them with one half so good a grace
> As mercy does. (ii.ii.59-63)

> Hark, how I'll bribe you . . . .
> Not with fond sickles of the tested gold,
> Or stones, whose rate are either rich or poor
> As fancy values them: but with true prayers,

That shall be up at heaven and enter there
Ere sunrise: Prayers from preserved souls,
From fasting maids, whose minds are dedicate
To nothing temporal.   (ii.ii.150-56)

Her prosperous art, with its otherworldly tenor, is decidedly not what is needed in the ailing world of the play.
The art which is needed in both *All's Well* and *Measure
for Measure* is this-worldly and human rather than otherworldly and divine, an art that works to reconcile the
merely natural with the properly supernatural in human
nature, not to lock up the former and cloister away the
latter. The ideal toward which these plays move is not
chastity, the personal ideal of Isabella, and of Diana in
All's Well, but "married chastity,"[6] the personal and social
ideal later embodied by Imogen in *Cymbeline*, whose bed-
chamber is adorned with images of Cleopatra and "Chaste
Dian" emblematic of the two sides of her nature, of the
moral oxymoron of married chastity itself.

If Isabella advocates the absolute divorce of the orders
of nature and grace in human life, Helena and the Duke
seek a closer communion between them, and the art they
finally employ is directed to that end. Rather than ministering to the sick human will from without or from above
(as the King, Isabella, and Angelo try variously and un-
successfully to do) Helena and the Duke set about curing
it from within. Though their end is different from that of
Hamlet—reform rather than revenge—the means they
adopt is very similar: to hold a mirror up to degraded

[6] The concept of "married chastity" is of course central to the third
and fourth books of *The Faerie Queene*, where its chief exemplar is
Amoret, but the term itself comes from "The Phoenix and the Turtle."

human nature, show it its own sinfulness, and thereby pre-cipitate a kind of self-discovery. Like "The Mousetrap" in *Hamlet*, the bed trick is staged in these plays as a form of shock treatment. (We might recall that after the play-within-a-play Claudius reveals in soliloquy his detestation of his own crimes almost to the point of repenting them— not at all what Hamlet had intended.) It may seem per-verse to talk of the bed trick in the same breath with "The Mousetrap" as an endeavor of art, but that is how its prac-titioners think of it:

> Why then tonight
> Let us assay our plot; which, if it speed,
> Is wicked meaning in a lawful deed,
> And lawful meaning in a lawful act,
> Where both not sin, and yet a sinful fact.
> (*All's Well*, iii.vii.43-7)

> He [Angelo] is your husband on a pre-contract:
> To bring you thus together 'tis no sin,
> Sith that the justice of your title to him
> Doth flourish the deceit.
> (*M. for M.*, iv.i.72-5)

The Duke stresses not only the legal justification of the bed trick but its poetic justice. Both Angelo, who insists throughout on a merciless legalism, and Bertram, who lays down seemingly impossible conditions for accepting Helena as his wife, are outwitted on their own terms. When Helena returns from supposed death wearing her husband's ring and carrying his child, she has in effect per-formed another miracle, the secular equivalent of her earlier recovery of the King. Not only is Angelo guilty of violating, like Claudio, the letter of the law by consummating his own "pre-contract" but the spirit as well, unlike Claudio, by committing adultery in his heart—a concept, we might recall, that evokes the same Scriptural context as the title of the play. The incredible fact that a man can mistake in bed the woman he detests for the woman he desires is not the difficulty but the point of the bed trick, a commentary on the reductiveness of lust in action which not even characters as self-deluded as Bertram and Angelo can misread. The bed trick is employed in these plays not as Shakespeare's way out of the dramatic dilemma he has gotten himself into, but as Helena's and the Duke's way of making Bertram and Angelo confront the moral dilemma they have gotten themselves into.

Helena and the Duke manage to avoid the sexual betrayal of *Troilus* through a *coup de théâtre* designed to restore the social integrity of their world and the personal identity of its inhabitants. But because the "bed trickery" they employ reflects—and reflects upon—the moral ambivalence at the very core of these plays, it is no mere *coup de théâtre* in the way the Friar's benign deception in *Much Ado* (employed to bring round another Claudio) is. Yet the art of Helena and the Duke seems less than wholly "prosperous," itself slightly tainted and imperfectly effective, compared to the "prosperous and artificial feat" (*Per.*, v.i.72) of Marina, Paulina, and especially Prospero in the romances to come. Part of the triumph of Prospero's art consists in his express recognition of its limits, in his acknowledgment of the resistance life offers to being transmuted into art at all, and especially into romance. A similar resistance, expressed not only through Bertram and Angelo but through Parolles, Lucio, and most of the low-life characters as well, makes itself felt in these plays (particularly in their long and painful recognition scenes) but it goes curiously unacknowledged by the stage managers themselves. Helena and especially the Duke seem blithely unaware that the self-discoveries they have precipitated represent only half the struggle toward self-recovery. "Is it possible he should know what he is," comments one of the captains present during Parolles' exposure, "and be that he is?" (iv.i.44-5). The answer, as the play goes on to show, is that it is only too possible, and we may wonder whether the same is not true for the principals as well. Bertram and Angelo doubtless come to discover of themselves, as a result of the humanist endeavors of Helena and the Duke, what others already know: "As we are ourselves, what things we are . . . ! Merely our own traitors." (*All's Well*, iv.iii.18-19) But that they are ripe for the self-recovery celebrated at the end of *The Tempest* is something that we, like Mariana, can only take on faith:

> They say best men are moulded out of faults,
> And, for the most, become much more the better
> For being a little bad.   (v.i.437-9)

Her tentativeness suggests there is good reason to doubt. For the problem comedies, unlike the romances, give little time on stage to the "heart sorrow" that alone signals the reform of the heart. Even Duke Vincentio, though described as "One that, above all other strifes, contended especially to know himself" (iii.ii.226-7), is never shown, as Prospero is shown, engaged in the strife for self-knowledge he demands of Angelo. Nor is the Duke aware, as Prospero is aware, of the limits of his role. In his zeal for poetic justice and romance endings, he marries off everyone, including himself, and by coupling the incorrigible Lucio with "a punk," makes a mockery of the institution. (Similarly in *All's Well*, the King is bent on doing the same for Diana at the end as he did for Helena at the beginning —we can only hope with happier results.) Sick desire is sacramentalized at the end of these plays, for better or worse, but hardly cured. Therein the patient must minister to himself.

These are disquieting conclusions to be sure, but our disquietude arises, I submit, not from the design *of* the plays but from the designs *within* the plays. One of the common errors in interpretation of the problem comedies has been to blur this distinction: "None of the plays is wholly satisfactory from a formal point of view . . . because of the working out of a serious moral problem in an action built of improbable device and lucky coincidence. The result is . . . to make the solutions seem trivial or forced."[7] The bed trick raises as many problems as it solves; the cure partakes too much of the disease; in sum, the designs of Helena and the King, of Isabella and the Duke, are unsatisfactory. The design of Shakespeare reveals that they are so. The playwright is no more identical with his stage managers, however sympathetic, than the play is equal to the sum of its plots. We are used to distinguishing in prose fiction between the novelist and the narrator whose judgment is not always to be accepted at face value. The dramatic equivalent of the unreliable nar-

[7] Madeleine Doran, *Endeavors of Art* (Madison, 1954), pp. 366-67.

rator is the fallible *architectus*, the figure we encounter in each of the problem plays and even to a lesser degree in *The Tempest*. The human capacity for projecting high designs and the equally human incapacity to realize them are combined in the same figure. The problem facing Helena, radically formulated near the beginning of her play, "That labouring art can never ransom nature / From her inaidable estate" (ii.i.116-18) is the problem facing all romancers. Helena and Vincentio gloss over that fundamental recalcitrance of life to the designs of art, and in so doing become bad romancers. For the first time in his career as a romancer Shakespeare faces that recalcitrance head on, and we catch him in the act of realizing that when romance comes too easily or overlooks too much, it is not worth having. The problem plays stand midway between the romantic comedies and the romances in more than a chronological sense. The resistance they offer to the wishes of the romantic imagination is greater than anything in the early comedies and comparable to much in the final romances; to increase it further is to enter the world of tragedy. At the same time they lack figures of vision and resourcefulness adequate to overcome that resistance; to provide them is to enter the world of the last plays.

CHAPTER 4

Baconian Tragedy

Woe to him who seeks to please rather than to appall.

—Melville

SHAKESPEAREAN comedy and romance generally moves toward the marriage of its principal characters; Shakespearean tragedy, toward their death. It is a mistake, however, on this basis to expect from his plays a generic purity and singlemindedness which few of them in fact possess. I do not mean simply that Shakespeare mingles kings and clowns, that *Lear* has its Fool and *Macbeth* its Porter (much to the chagrin of a neoclassicist like Voltaire) but that the world of a given play will often promise or threaten an outcome very different from the one it finally provides. Or Shakespeare may endow certain characters with a critical awareness of the kind of play they are in and with the power to affect its outcome by the attitudes they proceed to adopt. Two notable exceptions to the principle stated above are *Troilus and Cressida*, whose ending denies the fulfillment of either marriage or death by avoiding both alike, and *Antony and Cleopatra*, at the end of which marriage and death coincide in the minds of the protagonists: "Husband, I come." Both *Troilus* and *Antony* are set in classical antiquity; but the universe of the later work is made to vibrate with a prophetic Christianity and to hold out the hope of a posthumous reunion, so persistently do the lovers cling to their vision of themselves. Fortune tyrannizes over both actions, but whereas Cressida submits to the turning wheel, Cleopatra claims to transcend it. It is Caesar whom she scorns as "Fortune's knave." At the center of both plays is an inconstant woman; but in Cleopatra "vilest things become themselves," and we are forced to see grace in her frailty. It is as if Antony and Cleopatra had contemplated the fortunes of Troilus and Cressida and determined to avoid, by a mutual act of will, the futility of a repeat performance. *Troilus* may be Shakespeare's darkest comedy, but *Antony* is certainly his brightest tragedy. "For a tragedy," A. C. Bradley observed, "it is not painful," certainly not when compared with "the famous four."[1] Within the development of Shakespeare's career, *Antony* is the Roman archway dividing the mature tragedies from the final romances; it looks back onto one world and forward onto another and enjoys the best of both.

That Shakespeare's romances are imaginatively continuous as well as chronologically contiguous with his tragedies, although it remains to be adequately demonstrated, is now widely accepted. The corollary of such a view is that any of the tragedies should be more or less rich in romance elements, not only the plays at the end of the "tragic period" but those at the beginning. *Hamlet*, though identified in the popular mind with grinning skulls, dark soliloquies, and the quintessence of tragedy, implies at many points the possibilities of romance, and in so doing, sets the pattern for the tragedies to come. As inwardly rotten as the state of Denmark is soon revealed to be, there

[1] *Oxford Lectures on Poetry* (Bloomington, 1961), p. 282.

are moments when it might occur to someone seeing the play for the first time that all may yet be well. After the ghost's disclosure or the successful theatrical or the air-clearing harangue with his mother, Hamlet thinks as much himself. But it is with the final act that circumstances, which until now have gone from bad to worse, seem suddenly to take a turn for the better. The Hamlet who returns from two close calls with death on the way to England seems better qualified, morally and psychologically, to set right his disjointed world than the Hamlet of previous acts, seems closer both to the perfect courtier of Ophelia's description and to the chivalric warrior epitomized in his father, romantic ideals from which Hamlet, along with the rest of the Danish nobility, had fallen off.

Most of us would agree that the Hamlet of the last act knows himself better, that he returns from his perilous voyage, like a later romantic voyager, a sadder but wiser man, than the Hamlet of the first act. The matter of change in the tragic hero is a difficult one, but a matter of some importance to our understanding not only of Hamlet but of all the later plays, and I believe it has been generally misconstrued. Maynard Mack has pointed out as a recurrent feature of Shakespeare's tragic construction that the hero undertakes a journey prior to the crisis of the action, and when we next see him he appears to us to have changed.[2] In some of the tragedies, *Hamlet* and *King Lear* among them, the hero travels not merely to a different place but into a different imaginative environment, almost

[2] "The Jacobean Shakespeare: Some Observations on the Construction of the Tragedies," *Stratford-upon-Avon Studies 1*, edd. John Russell Brown and Bernard Harris (London, 1960).

into another dramatic mode, one that signals or reflects his inward reassessment and regrouping. Lear's heath and Hamlet's sea world correspond within their tragedies to the "green" or "golden" worlds of the earlier romantic comedies—the wood outside Athens, Arden, Belmont—where certain crucial transformations are set. Once the regenerative properties of Arden have been established, it seems that practically all a character has to do in *As You Like It* is blunder into the forest in order to be totally reformed. The interim settings of *Hamlet* and *Lear* also look forward to the radical shifts of scene in the final romances (the Welsh hills, pastoral Bohemia, Prospero's island) where the rising phase of a much longer action begins.

When we see Hamlet after his return, he not only looks different, I would suggest, but *sounds* different as well:

> Up from my cabin,
> My sea-gown scarfed about me, in the dark
> Groped I to find out them, had my desire,
> Fingered their packet, and in fine withdrew
> To mine own room again, making so bold,
> My fears forgetting manners, to unseal
> Their grand commission.   (v.ii.12-18)

T. S. Eliot has called attention to this passage as an example of Shakespeare's "quite mature" versification, and in its colloquialism, frequent enjambement, and metrical freedom it closely approaches the speech-music which characterizes the last romances. This liberation of the verse also reflects a new freedom in the sea world into which Hamlet voyages, away from the claustrophobic closeness of the Denmark Hamlet deems a prison, and above all, a new freedom to act. The old Hamlet, straitjacketed by overly precise reflection, dies at sea, and a new Hamlet, one who acts rashly but effectively, is born—or rather reborn, for we know from Gertrude and Ophelia that this is the man Hamlet used to be, a "do-er" before he became a mere actor. Into this sea world where anything can happen (for like the forests of the romantic comedies it is a world released to possibility, freed from the chain of causality and the demands of verisimilitude) Hamlet sails, when—lo and behold!—a pirate ship appears on the horizon, giving him yet another opportunity for rash and soldierly action. He boards it and finds himself, like Valentine in the forest of *Two Gentlemen of Verona*, among a band of "thieves of mercy" (iv.vi.21). The whole episode is right out of the *Aethiopica* or *Apollonius of Tyre* or the *Ephesiaca*, that is, right out of the kind of romance material Shakespeare reworked for the romantic comedies and last plays.

But given the similarities between this phase of the tragic action and that of his romantic plays, the differences are even more telling. What Shakespeare has done in *Hamlet* (and it is a technique he will exploit still more relentlessly in *Lear*) is to introduce the conventions, and thereby raise the expectations, of romance at a crucial point only to dash them with a vengeance a moment later. Just when we have reason to believe all may yet turn out for the best, things are revealed to be worse than ever. Edmund is defeated by his brother in single combat and with his dying breath resolves to do "some good. . . . Despite of mine own nature." His last-minute romantic reformation raises our hopes; then they are dashed once and for all when Lear enters with Cordelia in his arms. It is as though Shakespeare invokes conventions of romance at such a point in order to repudiate them, to expose their inadequacy or outmodedness within the world of tragic experience and thereby bring home the essential quality of that experience. Hamlet arrives safely home after his "hairbreadth scape" from death with a new power of action and self-knowledge just in time to witness the funeral of Ophelia, whom he now knows he loved, but knows too late. On the way to victory in his duel with Laertes (and it might momentarily seem in his larger duel with Claudius) he learns that one sword is unbated and envenomed, that he is already a dead man, and victory turns into defeat. The situation in *Hamlet* has deteriorated too far to be repaired. Shakespeare seems to say there will be no wishful deliverances from a world which remains "harsh," in *Lear* "tough," to the bitter end, harsher and tougher than anyone had previously imagined.

It is only within so harshly conditioned a universe that the nature and extent of change in the tragic hero can be understood. It is all too easy in our naive trust that, as Tennyson put it, "somehow good / Will be the final goal of ill," that wisdom, if nothing else, must issue from suffering, to overstress the purgative and redemptive aspect of Shakespearean tragedy. Perhaps it is not too far from the truth to say that comparatively little has been written on the romances, because so much of what properly applies to them has been misapplied to the tragedies. Bradley, for example, stopped himself just short of retitling the greatest of them "The Redemption of King Lear." Of Hamlet in the last act we may say that the sometime scourge of God now conceives of himself more temperately as a humble pawn of providence. Yet we do not know whether heaven is really ordinant, nor whether flights of angels sing Hamlet to his rest, nor whether the "felicity" he speaks of to Horatio consists in some form of immortality or the silence of the grave. Although his renewed competence to act is not in doubt (we even learn, as Hamlet awaits the king's invitation to the duel, that he has resumed his long-neglected "custom of exercises") it returns only after it is too late to do much good. In his few brief exchanges with his mother, I think we may fairly detect, for whatever it is worth, a change from his behavior toward her during "The Mousetrap," a new courtesy and concern.

But these are the only outward signs of inward change that, as far as I can tell, Shakespeare has definitely provided—just enough to make us realize how incomplete Hamlet's change has been. If there are others, they are so elusive or equivocal that we are left, not with restored faith in man's capacity to remake himself, but with a new awareness of the iron limitations on that capacity: "Virtue cannot so inoculate our old stock but we shall relish of it." Maynard Mack, among others, believes that the burial of Ophelia "tears from him a final cry of passion" and "the striking contrast between his behavior and Laertes's reveals how deeply he has changed."[3] I would

---

[3] "The World of *Hamlet*," *Yale Review*, XLI (1952), 522. I stress my differences with Mack on this particular point and the larger view

suggest that this scene in fact reveals the opposite: how in-completely Hamlet has changed. For Shakespeare has his tragic heroes, at crucial moments in their closing scenes, relapse into their former selves. Lear reveals in the last act a capacity for self-deception—"This feather stirs; she lives!"—and rash judgment—"A plague upon you, mur-derers, traitors all!"—reminiscent of that which character-ized him in the first. Are not Hamlet's graveside antics "a trick of the old rage," a momentary reversion to his earlier self-righteous posturing and self-indulgent play acting? Does he not tear whatever passion he now feels to tatters? Change not only comes too little and too late, but when it does come it is not abiding. After having dealt so roughly in *Hamlet* with the humanist vision of a universe ulti-mately benevolent and a human spirit infinitely redeem-able (the vision which informs his romantic plays), Shake-speare cannot fall back on it with much assurance. Hamlet can no more make amends for his criminal insanity toward the family of Polonius than Claudius can repent of his crimes. Leontes and Alonzo will be able to do both.

The complementary principles of Shakespearean com-edy and romance on the one hand and tragedy on the other were advanced during Shakespeare's lifetime, the former by Sir Philip Sidney and the latter by Sir Francis Bacon. While rehearsing many of the same Renaissance common-places as Sidney, Bacon assigns so different a value to the key concepts of "pleasure," "nature," and "making" as to call the value and validity of poetry itself into question:

---

of the tragedies it reflects, only because his statement of that view seems to me to crystallize the issues at stake better than any other.

Poesy is a part of learning in measure of words for the most part restrained, but in all other points extremely licensed, and doth truly refer to the Imagination; which, being not tied to the laws of matter, may at pleasure join that which nature hath severed, and sever that which nature hath joined, and so make unlawful matches and divorces of things. . . . Poetry is . . . one of the principal portions of learning, and is nothing else but Feigned History, which may be styled as well in prose as in verse.

The use of this Feigned History hath been to give some shadow of satisfaction to the mind of man in those points wherein the nature of things doth deny it; the world being in proportion inferior to the soul; by reason whereof there is agreeable to the spirit of man a more ample greatness, a more exact goodness, and a more absolute variety, than can be found in the nature of things. Therefore, because the acts or events of true history have not that magnitude which satisfieth the mind of man, poesy feigneth acts and events greater and more heroical; because true history propoundeth the successes and issues of actions not so agreeable to the merits of virtue and vice, therefore poesy feigns them more just in retribution, and more according to revealed providence; because true history representeth actions and events more ordinary and less interchanged, therefore poesy endueth them with more rareness, and more unexpected and alternative variations. So as it appeareth that poesy serveth and conferreth to magnanimity, morality, and to delectation. And therefore it was ever thought to have some participation of divineness, because it doth raise and erect the mind, by submitting the shews of things to the desires of the mind; whereas reason doth buckle and bow the mind unto the nature of things.

Bacon warns us elsewhere that poetry is "as a dream of learning," that "it is not good to stay too long in the theatre," and that "as for poesy, it is rather a pleasure or play of the imagination, than a work or duty thereof." And most characteristically of all, he writes in the plan to *The Great Instauration*: "And all depends on keeping the eye steadily fixed upon the facts of nature and so receiving their images simply as they are. For God forbid that we should give out a dream of our own imagination for a pattern of the world."[4] Shelley maintained that "Lord Bacon was a poet," even though Bacon conceived of himself as a philosopher and historian. His fascination with parables in *The Wisdom of the Ancients*, his unfinished science-fiction; *The New Atlantis*, and his great labor of effective mythmaking, *The Advancement of Learning*, may all conspire against him to confirm Shelley's pronouncement that he is a poet in spite of himself. He is certainly a principal legislator of the modern world, if not an unacknowledged one. But if Bacon is a poet, he is one who was inclined to write off poetry as dream and wish fulfillment.

Yet not all forms of poetry are equally vulnerable to a criticism springing from Baconian premises. If Shakespeare's romantic comedies are failures or frivolities by

---

[4] Quotations from Bacon, in order, are to *Selected Writings of Francis Bacon*, ed. Hugh G. Dick (Modern Library, New York, 1955), pp. 243-4, 247, 284, 451, and *The Works of Francis Bacon*, ed. James Spedding, et al. (London, 1874), VIII, 470.

Baconian standards, Ben Jonson's satiric comedies must be deemed successes. Jonson greatly admired Bacon personally, and I suspect Bacon would have admired Jonson's plays, for Jonson's principles and practice illustrate a mimetic empiricism that accords well with the scientific empiricism of Bacon. "The true Artificer," writes Jonson, "will not run away from nature, as hee were afraid of her, or depart from life and the likeness of Truth."[5] Jonson was in fact abused in his own time as "a meere Empyrick, one that getts what he hath by observation, and makes onely nature privy to what he endites" and as "so slow an Inventor, that he were better betake himselfe to his old trade of Bricklaying; a bould whorson, as confident now in making of a booke, as he was in times past in laying of a brick."[6] Jonson is of course no *mere* empiric, for in literature as well as science pure observation is as impossible as invention is necessary. Yet the jibe, for all its wantonness, contains a grain—and no more than a grain—of truth. However tirelessly Jonson insists on the primacy of holding the mirror up to nature, he is no less proud of his skill at constructing comic plots in imitation of classical models. To this extent he is like a good bricklayer, conforming his artifact to a regular, prior, and extrinsic plan—a plan that, whatever relation it bears to nature, certainly derives from the art of new comedy. The classic distinction between "bitter" Jonsonian and "sweet" Shakespearean comedy doubtless suggests a basic temperamental difference between the two

[5] "Timber, or Discoveries" in *Critical Essays of the Seventeenth Century*, ed. Joel E. Spingarn (Oxford, 1908), I, 23.

[6] *The Return from Parnassus*, Part Two, I.i.294-9. *The Three Parnassus Plays*, ed. J. B. Leishman (London, 1949), p. 244.

men, but it also reflects the different comic traditions that each exploited and extended through his work.

The Jonsonian tradition of new comedy handed down from classical Rome to Renaissance Italy might be termed, to adopt a phrase from *Epicoene*, "comedy of affliction"; the Shakespearean tradition has its real beginning in the drama of the medieval church. I have called it comedy of amendment, or to adapt a key word from *As You Like It*, comedy of atonement. To atone, as Hymen reminds us, means to become at one, which describes the typical movement of character and society in Shakespeare's comic plots. In his one reworking of a classical comedy, not only are the characters of *The Comedy of Errors* morally upgraded far above their Plautine prototypes in the first place, but the society of Shakespeare's play is a much healthier one by the end than it was at the beginning—something that cannot be said for the *Menaechmi*. Although Jonson's comedies end more or less happily, their happiness consists more in the exposure of human wickedness than in the celebration of human goodness. When Shakespeare excludes one of his few rigid or "humorous" characters (Shylock, Jaques, Malvolio) from the concluding harmony, it works to lend credibility to his comic vision by implying that not quite everyone is capable of reform. Jonson never faces this problem, for rarely is anyone reformed in his plays.[7]

---

[7] There are a few exceptions, the most remarkable of which is the miser Sordido in *Every Man Out of His Humour*, "by wonder changed" (III.ii) after being saved from suicide. His "dishumouring" comes as quite a shock, an almost Shakespearean moment in a play built on un-Shakespearean premises. Though Jonson cites a precedent in Plautus for the scene, it also has many parallels in morality tradition. Jonson, in fact, often draws upon morality models, explicitly in *The*

Not even in what has been traditionally considered one of his "sweetest" comedies, *Epicoene*, is there any attempt to reform Morose. Once the "good" characters have tricked him into rewriting his will, he is dismissed with a few harsh words. In Jonson's dramatic world almost everyone remains as he was. Jonson thus creates, even in the act of writing comedy, the illusion that he has refused to submit "the shews of things to the desires of the mind," that he has kept his "eye steadily fixed upon the facts of nature," and that he is determined "not to invent fables and romances of worlds, but to look into, and dissect the nature of this real world."[8]

Shakespeare's problem comedies, if there is any truth in my view of them, represent a slight shift in the direction of Jonson. But it is in the great tragedies that Shakespeare goes well beyond even Jonson in mimetic empiricism. The last thing Shakespearean tragedy can be charged with is giving "some shadow of satisfaction to the mind of man in those points wherein the nature of things doth deny it." In fact, they have more often been charged with the opposite. Thomas Rymer was outraged by the absence of "poetical justice" (a phrase he coined) in *Othello* and

---

Devil Is an Ass and *The Staple of News*, just as Shakespeare does upon Roman comedy. The crucial difference is that Jonson adopts from the moralities the array of unchanging vicious types who surround the morality hero; Shakespeare, the redeemable hero himself. The other notable exception to my generalization about Jonson's characters is Justice Overdo in *Bartholomew Fair*, whose rigidity softens in the uncharacteristic festivity that concludes that play.

[8] Preface to *The Advancement of Learning*. Quoted in Basil Willey, *The Seventeenth Century Background* (New York, 1953), p. 33.

blasted its author for, among many other things, failing "to expose the Monster Iago, and after show the Divine Vengeance executed upon him."[9] Although Iago finally is exposed, the fact that his punishment is postponed until after the play and that he means to keep silent even then denies us even the small satisfaction of watching him suffer for his crime. It is the denial of any consolatory or compensatory justice that moved A. C. Bradley to call Othello's persecution and murder of Desdemona, "unless I mistake, the most nearly intolerable spectacle that Shakespeare offers us."[10] Of course there is no dearth of such moments in Shakespearean tragedy, and it is difficult to say which is the worst. Scarcely more tolerable than the scene that horrified Bradley is the murder of Macduff's family in *Macbeth*, a scene that germinates in Shakespeare's imagination from one casual sentence in Holinshed, or worse yet, Lear's final entrance with Cordelia, for which there is no precedent whatever in his sources. Shakespeare's working principle in the tragedies is to exclude nothing pitiable or terrifying that he finds in his historical sources and often to invent pitiable and terrifying material of his own.

Among the tragedies, *King Lear* has seemed to many the most scarifying of all. Dr. Johnson found "the extrusion of Gloucester's eye . . . an act too horrid to be endured in dramatic exhibition," and the death of Cordelia "in a just cause, contrary to the natural ideas of justice,

---

[9] "A Short View of Tragedy" in *Critical Essays of the Seventeenth Century*, ed. Spingarn, II, 254.

[10] *Shakespearean Tragedy* (New York, 1955), p. 147.

to the hope of the reader, and what is yet more strange, to the faith of the chronicles." Johnson is worth quoting at length:

> A play in which the wicked prosper and the virtuous miscarry may doubtless be good, because it is a just representation of the common events of human life; but since all reasonable beings naturally love justice, I cannot easily be persuaded that the observation of justice makes a play worse, or that if other excellencies are equal the audience will not always rise better pleased from the final triumph of persecuted virtue.
>
> In the present case the public has decided. Cordelia, from the time of Tate, has always retired with victory and felicity. And, if my sensations could add anything to the general suffrage, I might relate, I was many years ago so shocked by Cordelia's death that I know not whether I ever endured to read again the last scenes of the play till I undertook to revise them as an editor.[11]

Yet Bacon asserts that poetry feigns the issues of actions "more just in retribution, and more according to revealed providence" than history, which presents them "not so agreeable to the merits of virtue and vice." In the case of *King Lear* it is history that offers a Hollywood ending, which, to Johnson's bewilderment, Shakespeare rejects as too good to be true. The ending Shakespeare does provide, Johnson is in effect saying, is too true to be good.

As both Bacon and Johnson seem to be aware, poetic

---

[11] *Samuel Johnson on Shakespeare*, ed. W. K. Wimsatt, Jr. (New York, 1960), p. 98.

justice is the literary equivalent of theodicy; commitment
to the former reflects confidence in the latter. The characters of *King Lear* actively search for a theodicy, for some
sign or evidence of divine justice in their world, but the
ending of the play leads us to suspect that they search in
vain:

> If that the heavens do not their visible spirits
> Send quickly down to tame these vilde offences,
> It will come,
> Humanity must perforce prey on itself
> Like monsters of the deep.   (IV.ii.46-9)

> Think that the clearest Gods, who make them honours
> Of men's impossibilities, have preserved thee.
>   (IV.vi.73-4)

> The gods are just, and of our pleasant vices
> Make instruments to plague us.   (v.iii.170-71)

> Why should a dog, a horse, a rat have life
> And thou no breath at all?   (v.iii.306-7)

Most of the principals in *Lear* offer theories of the universe
they inhabit, and they divide more or less evenly into two
groups: the exponents of a universe essentially ordered
and just and the exponents of a universe manifestly lawless and amoral. These two groups correspond not only
to the "good" Lear-Cordelia-Gloucester-Edgar, and the
"bad" Goneril-Regan-Edmund, parties within the play but
also to the main schools of criticism on it: those who contend that the suffering presented in the play is somehow
redeemed or redemptive (and who generally admit some
sort of Christianity into its universe) and those who insist

on the gratuitousness and "absurdity" of its suffering (and often concomitantly on the paganness of its setting).[12]

The view which sees redemptive suffering in *Lear* (and which originates in Victorian optimism) especially needs to be retired—not on the fashionable but sentimental grounds that Dachau and Hiroshima have shown us the true meaning of Shakespeare's play, but on the grounds that the repudiation of optimistic world views is part of the very structure of Shakespeare's tragedies and central to their tragic effect. For difficult though it may be to bear in mind, as the words "tragic" and "tragedy" are applied to events in our world with depressing frequency, the "tragic universe" is properly speaking a fiction, as much an imaginative construct as the more recognizably fictive universe of romance. It is particularly easy to forget this in the case of *Lear*, owing perhaps to the fullness and richness of its world, and to discuss it as if it *were* the world we inhabit rather than a great imitation of it. One or the other of the views cited above might be justified if the play consisted of the story of Gloucester or the story of Lear alone, for each view fits one or the other plot but not both. The function of the subplot in *Lear* and its relation to the main plot have been long and widely misconstrued. It is

---

[12] My somewhat maverick contentions about *Lear* find some support in William R. Elton's study of the play's Renaissance theological content and context, *King Lear and the Gods* (San Marino, 1966). To the list of optimist, though not explicitly Christian, readers of Lear contained in his opening chapter, I would add the following: Maynard Mack, *King Lear in Our Time* (Berkeley, 1965), esp. pp. 83-117, and Paul A. Jorgenson, *Lear's Self-Discovery* (Berkeley, 1967). To his list of pessimist readers: Jan Kott, *Shakespeare Our Contemporary* (New York, 1964), pp. 127-68.

there, I would suggest, not primarily "to enact and express a further aspect of the Lear experience,"[13] but to enact and express an essentially different kind of experience from that of Lear.

Lear's initial belief in a firmly ordered and just universe is called into question by his experience and shaken to its very foundation. Gloucester and Edgar hold a similar view of things, but their experience, painful as it is, serves rather to confirm such a view and moves them to utter simplistic, even pietistic, sentences on divine justice. Even Gloucester's outcry on the wanton sadism of the gods is spoken out of that despair which precedes reformation and betrays an inverse sentimentality in which the tougher and finer nature of Lear never indulges. Unlike most critics of the play, I have never found Gloucester and Edgar very appealing—hardly more so, in fact, than Polonius and Laertes, with whom they share a common function within their respective plays: to enact a recognizably conventional kind of "tragedy" and thereby throw the more intractable experience of Hamlet and Lear into stark relief, endow it by contrast with the depth and complexity of life itself. The Polonius subplot in *Hamlet* turns out to be a simple tragedy of revenge with the stock revenger Laertes as protagonist. The Gloucester subplot, with its black-and-white symmetries of good and bad, lawful and illegitimate, "natural" and "unnatural" sons and its heavily moralistic scheme of sin and retribution, is as simplistic as any of the

---

[13] L. C. Knights, "The Question of Character in Shakespeare," *More Talking of Shakespeare*, ed. John Garrett (London, 1959), p. 66. Quoted with approval by Maynard Mack, *King Lear in Our Time*, p. 71.

neat little "tragedies" of the *de casibus* tradition culminating in *A Mirror for Magistrates*. Although both Lear and Gloucester are more sinned against than sinning, it is only Gloucester to whom the moral category of "sin" applies at all, and only Gloucester whose punishment is directly, albeit Dantesquely, appropriate to his sin. Whereas Gloucester is clearly enlightened to his earlier moral blindness as a result of his physical blinding, clearly repents of his transgressions, and passes away clearly a sadder but wiser man than he was before, none of these are clear in the case of Lear. The Gloucester universe has a moral transparency and a rough justice which the Lear universe does not. If one wishes to find a Christian world view positively employed in *King Lear*, the place to look for it is in the Gloucester subplot, the form and significance of which are medieval, morality derived, and not really tragic at all.

To turn to the main plot is to enter a dramatic universe of an altogether different cast. Whereas the experience of Gloucester, Edgar, and even Edmund works ultimately to "show the heavens more just," that of Lear shows nothing of the kind. The moralistic world view which buoys up the stripped and banished Edgar and which Gloucester's fortunes would seem to bear out is about as relevant to Lear's situation as are Poor Tom's mutterings about sin and foul fiends. Rather than illustrating a traditional Christian pattern of sin and retribution, contrition and repentance, and suffering and redemption, the Lear plot develops into a photographic negative of such a pattern. Instead of a tidy Christian scheme of sin and its wages, Lear's career yields up only a causeless and seemingly endless round of punishment. Instead of a new spiritual strength and self-knowledge as the outcome of suffering, we see mainly madness and exhaustion. The neat symmetry of one good and one evil son gives place to the telling, if often overlooked, disproportion of two evil and one good daughter (here the chronicles play into Shakespeare's hands). The basic assumptions of the Gloucester plot (of man's unfailing potential for amendment, of the essential goodness of the created universe, and of its ultimately self-righting moral economy) are all relentlessly questioned by Lear: Is man no more than this . . . ? Is there any cause in nature that makes these hard hearts? Why should a dog, a horse, a rat have life, and thou no breath at all? The relation of the Gloucester plot to the Lear plot (given a basic parallelism which makes its divergences all the more striking) becomes one of thesis to antithesis; the one holds out a wishful and comforting illusion of things as we would like them (especially in our misery) to be; the other dispels it with a scarifying vision of "the thing itself"—much as Lear naked on the heath is the reality of which Edgar is merely an imitation. This is not to imply that Lear does not try to cast his own experience into the mold of Gloucester's. Lear is, as any suffering man would be, desperate for release—"Come, let's away to prison; / We two alone will sing like birds i' th' cage"—and for redemption:

> This feather stirs; she lives! If it be so,
> It is a chance which does redeem all sorrows
> That ever I have felt. (v.iii.265-7)

But Lear's desire for a romance ending, however closely it echoes our own, is not to be pathetically confused with the ending Shakespeare provides.

Although not all the criticism of *King Lear* over the past century has expressed the position of Job's comforters, its dominant strain has been one of optimism, however qualified. Every conceivable shred of evidence that the play represents the triumph of humanity as much as its defeat has been salvaged from the general holocaust and put on display. We are told that within the immensities and intensities of evil and suffering abide not only the large-scale loyalty, endurance, and forgiveness of Kent, Edgar, and Cordelia but the small-scale decency of Cornwall's servant—even if his attempt to save Gloucester's one remaining eye is immediately frustrated and payed for with his life. We are told that despite the reechoing theme of social and familial breakdown, the bonds which hold humanity together are reaffirmed—even if the families and society concerned are themselves decimated in the process of affirmation. We are told that the characters who deny those bonds, who exist as islands, whose "reason" is amoral and whose "nature" is brutal, ultimately destroy themselves—even if they take the good and the innocent along with them. We are told that Edmund in the end cannot help doing some good "Despite of mine own nature"— even if his last-minute reformation comes too late and the hopes it has raised are immediately dashed when Lear enters with the hanged Cordelia in his arms. Shakespeare in *King Lear* repeatedly holds out hope with his left hand only to take it back with his right; raises romantic expectations only to defeat them with tragic actualities. The play is full of false dawns.

Probably the greatest romanticization of the play, and one that we have yet to work ourselves entirely out from under, is that of A. C. Bradley: "Should we not be at least as near the truth if we called this poem The Redemption of King Lear, and declared that the business of 'the gods' with him was neither to torment him, nor to teach him a 'noble anger,' but to lead him to attain through apparently hopeless failure the very end and aim of life?"[14] At last it is out: Lear's is a fortunate fall, and his play is Shakespeare's *Oedipus Coloneus* or *Samson Agonistes*. Like Johnson, Bradley feels that Shakespeare's ending is neither dramatically inevitable nor emotionally supportable; but whereas Johnson candidly admits his preference for the romantic version of Nahum Tate while recognizing that it is a different play, Bradley writes of Shakespeare's play as if it were Tate's. It is not that Bradley is wrong in discerning the seeds of romance in Shakespeare's ripest tragedy but in seeing them as having already sprouted. More remarkable than that Tate's *Lear* held the boards for 150 years is the fact that Shakespeare's lent itself so readily to romantic revision. The opening scene of Lear's division of the kingdom and trial of his daughters' love is problematic only to those who fail to perceive its consistency with the romance aspect of much of the subsequent action. When the storm-tossed Lear awakens to music in the presence of his long-lost daughter and says, "You do me wrong to take out of the grave," his figurative resurrection brings us very close to the world of the romances to come, where literal

[14] *Shakespearean Tragedy*, p. 228.

resurrections are possible. But whereas Marina in *Pericles* will lift her father out of the life-in-death of his sackcloth and ashes into a well-earned and conclusive prosperity, the reunion of Lear and Cordelia proves but a false dawn, as her army is beaten and his dreams of song-filled imprisonment are dispelled by still another and final separation. Cordelia herself, "one daughter / Who redeems nature from the general curse / Which twain have brought her to" and whose "heavenly eyes" weep "holy water," is, like the marvelous maidens of the last romances, as much a personified principle of faith-in-love as a flesh-and-blood daughter; while her fleeting redemption of Lear, like Marina's of Pericles, suggests another romantic story and another redemption by another child of man. But whatever Christian associations adhere to the action of Lear and Cordelia (and Shakespeare has deliberately omitted the Biblical parallels and allusions to "heavenly joys" which stud the old play of *King Leir*) work ironically.

Whether or not we insist on the pre-Christian setting of *Lear*, the fact is that whatever fleeting recollections (or anticipations) of the atonement and the apocalypse surround Lear and Cordelia, she does not redeem all sorrow and her death—once again pathetically—is not "the promis'd end" as Kent would have it. To an audience familiar with the Christian story it must remain another false dawn. Even the sudden reformation of Edmund is right out of romance: it recalls the conversions of Oliver, Duke Frederick, and Proteus in their forest worlds and prefigures Iachimo's in the Welsh hills of *Cymbeline*. With Edmund's motiveless reformation we are again briefly transported outside the consequential world of tragedy (if anything, it leads us and the characters of the play to expect a romantic aversion of catastrophe) until Lear's final entrance plunges us (and them) back into it, for Shakespeare does not relinquish his Baconian principles at the eleventh hour. The elements of romance which are so abundant in *King Lear*, and which made Tate's task of revision half-done before he began, are all finally in the service of tragic effect. If *Lear* takes us, in Bradley's words, "beyond the strictly tragic point of view," it does so only to invalidate any point of view other than the strictly tragic. In so doing, *King Lear* becomes a kind of definition in action of Shakespearean tragedy.

It should be evident from the case of *King Lear* that romance is not simply a literary genre in which Shakespeare worked at the beginning and end of his career and had no use for in between, but a mode of perceiving the world which helps to shape most of his work, even his mature tragedies. In *Othello*, for example we are presented with a protagonist whose past history reads like a synopsis of the *Aethiopica*, who has run the gamut of romantic trials, and who would seem to have emerged "all in all sufficient." (iv.i.265) But the very qualities that make Othello so eminently sufficient in the romantic spheres of love and war—his power of unreflecting action—also render him hopelessly inadequate in the world of hidden motives and dark innuendo created by Iago. Othello is as competent to handle Brabantio's public accusations, the Turkish crisis, and the brawl in Cyprus as he is incompetent to see beneath appearances into the reality of Iago, Cassio, and Desdemona. (Just as the magisterial Othello would have no problem in Hamlet's position, neither

would the perspicacious Hamlet in Othello's.) The play
establishes Othello's romantic authority early, as Brabantio
is disarmed, the tempest en route to Cyprus weathered,
and the Turkish threat dispersed, but only to set the stage
for his romantic inadequacy, helpless as he is to put down
the tempest aroused in his mind and heart. Shakespearean
tragedy characteristically places its heroes in situations
which require nothing less than a radical transformation of
the self. Othello's failure to remake himself is typical of
most of the tragic heroes. In his final speech, whether or
not he is trying simply to "cheer himself up," he recol-
lects a deed of derring-do from his past to resurrect and
validate his conception of himself as a brave and noble
hero of romance, a role whose inadequacy at this point is
dramatically obvious to everyone except him. One reason
critics are tempted to "redeem" Shakespeare's tragic heroes
is that most of them try so hard to redeem themselves.

Only a character so passionately, so incorrigibly given
to romanticizing himself and his world could invest the
loss of a handkerchief (he has already associated it with
far-away places and magical charms) with such momentous
import and dire consequence. Thomas Rymer, who reduced the handkerchief (along with much else in the play)
to mere domestic "linen," failed to take this into account
when he complained that such a "trifle" should produce
such monstrous effects. But aside from the fact that the
handkerchief is no trifle to Othello, Shakespeare's tragedies
often seem to turn on essentially romantic accidents or co-
incidences. Richard II, delayed by a storm, returns from
Ireland one day too late to defeat Bolingbroke; an un-
timely rumor of plague prevents Friar John from deliver-

ing his message to Romeo, who in turn kills himself an instant before Juliet wakes up; Cassius commits suicide on the false report that Titinius has been taken by the enemy; Edmund reforms—"Great thing of us forgot!"— a few seconds too late to revoke his order of execution on Cordelia. Such accidents may be heart-lifting as well as heartbreaking (Hamlet's blundering onto Claudius' death-warrant aboard ship and his subsequent encounter with the pirates, or Timon's stumbling upon gold in the forest outside Athens) and seem to promise a new and welcome turn of events. That Shakespeare's tragedies extend this hospitality to the coincidental, the unforeseen, the improbable (to that aspect of experience which traditionally forms the province of comedy and romance) becomes a source of strength rather than weakness, an important aspect of their ultimate fidelity to life. Their implicit recognition that messengers do not always arrive too late, that events may take a happier turn at any point, that Othello may yet come to his senses in time to stop himself from strangling Desdemona, makes their catastrophes all the more terrible when they do come, and their universes that much bleaker. Shakespearean tragedy maintains the possibility of a romantic outcome right to the bitter end, as a feather seems to stir at Cordelia's lips and Desdemona awakens from death just long enough to exonerate her husband with her final breath.

If Hamlet, Othello, and Lear are desperate for redemption in their closing speeches (even to the point of falsifying their experience to attain some semblance of it) Macbeth, in his closing speeches, is just plain desperate. Yet the universe of *Macbeth*, ironically, proves to be in certain respects closer to the universe of romance than those of the earlier tragedies. For the moral degeneration of Macbeth takes place in a universe where regeneration—personal, social, and cosmic—is not merely an ever-present possibility but a dramatized reality. Among the several alter-egos of Macbeth—"the merciless Macdonwald," Banquo, and even Malcolm—there is the Thane of Cawdor, whose career forbodes that of the inheritor of his title in everything but its ending. Whereas the first Cawdor confesses, repents, and asks pardon for his crimes so that "nothing in his life / Became him like the leaving it" (I.iv.8-9), the second dies unrepentant and unredeemed. As Macbeth becomes further and further alienated from human community, Malcolm becomes associated with an English king of superhuman virtue, who cures the sick with his touch, who "hath a heavenly gift of prophecy, / And sundry blessings hang about his throne / That speak him full of grace" (IV.iii.157-9): the angelic anti-type to the now demonic Macbeth. The moral distance between Malcolm (along with Edward the Confessor) and Macbeth is the measure of the latter's own lost possibilities, lost possibilities of friendship and love fully recognized and enumerated by Macbeth himself. On the social and political levels the tragical history of Macbeth's reign is played off against the budding historical romance of Scotland—to flower finally, it is strongly hinted, in the reign of James I. As Macbeth comes to see his life in images of blight and sterility, the natural forces he has murdered in himself revive within the realm at large in the form of a pious and legitimate king at the head of an army of moving trees and have their vindication. The rebirth of a natural world which had seemed "dead" to Macbeth anticipates the rebirth of nature toward the end of *The Winter's Tale*, a process which sweeps up the penitent Leontes with it but from which the unrepentant Macbeth has cut himself off.

But if Shakespearean tragedy characteristically takes shape against a background of romance, it is in the three classical tragedies between *Lear* and *Pericles* that romance begins to move into the foreground and that the transition from tragedy to romance within his own career, from a Baconian to a Sidneian poetics, becomes clearly visible. Whereas the earlier tragedies undercut the romantic gestures and attitudes of their heroes—Hamlet's fifth-act professions of love and good faith toward Ophelia and Laertes, Lear's desire for song-filled imprisonment with Cordelia, the bravura of Othello's suicide-speech—and insist on their futility, *Coriolanus*, *Timon of Athens*, and *Antony and Cleopatra* all but invite them. The worlds of these plays, even more than that of *Macbeth*, turn almost benign as the evil formerly embodied in Claudius, Iago, Goneril, and Edmund disappears, and the chief obstacle to a romantic outcome becomes the tragic hero himself. Coriolanus, Timon, and Antony all have opportunities to salvage some semblance of victory out of defeat, to remake themselves from within and reconcile themselves to their worlds; only Antony succeeds in doing so. The stage has been set for the romances.

"*Coriolanus*," writes A. C. Bradley, "is as much a drama of reconciliation as a tragedy" and "marks the

powers of repentance and forgiveness that charm to rest
the tempest raised by error and guilt."[15] In his desire to
smile through his tears, Bradley once again mistakes the
romantic potential of *Coriolanus* for the actuality. Coriolanus is indeed offered a grand opportunity for repentance
and forgiveness—the scene in which he is entreated and
finally persuaded by his mother to spare Rome—but only
after repentance and forgiveness are no longer really possible for him, as he himself in a rare moment of introspec-
tion and insight realizes. All he can bring himself to do is
retreat from the position in which he has so singlemindedly
entrenched himself:

> You have won a happy victory to Rome;
> But for your son—believe it, O, believe it!—
> Most dangerously you have with him prevailed,
> If not mortal to him. But let it come.
>
> (v.iii.186-9)

Whereas Prospero is able to turn *The Tempest* from a
tragedy of revenge into a romance of reconciliation by
casting himself into a new part—"The rarer action is in
virtue than in vengeance"—Coriolanus is unable to embrace the role of reconciler urged by his mother and behaves after his submission like "a man by his own alms
empoisoned, / And with his charity slain." (v.vi. 11-12)
To the extent that *Coriolanus* is profoundly pessimistic
about the ability of a particular man to remake himself in
the middle of the journey, it remains the last of the tragedies rather than the first of the romances.

---

[15] "Coriolanus," British Academy Shakespeare Lecture (1912), reprinted in *Coriolanus*, ed. Reuben Brower (Signet Shakespeare, New
York, 1966), p. 263; *Shakespearean Tragedy*, p. 75.

The play raises this (as I think) central concern of Shakespearean dramaturgy in a very pure form by repeatedly placing a hero chronically unable to change into positions which require him to do so. Shakespeare has Coriolanus change costume twice during the course of the play, while each occasion serves to demonstrate his essential rigidity. He is painfully ill-at-ease in both the ritual gown of humility before the people and the "mean apparel" (a still more mortifying version of the gown of humility) in which he appears as an outcast before Aufidius' festive house and delivers his second and last soliloquy. His banishment and humiliation fail to trigger even the fitful flashes of self-awareness that Lear experiences on the heath. Coriolanus, as the dramatic stress on his name suggests and nearly everyone in the play remarks sooner or later, can conceive of himself only as a soldier and feels at home only in armor at the head of his troops. As in the earlier tragedies, Shakespeare surrounds his inflexible hero with characters to whom role-playing is second nature: the politician Menenius, the Machiavellian Aufidius, and even the austere Volumnia, who knows how to act when it is expedient. When called upon by Cominius to abandon his vindictive designs on Rome, Coriolanus "was a kind of nothing, titleless" (v.i.13), and when Virgilia later appeals to him, he compares himself to "a dull actor now, / I have forgot my part and I am out." (v.iii.40-41) When the earlier tragic heroes try to be something other than themselves (Brutus, a conspirator; Hamlet, a revenger; Macbeth, a usurper) the results are invariably disastrous, and in their final speeches and postures they try to reclaim something of their former integrity and identity. Coriolanus does much the same thing in his final speech on fluttering the Volscians in Corioli; but with a difference. Whereas Othello and Macbeth realize that a priceless part of themselves has been lost, a "pearl" or a "jewel" cast away, Coriolanus remains curiously unaware that in seeking to preserve his integrity he has destroyed it; in remaining the soldier he has betrayed the son of Rome. His tragic inflexibility is presented as a kind of arrested development. It is as her boy that his mother persuades him to relent; his son chases butterflies with the same determination that his father hunts down fleeing troops; and "boy" is the final, irresistible taunt with which Aufidius works his downfall. But aside from his peculiar self-ignorance, Coriolanus is the last of the purely tragic heroes, all of whom may be said to die of inflexibility. In the case of Coriolanus, his death by the swords of the Volscian conspirators is in a sense redundant, since he virtually annihilates himself when he violates his principle of being and relents.

It makes no difference, for my purposes, whether *Timon of Athens* was written at the time of Lear or at the time of *Antony* and *Coriolanus*. The monolithic rage of its hero and its theme of "ingratitude" link it to the earlier tragedy, while the subplot of Alcibiades' exile and return, derived from Plutarch and illustrating reconciliation, connect it with the later ones. Timon, unlike Alcibiades, dies unreconciled either with the society of Athens or with humanity at large. What the malcontent Apemantus says of him remains true to his bitter end: "The middle of humanity thou never knewest, but the extremity of both ends." (IV.iii.301-2) Timon changes from one personified abstraction, Philanthropos, to another, Misanthropos, as a

result of a simple and complete reversal of fortune. Fortune, in the senses both of worldly wealth and position
and the goddess who administers them, is the shaping
power of the plot. Her wheel, as in *Lear*, comes full circle,
though it is Fortune's Hill rather than her wheel which
is discussed by a poet and a painter, both time-servers themselves, in the opening scene, and which becomes a paradigm
of Timon's subsequent career:

Poet. When Fortune in her shift and change of mood
    Spurns down her late beloved, all his dependants
    Which labour'd after him to the mountain's top
    Even on their knees and hands, let him sit down,
    Not one accompanying his declining foot.
Pain. 'Tis common.
    A thousand moral paintings I can show
    That shall demonstrate these quick blows of Fortune's
    More pregnantly than words.   (i.i.86-94)

The goddess Fortune presides over more than one Elizabethan dramatic romance, and the revolution of her wheel
also forms the parabolic pattern of tragedy for every
tragedian from Chaucer's monk through Marlowe. That
pattern continues to exist as a kind of fossil in most of
Shakespeare's tragedies, but in the action of *Timon* the
fossil comes sluggishly to life.

    Like a hero of romantic comedy, Timon gains insight
through misfortune early and at the relatively light cost
of a few thousand drachmas. Early in the play he sees the
moral implications of his bankruptcy: "And in some sort
these wants of mine are crown'd / That I account them
blessings; for by these / Shall I try friends." (ii.ii.185-7)

But he is deluded about the outcome of that trial, thinking still that "I am wealthy in my friends." He tells his steward, who is as sensible and loyal as Kent, "You shall perceive how you / Mistake my fortunes." When they meet again the Steward announces that the midpoint of the romance cycle has been reached, that the wheel has come half-circle: "My dearest lord, bless'd to be most accurs'd, / Rich only to be wretched—thy great fortunes / Are made thy chief afflictions." (iv.ii.42-4) Thrown back on nature, Duke Senior can moralize that the uses of adversity are sweet, can find "tongues in trees, books in the running brooks / Sermons in stones, and good in everything" (*A.Y.L.*ii.i.16-18). Thrown back on nature, Lear too can say, "The art of our necessities is strange, / And can make vile things precious," even though the elements he confronts on his blasted heath are far less benign than those of the Forest of Arden.

When Timon decides that he "will to the woods, where he shall find / Th'unkindest beast more kinder than mankind" (iv.i.35-6), he casts himself in the role of a romance hero about to enter a world closer to the Duke's forest than to Lear's heath. The wood outside Athens to which he retires recalls, in fact, another wood outside Athens, that of *A Midsummer Night's Dream*. Shakespeare's return to the forest at this late date in his career is also a return to the poetics of forest comedy. The green world of Shakespearean comedy is, of course, closely related to the "golden world" of Sidney's *Apology*. The "golden world" is also a phrase from *As You Like It*, where, whatever real French forest it suggests, Arden combines many of the wonderful features of Arcadia and Eden. Shakespeare's forest comedies are also pastoral romances in which the benignity of nature calls forth the natural benignity of man, where the evils of civilization are purged, and where society regains something like a prelapsarian integrity. As Duke Senior puts it: "Here we feel not the penalty of Adam," while Old Adam himself disappears after leading Orlando into Arden. The forest into which Timon retreats from decadent Athenian society is just such another romantic world of inexplicable shifts of fortune, humane brigands, and instantaneous personal reformations. Timon's first act is to dig for roots and come up instead with gold. The sudden dissipation of a fortune is momentarily redressed by the still more sudden finding of one. Like Valentine in the forest world of *Two Gentlemen of Verona*, Timon encounters a band of kindly thieves. The play seems suddenly to have turned, if I may crack the wind of a poor Polonian phrase, into pastoral tragedy. For Timon seems to have learned in the interim that gold, outside of fallen society, is unnatural and useless to man, and he cries out for "Roots, you clear heavens!":

> Why should you want? Behold the earth hath roots;
> Within this mile break forth a hundred springs;
> The oaks bear mast, the briers scarlet hips;
> The bounteous housewife nature on each bush
> Lays her full mess before you. Want? Why want?
> (IV.iii.420-24)

Although the First Bandit counters Timon's romantic primitivism and its vegetarian diet with skepticism—"We cannot live on grass, on berries, water, / As beasts and birds and fishes"—they are nonetheless persuaded to re-

nounce their thievery. The whole scene looks backward
to the conversion of the gentlemen-thieves of *Two Gentlemen* (and those of Oliver and Frederick in Arden) and
simultaneously forward to Marina's conversion of the
clientele of the Mytilenian brothel in *Pericles*.

The ending of *Timon* is divided between tragedy and
comedy, between the bitter malediction of Timon's epitaph
and Alcibiades' closing speech on "faults forgiven." It is as
if the tragic and romantic potential of Coriolanus' decisive
act were separately enacted in the mainplot and subplot
of this play, as Alcibiades chooses a qualified forgiveness—
"the olive with the sword"—and Timon clings to his im-
potent vindictiveness. Like a hero of romance, Timon
comes to see that worldly substance is but shadow, that his
curse has proved a blessing in disguise, and that the ruins
of Fortune compose the architecture of a higher providence:

> My long sickness
> Of health and living now begins to mend,
> And nothing brings me all things.
> (v.i.185-7)

But if Timon perceives, in Hermione's words, that the
action he now goes on is for his better grace, he is unable
to act out the new role demanded of him, to affirm, with
Prospero, that the rarer action is in virtue than in vengeance. He rejects the offered reconciliations of Alcibiades
and Athens alike. The chief difficulty of the play, I would
suggest, is that it imposes a tragic ending on an action whose
inward logic is toward a romantic reconciliation; it fails
to realize fully either potentiality of an action that offers
both.

Antony and Cleopatra is a tragedy and a romance at
once. Not only do the possibilities of both forms coexist
in *Antony*, but both are fully realized. Although the stuff
of tragedy is present in abundance—disastrous reversals of
fortune, military defeats, personal and political betrayals,
a double suicide—an unusually ample place is accorded
within the play to a point of view which "shackles accidents and bolts up change," which sees mirth in grief and
gain in loss:

> If there were no more women but Fulvia, then had you
> indeed a cut, and the case to be lamented. This grief is
> crowned with consolation: your old smock brings forth
> a new petticoat, and indeed the tears live in an onion
> that should water this sorrow.   (i.ii.167-72)

Nor is it only in the witty and detached overview of
Enobarbus that these odds are made even. Menecrates
counsels Pompey in a more serious vein that his designs
may ultimately be served rather than foiled by the union
of Antony and Octavius. "We, ignorant of ourselves,"
Menecrates points out, "Beg often our own harms . . . so
find we profit / By losing of our prayers" (ii.i.5-8)—a
paradox which also describes the lovers' situation at the
end. Their defeat and death turn by the slighest shift
of perspective into their victory and apotheosis:

> My desolation does begin to make
> A better life: 'tis paltry to be Caesar:
> Not being Fortune, he's but Fortune's knave,
> A minister of her will.   (v.ii.1-4)

The tragedy of Fortune implicit in *Antony* is transcended
even as it is realized. Antony's suicide in the high Roman

fashion enables him to stay once and for all the inevitably ebbing tide in the affairs of men and affirm his identity in death—"a Roman by a Roman valiantly vanquished." The fact that his suicide is accidentally bungled proves in this play to be no false dawn, as it might have been in another. It frees the Egyptian Antony from the stern expectations of his Roman identity and allows time for a final reunion and reconciliation with Cleopatra as well as the consolidation of their love in a kind of marriage. Their love turns out to be the only relationship in the play which finally does not "rot itself with motion," as they embrace death as bridegroom and bride and depart this "dull world" for a pastoral underworld "Where souls do couch on flowers." Antony and Cleopatra convince us by their final words and deeds, as Timon and Lear do not, that for them vile things are precious, curses have proved blessings in disguise, misfortune has been truly fortunate.

They can do so only because virtually everything in the world of this play is throughout presented, to appropriate a phrase of Macbeth's, "in a double sense," preeminently the lovers themselves. We are caught, like Antony himself during the early acts, between the equally attractive and repulsive worlds of Rome and Egypt; between a sober, if sometimes hypocritical, Roman morality and an enchanting, and often sleazy, Egyptian amorality; between Octavius' self-disciplined will to power and Cleopatra's self-indulgent will to flower. The lovers do not escape being judged by Roman norms, though their inadequacy as norms is generally implied. Antony's "faults, in him seem as the spots of heaven" (i.iv.12), while in Cleopatra "vilest things / Become themselves . . . that the holy priests /

Bless her, when she is riggish." (ii.ii.238-40) Caesar may be "the Jupiter of men" but Antony is the "god of Jupiter," the "immortal phoenix," "plated Mars," a "Jove," and "Herculean Antony." Cleopatra is "Juno" to Antony's Jove, "Venus" to his Mars, and above all Isis, goddess of the earth and moon, fertility and chastity at once. They are all too human or semi-divine, are bound together in degrading lust ("a strumpet's fool") or transcendent love ("There's beggary in love that can be reckoned"), according to the loyalties of the observer. If we adopt a strictly Roman perspective, their play becomes a tragedy of self-indulgence—"All for Love"—and self-delusion as the lovers vainly strive to see themselves as gods. But the Roman perspective is difficult to maintain when even the most skeptical and hardheaded of Romans must repeatedly resort to romantic hyperbole and oxymoron to do justice to Cleopatra in describing her and himself dies of a broken heart when he follows the politic Roman way and betrays his own love for Antony. If we accept the lovers at their own final evaluation and see their experience from the over-view they claim to attain, the play becomes a romance ("The World Well Lost"); yet we must also acknowledge that it is Caesar who remains to deliver the last word. Not only the character of Cleopatra but the play itself has the infinite complexity of a transcendent paradox, which in Dryden's version is split tendentiously into thesis and antithesis.

To the extent that both Antony and Cleopatra have, so to speak, one foot in the natural order and one outside it, that they are subject yet superior to chance and change, their play embodies the poetics of Sidney and Bacon at once. Enobarbus' account of Cleopatra on Cydnus, "where

we see / The fancy outwork nature," might serve to describe the Egyptian setting she dominates and the kind
of imagination that reigns there. What Antony in his
Roman mood terms "the strong necessity of time" (1.iii.42)
as well as the realistic limitations of space have no authority in Egypt. In this nighttime world of music, love, revelry, and dressing-up, the pleasure, not the reality, principle
reigns. Age cannot wither Cleopatra, though she is push-
ing forty and has borne numerous children, and she is
endowed by Octavius with the power to "nod" her lover
across the seas from Rome. Her moods all but determine
the weather of the place. "We cannot call her winds and
waters sighs and tears," Enobarbus justly remarks, "they
are greater storms and tempests than almanacs can report . . . . She makes a shower of rain as well as Jove."
(1.ii.149-53) If Antony and Cleopatra are as gods in Egypt,
they recreate reality after their own desires by a kind of
divine fiat: "Let Rome in Tiber melt"; "Melt Egypt into
Nile." The poor messenger who brings news of Antony's
marriage is forced by Cleopatra to bend reality to the desires of her mind, to bring forth a second Octavia such as
never was in nature: dull of tongue, low-browed, and
dwarfish. Whereas Cleopatra treats messengers with Olym-
pian whimsy—"Some innocents 'scape not the thunder-
bolt" (ii.v.77)—Caesar and the Romans regard them
merely as a source of military intelligence.

If Egypt embodies the art of the impossible, Rome as
the setting for imperial power politics embodies in every
sense the art of the possible. When Samuel Johnson praised
Shakespeare for representing "the real state of sublunary
nature," he might have had the Rome of this play in mind,
for Rome corresponds to the world as Bacon and Jonson

conceive it, as we conceive of it in everyday consciousness: a hard, unyielding, brazen reality whose one certainty is flux and where human affairs are subject to the ceaseless roll of Fortune's wheel as surely as the "varying shore" is to the tides. But Egypt is no less "real." Antony can transcend his desire for revenge on the Cleopatra who betrays him, she can become all fire and air and leave her other elements behind to baser life, only because the "other world" of Egypt, where one can dress up and be anything one wants and where the impossible can occur, is granted an equal imaginative status in the play with the tragic center of Rome. No such place (Timon's wood excepted) exists in the earlier tragedies. To find such a place we must go back to the forest world of *A Midsummer Night's Dream* (and the other early comedies), where "fancy" proves itself at least as real and potent a force in human life as the "cool reason" of Theseus, or to the tavern world of the comical *1 Henry IV*, where another prince of the world hides out from the realities of power politics only to emerge with a better and richer sense of his own identity. For all the inescapability of Rome and what it represents, *Antony and Cleopatra* begins and ends in Egypt. "Of all Shakespeare's historical plays," writes Coleridge, "*Antony and Cleopatra* is by far the most wonderful. There is not one in which he has followed history so minutely, and yet there are few in which he impresses the notion of angelic strength so much."[16] Given that he exaggerates Shakespeare's fidelity to history, Coleridge

[16] *Shakespearean Criticism*, ed. T. M. Raysor (Everyman's Library, London, 1960), I, 77.

seems to discern the high tension of poetic strategies within
the play, each qualifying and validating the other.

When Timon commends the Athenian Senators who
visit him in the woods "To the protection of the prosperous
gods, / As thieves to keepers" (v.i.182-3), he pretty well
sums up the state of relations between man and the gods in
most of Shakespeare's pre-Christian plays. But in *Antony*,
with its tantalizing references to a "new heaven, new
earth," to a *Pax Romana* when "the three-nook'd world /
Shall bear the olive freely," and to Herod of Jewry, we
may perhaps be excused if we imagine the lovers in their
final scenes breaking through the limits of tragical history
into the apocalyptic order of romance, the order proclaimed
at the end of *Cymbeline* where the power of faith and
love makes the relations of men and gods more than that
of thieves to keepers. Or perhaps to entertain such a notion is to dream:

Cleopatra. You laugh when boys or women tell their
    dreams,
  Is't not your trick?
Dolabella.   I understand not, madam.
Cleopatra. I dreamt there was an Emperor Antony.
  O such another sleep, that I might see
  But such another man!
Dolabella.   If it might please ye,—
Cleopatra. His face was as the heavens, and therein stuck
  A sun and moon, which kept their course, and lighted
  The little O, the earth.
Dolabella.   Most sovereign creature—

Cleopatra. His legs bestrid the ocean, his rear'd arm
  Crested the world: his voice was propertied
  As all the tuned spheres, and that to friends:
  But when he meant to quail, and shake the orb,
  He was as rattling thunder. For his bounty,
  There was no winter in't: an autumn 'twas
  That grew the more by reaping: his delights
  Were dolphin-like, they show'd his back above
  The element they lived in: in his livery
  Walk'd crowns and crownets: realms and islands were
  As plates dropp'd from his pocket.
Dolabella.   Cleopatra!
Cleopatra. Think you there was, or might be such a man
  As this I dreamt of?
Dolabella.   Gentle madam, no.
Cleopatra. You lie up to the hearing of the gods.
  But if there be, or ever were one such,
  It's past the size of dreaming: nature wants stuff
  To vie strange forms with fancy, yet to imagine
  An Antony were nature's piece, 'gainst fancy,
  Condemning shadows quite.   (v.ii.74-100)

Dolabella the Roman may or may not laugh as Cleopatra, in unfolding her dream of this king of kings, runs away from nature. Bacon, who pays full tribute to the reality principle, would certainly have smiled.

Shakespeare left behind no statement of principles in his own person. But through the mouths of two of his characters he expresses both the Sidneian and Baconian poetics. Though Theseus, like Bacon, finds "cool reason" his métier and groups poets with lovers and madmen, his analysis of the imaginative function—to body forth the forms of

138

things unknown, turn them to shapes, and give to airy nothing a local habitation and a name—accords perfectly with the dramatic premises of the romantic comedy in which he appears. Hamlet, on the other hand, finds himself in a world where dreams are ruthlessly dispelled, and his advice to the players expounds, appropriately enough, a lifelike tragic *mimesis*. When Theseus comes to choose among the various plays in Peter Quince's repertory, he rules out a "satire keen and critical" as not sorting with a nuptial ceremony. He then comes upon "a tedious brief scene of young Pyramus / And his love Thisby; very tragical mirth." "Merry and tragical? tedious and brief?" he asks, "How shall we find the concord of this discord?" His Master of the Revels answers that the play, though brief in length, is tedious in quality, and though Pyramus kills himself, the ineptitude of its actors makes it comic. *Antony and Cleopatra* is neither brief nor tedious but it does celebrate two suicides which are also a marriage, and it is merry and tragic at once. The concord of this discord has been found.

PART III

THE ROMANCES

CHAPTER 5

This Great Miracle:
Pericles

To let the follies and license of a few detract from the
honour of parables in general is not to be allowed; being
indeed a boldness savouring of profanity; seeing that
religion delights in such veils and shadows, and to take
them away would be almost to interdict all communion
between divinity and humanity.

—Bacon

THE PLAY OF *Pericles* in process of being exhumed from
the Ossa of problems under which it has long been buried.
The text has been a fundamental and abiding problem, a
quarto so bad it is impossible at certain points in the play
even to guess what Shakespeare wrote, if indeed he wrote
it. For there has also been a long-standing problem of
authorship, arising from the omission or exclusion of
Pericles from the first folio and the change of style between its second and third acts. But even though speculation of divided authorship has now been seriously challenged,[1] both on the textual grounds that its change of
style may result simply from the differing competence of
two reporters and on the critical grounds that an underlying
poetic coherence may be discerned between its two halves,

[1] See G. Wilson Knight, *The Crown of Life* (London, 1947), pp.
32-75, and Philip Edwards, "An Approach to the Problem of *Pericles*,"
Shakespeare Survey 5 (London, 1952), pp. 25-49.

there remains a still larger problem of interpretation. Given that the play is consistent in detail, what are we to make of a self-consistency so strange and archaic? Granted that Shakespeare did write the entire play, how do we account for this radical change in his poetic and dramatic practice? For it is not only the verse of the first two acts that, as one critic has remarked, seems earlier than the earliest Shakespeare we have,[2] but the dramatic technique of the play as a whole. How do the naive and stagey features of *Pericles* (its Chorus, dumb-shows, theophany, gnomic verse, episodic structure, and black-and-white characterization) work together to produce a coherent effect, and what kind of an effect do they produce? For these features are not confined to the opening acts but occur throughout the play. If we are willing to grant Shakespeare's authorship of the entire play, we should also be willing to grant that at this late date in his career he knew what he was doing. To postulate a euphoric Shakespeare, an exhausted Shakespeare, a senile Shakespeare, a newly converted Shakespeare, or (most recently) an experimental Shakespeare simply will not do,[3] partly because such quasi-biographical speculations throw no real light on the play itself and partly because they fail to explain, or even engage, the historical problem of *Pericles*: the fact that this least pop-

[2] See Hardin Craig, "Shakespeare's Bad Poetry," *Shakespeare Survey* I (London, 1948), pp. 51-6. Craig also argues that Gower's speeches are probably by Shakespeare.

[3] The views, in order, of Edward Dowden, *Shakspere: His Mind and Art* (New York, 1880), pp. 336-82; Lytton Strachey, "Shakespeare's Final Period," *Books and Characters* (New York, 1922), pp. 49-70; E. K. Chambers, *Shakespeare: A Survey* (London, 1925), pp. 49-70; and E.M.W. Tillyard, *Shakespeare's Last Plays* (London, 1938), pp. 22-4.

ular of Shakespeare's plays was in its first days among his most popular.

When Ancient Gower walked onto the stage as Chorus, a Jacobean audience would have been immediately aware of the archaism of the device. The convention of the poet as Chorus had been all but swept aside by the momentum of increasing naturalism, and plays at this point in the development of the drama often began in mid-dialogue: "Tush, never tell me!" "Nay, but this dotage of our general's." The convention of poet as Chorus originates in the medieval religious drama, specifically in the 'saint's play, of which lamentably few have survived in English despite their widespread popularity. The late fifteenth-century *Conversion of St. Paul* illustrates the technique. There the *Poeta* introduces and recapitulates each scene, apologizes for breaks and leaps in the action, but most importantly, acts as moral interpreter to the audience. Even if Shakespeare happened to be unacquainted with this particular play, similar miracle or saint's plays were performed late into the sixteenth century on their appropriate festival days. A few plays produced shortly before *Pericles* employed the choric device primarily to compress a sprawling romantic action, and Shakespeare had already used a choric narrator for much the same purpose in *Henry V*. But in none of these precedents is the main function of the Chorus moralistic and didactic.[4] In this conspicuous ele-

---

[4] F. D. Hoeniger cites Barnabe Barnes' *The Divil's Charter* (1607) and John Day's *The Travailes of the Three English Brothers* (1607). He sees a closer resemblance than I do between their choruses and that of *Pericles*, though there is no reason why they could not have employed the device similarly. See *Pericles* (New Arden Shakespeare, Cambridge, Mass., 1963), p. xxi. I am indebted to his introduction

ment of his role Gower is closer to the medieval *Poeta*, and in his constant moralizing over the action he presents, Shakespeare deliberately preserves his identity as a child of the Middle Ages, Chaucer's "moral Gower."

Obviously Shakespeare would not cultivate an archaic medievalism at this stage in his work without sophisticated ulterior motives. Gower's opening speech frankly announces his designs on us:

> To sing a song that old was sung,
> From ashes ancient Gower is come
> Assuming man's infirmities,
> To glad your ear, and please your eyes.
> It hath been sung at festivals,
> On ember-eves and holy ales;
> And lords and ladies in their lives
> Have read it for restoratives:
> The purchase is to make men glorious,
> *Et bonum quo antiquius eo melius.*
> If you born in these latter times
> When wit's more ripe, accept my rimes.

The imitation of Gower's jingly rhymes, antiquated diction, and unabashed didacticism is itself skillful, as is Shakespeare's unfolding of the chief motives of the play—resurrection and restoration—within the first eight lines. The proverbial Latin tag, the emphatic contrast between "these latter times" and "a song that old was sung" (a contrast embodied in the resurrected Gower himself) serve to surround the tale with an air of revered antiquity. The "festi-

---

for first drawing my attention to the influence of the miracle play. See pp. lxxxvi-xci.

vals," "ember-eves," and "holy ales" on which it has been sung are all occasions in the Church calendar. Shakespeare is telling us through the shorthand of dramatic convention that the action we are about to witness is a timeless parable for our spiritual recreation (in both senses of the word) and that to learn from it we must first unlearn our sophisticated notions of dramatic story telling. Aware of the difficulties that this request involves, he makes Gower self-consciously humorous in his demand, has him voice (and hopefully dissipate) the audience's own impulse to scoff at such a tale. Like the chorus of Time in *The Winter's Tale*, Gower's speeches are not offered as great dramatic poetry but as dramatically appropriate poetry calculated to persuade us to accept certain impossibilities, to establish on the spur of the moment a convention crucial to our acceptance and understanding of what is to follow. In Gower's case the convention was partly established in the mind of the audience already, familiar as it must have been with an earlier drama.

What follows in the first scene begins to explain the choice to resurrect a dead poet and a dead convention. Pericles, full of hope and bent on adventure, seeks to wed the daughter of King Antiochus. About to attempt the inevitable riddle on which marriage or death depends, he prays to the gods:

Pericles. You gods, that made me man, and sway in love,
  That have inflamed desire in my breast
  To taste the fruit of yon celestial tree
  Or die in the adventure, be my helps,
  As I am son and servant to your will,

To compass such a boundless happiness!
Antiochus. Prince Pericles—
Pericles. That would be son to great Antiochus.
Antiochus. Before thee stands this fair Hesperides,
    With golden fruit, but dangerous to be touch'd;
    For death-like dragons here affright thee hard.
    Her face, like heaven, enticeth thee to view
    Her countless glory, which desert must gain.

(I.i.20-32)

The situation corresponds, with a difference, to that of the three caskets in *The Merchant of Venice*, or more generally, to that of the quest-romance or the Petrarchan lyric. There the young lover conventionally adopts religious vocabulary to express his highest aspirations and finest feelings—the vocabulary of Morocco and Aragon in the earlier play.

This would seem to be the language of Pericles and Antiochus, in which the princess becomes an earthly paradise where "golden fruit" hangs on a "celestial tree" guarded from the unworthy by "death-like dragons." The all-important difference is that their romantic-religious vocabulary is in deadly earnest and rings with portentous echoes of temptation and fall. Antiochus' daughter, whose beauty "enticeth" Pericles to "view," "touch," and "taste," comes to represent in the course of the scene, not that good which rewards romantic *virtù*, but that evil which tests moral virtue. Like a man who thinks he has come to a wedding only to learn he has blundered into a funeral, Pericles begins to exchange the conventions of one sort of world for those of another—and so do we:

Antiochus, I thank thee, who hath taught
My frail mortality to know itself,
And by those fearful objects to prepare
This body, like to them, to what I must;
For death remember'd should be like a mirror,
Who tells us life's but breath, to trust it error.
I'll make my will then; and, as sick men do,
Who know the world, see heaven, but feeling woe
Gripe not at earthly joys as erst they did.

(1.i.42-50)

Although his claim to self-knowledge is premature (the state he describes will not be realized until the last act), he speaks and behaves like the protagonist of a morality play. Pericles is presented as a kind of Everyman, derived from his medieval predecessor through the figure of Juventus in Tudor interludes, whose outline is visible in the worldly Bassanio of *The Merchant of Venice*. But if Bassanio is a wholly secularized and naturalized version of this figure, Pericles is not and signals a return on Shakespeare's part to an older dramatic mode. Unlike his medieval prototype, however, Pericles is not lusty or culpable but eminently virtuous. Yet his recognition of the incest writ large in the riddle is presented as a kind of fall, if only from innocence into knowledge, and his play too will be concerned with redemption.

The morality-related world of the opening scene is further developed in the next two episodes, which deal with Pericles' public charity at Tharsus and his wooing of Thaisa at Pentapolis. Antiochus, whose name and eventual fate within the play recall the Macedonian king of the Apocrypha (2 *Mac.* ix. 9), could be any number of corrupt and prideful rulers out of the medieval drama: Herod, Tiberius, Mundus himself. Cleon, the governor of Tharsus, whose pride and plenty have changed in the course of worldly affairs to poverty and famine, is right out of the same tradition. The point is not that Antiochus and Cleon are the "lust-dieted and superfluous man" of *King Lear* made flesh, but that the morality figures which lurk behind the flesh-and-blood characterizations of *Lear*, and which are visible there only in outline, have now been brought out onto the open stage.[5] Antiochus' daughter, nameless and mute for most of the scene, is more a personified abstraction than a character, more like a Nice Wanton or the nameless daughter seduced by her father in the fragmentary miracle play *Dux Moraud* than like any previous Shakespearean character. Dionyza, whose real nature will soon be revealed when she tempts Cleon into having Marina murdered, is not so much the pale shadow cast by Lady Macbeth as the much older figure of Hypocrisy who lies behind Lady Macbeth, one of several morality personifications who hides envy behind a mask of gratitude.

Pericles not only divides its cast right down the middle

[5] *The Crown of Life*, pp. 41-2. Throughout his pioneering study of the play, Knight remarks on the similarity between characters in *Pericles* and those of the preceding tragedies. The source of these resemblances, as I try to show in the course of this chapter, is not so much in the recapitulatory quality of *Pericles* or its celebrated archetypal and mythic quality as in the medieval and morality derived structure and characterization it shares with the tragedies, particularly with *Lear*. For a fascinating discussion of the "homiletic structure" of *Lear*, see Maynard Mack, *King Lear in Our Time* (Berkeley, 1965), pp. 45-80.

into sheep and goats, the good and the wicked, after the fashion of the earlier religious drama, but like that drama sets up elaborate moral patterns of contrast and similarity between them. Antiochus' courtier turned assassin, Thaliard, contrasts with Helicanus, whom Pericles tests and finds loyal and true. If "Good Helicane" tends to remind critics of Kent, it is not because he is based on Kent but because Kent is based on Helicanus, that is, on the good counselors like him in the pre-Shakespearean drama going all the way back to *Gorboduc* and beyond. Antiochus' incestuous daughter, whom Pericles disastrously woos, is the moral antitype to Simonides' virtuous daughter Thaisa, whom he successfully woos and weds, as well as to Marina, who is not "appareled *like* the spring" (1.i.13) nor looks "*As* heaven had lent her all his grace" (1. Chorus, 24), but possesses those regenerative powers in earnest. The vicious Antiochus also contrasts in his public role of king (he is repeatedly referred to as a "tyrant") with the responsible ruler Pericles, as we see him back at Tyre—Gower, as is his wont, moralizes on the opposition between "a mighty king" and "A better prince and benign lord" (II. *Prologue.* 1-3)—and then with "the good Simonides," whose virtues as a prince are remarked on by several of the characters present at his feast.

This brings up another feature of the play also unprecedented in Shakespeare: the way characters are in the habit of moralizing upon their own and one another's conduct and speeches. Although it is second nature to Gower, he is by no means the only character who bears this peculiar relation to the lines he speaks. We have already heard Pericles draw an extended moral on his situation before attempting Antiochus' deadly riddle. It is as though he had momentarily stepped outside his role, seen that his situation resembled that of the protagonist in a morality play on the summoning by death, and made a speech appropriate to the occasion on the theme of *contemptus mundi*. Cleon and Dionyza do the same thing when their city is stricken with famine:

> O, let those cities that of plenty's cup
> And her prosperities so largely taste,
> With their superfluous riots, hear these tears!
> The misery of Tharsus may be theirs.
>
> (i.iv.52-5)

Such a speech can hardly be defended as psychologically appropriate to the ruined king who speaks it; but given the didactic and parabolic orientation of this play, as Gower has announced it in his prologue, it is highly appropriate to the speaker and context: a dramatic *exemplum* illustrating the themes of *contemptus mundi* and *caritas*. Similarly when Pericles is washed up on the coast of Pentapolis and overhears some fishermen making and expounding parables to the effect that whales are to schools of fish as rich misers are to society, he remarks, "A pretty moral," and continues aside (presumably for our benefit): "How from the finny subject of the sea / These fishers tell the infirmities of men." (ii.i.48-50) When he later appears at the feast of Simonides, meanly clad and bearing a withered branch green only at the top with the motto *In hac spe vivo*, Simonides comments to Thaisa: "A pretty moral; / From the dejected state wherein he is / He hopes by you his fortunes yet may flourish." (ii.ii.44-5) Either

Thaisa cannot read Latin or the playwright wants to make sure the moral comes across to the audience. I submit that the latter is the more likely.

The formula operating here is that of fulfilled expectation, and the more often fulfilled, it would seem, the better. *Pericles* not only contains little in the way of narrative surprise or psychological suspense, like the religious drama, but often has its characters repeat themselves in a manner that recalls that drama, the Croxton *Play of the Sacrament* for example:

> Jew Jonathas thys ys my name,
>> Jazon & Jaydon thei waytyn on my wylle,
> Masfat & Malchus they do the same,
>> As ye may knowe, yt ys bothe rycht & skylle.
>> I telle yow alle, bi dal and by hylle,
> In Eraclea ys noon so moche of myght.
>> Werfor ye owe tenderli to tende me tylle,
> For I am chefe merchante of Jewes, I telle yow
>> by ryght.[6]

There is nothing here that the audience does not already know from the prologue. Nor would the audience of a miracle play have the slightest uncertainty as to how such a play will end. Jonathas the Jew will of course be converted, so that the more he boasts before his conversion the better. Similarly in *Pericles*, we know that all will end well (Gower leaves us in little doubt of that), our pleasure is simply in seeing it all work out. Gower uses his foreknowledge to this end, for his method is first to tell us

---

[6] *Specimens of the Pre-Shakespearean Drama*, ed. John Matthews Manly (Boston, 1897), I, 246.

what will happen in a scene and then to show us the thing itself.

The first two acts are taken up mainly with representing princely and social virtue in action. Pericles had disclosed to Helicanus after his misadventure at Antioch that there "I sought the purchase of a glorious beauty / From whence an issue I might propagate / Are arms to princes and bring joys to subjects." (i.ii.72-4) He expresses the concern worthy a good prince about leaving his realm without a ruler before he embarks for Tharsus, where his act of "princely charity" wins him the "purchase" of a different kind of "glory." At Pentapolis, where Pericles again seeks a queen and heir for the good of his kingdom, Simonides repeatedly holds forth on what becomes a worthy prince—so much so that he reminds Pericles of his father, whose princely glory caused others to "vail their crowns to his supremacy." (ii.iii.43) Pericles distinguishes himself at the public spectacle of Simonides' feast by his skill in the public arts of jousting, music, and dance and proves himself, in Simonides' words, "her [art's] labored scholar." (ii.iii.17) The moral contrast with Antiochus also occurs on the public level (Pericles refers to him as a "tyrant" and Gower didactically enforces that contrast by referring to Pericles as "a better prince and benign lord." (ii. Prologue. 3) Antiochus' sin is fittingly revealed and punished in full sight of his subjects. I would tentatively suggest that the gnomic quality of the verse in the first two acts may in fact have less to do with incompetent reporters or collaborators than with the public nature of the action represented, as well as with a deliberate effort to return to archaic modes of dramatic representation. How much more stiff and jingly, after all, are the speeches of Pericles, Cleon, Helicanus, and Simonides than the closing speeches of Prince Escalus in *Romeo and Juliet* and Lodovico in *Othello* or the closing couplets of Edgar in *Lear?* Public moralizing in Shakespeare is often sententious. Whatever the truth of this point (and I do not press it), the sea change that comes over Shakespeare's versification in the third act corresponds to a shift in the play's center of gravity and interest from Pericles as prince to Pericles as man, husband, and father.[7] By the end of the second act the public plot has run its course. Antiochus' threat to the person and realm of Pericles has been dispelled. Pericles, foiled once in his wish to secure his succession, is now married and ready to resume his throne, the heir he had hoped for now on the way. It is the private man who remains to be tested.

But if the quality of the verse changes from the second to the third act, Shakespeare's mode of dramatic representation remains essentially the same: archaic, parabolic, and didactic. The great scene that announces the distinctive speech-music of the final romances, in which Thaisa dies and Marina is born, presents Pericles' situation against the backdrop of the gigantic rhythms of nature and its language relates the death of his wife and birth of his daughter—described as "this piece / Of your dead queen" and "this fresh-new seafarer" (iii.17-18, 41)—to mankind's universal experience of birth and death:

> A more blustrous birth had never babe;
> Quiet and gentle thy conditions! for

[7] See G. A. Barker, "Themes and Variations in Shakespeare's *Pericles*," *English Studies*, XLIV (1963), 401-44.

Thou art the rudeliest welcome to this world
That e'er was prince's child. Happy what follows!
Thou hast as chiding a nativity
As fire, air, water, earth, and heaven can make,
To herald thee from the womb.   (iii.i.28-34)

The circumstances of Marina's birth are extraordinary to be
sure; yet her birth is distinguished from that of all men
only in the degree of its difficulty and is described more
as a paradigm of human childbirth than as a special case.
G. Wilson Knight is surely right that "the storm is general-
ized; the child's birth shown as an entry into storm-tossed
mortality recalling the crying child of old Lear's lunatic
sermon."[8]

But Marina, even at this early stage of her career, recalls a much older figure than Lear's crying child. In the
fifteenth-century *Mundas et Infans*, for example, the child
enters and delivers these lines:

Fourty wekes my moder me founde,
    Flesshe and blode my fode was tho;
Whan I was rype from her to founde,
    In peryll of dethe we stode bothe two.

. . .

Fourty wekes I was frely fedde
    Within my moders wombe;
Full oft of dethe she was adred
    Whan that I sholde parte her from.[9]

Marina's later recollections of the day of her birth are
hardly more credible, in naturalistic terms, than Infans'
account of her prenatal life:

[8] *The Crown of Life*, p. 53.   [9] *Specimens*, ed. Manly, I, 354-5.

Born in a tempest, when my mother died,
This world to me is as a lasting storm,
Whirring me from my friends.   (iv.i.17-20)

When I was born the wind was north.
                                    (iv.i.51)

                When I was born . . .
Never was waves nor wind more violent;
And from the ladder-tackle washes off
A canvas-climber.   (iv.i.58-61)

What these lines may lack in psychological propriety they
more than make up for in figurative potential. It is to a
mode of drama that cultivates the latter at the expense of
the former that we find Shakespeare returning in *Pericles*,
even in that part of the play where his authorship has not
been in question.

    In Shakespeare's earlier work, characterization may be
seen as the product of two distinct forces: the impulse to
create notable images of virtue and vice that take their
places within the moral vision of the play as a whole, and
the need to reflect psychological and social reality in the
effort to make the play an imitation of life. Although there
may be no conflict between these impulses in theory (Hamlet includes showing scorn her own image and the age her
form and pressure under his definition of the true purpose
of playing, and the Painter in *Timon* sees no contradiction
between making moral paintings and making lifelike ones),
there is often a certain tension between the two in practice. Prince Hal's first soliloquy, to take one of many possible examples, serves to alert us to the moral reformation his play will illustrate, but it is hard to say what his

state of mind is in delivering it. The failure to perceive
that Shylock's social identity as Jew and usurer is largely
a means of rationalizing and motivating the behavior required of him by his moral role as comic Vice has led many
to accuse Shakespeare of anti-Semitism. In *Pericles* the
impulse to hold the mirror up to nature all but gives way
to the impulse to create a moral vision. Characters in this
play repeatedly speak and act, not as they would in life—
why should Marina recount the story of her birth to
Leonine?—but as the moral vision of the play, with its
pattern of contrasts and symmetries, demands.

Cerimon is a case in point. Like Friar Laurence in *Romeo
and Juliet*, he functions as medical and spiritual healer,
albeit more successfully within the romantic action of
Pericles than his tragic counterpart. Both figures are in-
troduced practicing their art; Friar Laurence soliloquizes
on the theory and practice of herb medicine, and Cerimon
delivers a long monologue on its moral status and justification:

> I hold it ever,
> Virtue and cunning were endowments greater
> Than nobleness and riches; careless heirs
> May the two latter darken and expend,
> But immortality attends the former,
> Making a man a god. 'Tis known I ever
> Have studied physic, through which secret art,
> By turning o'er authorities, I have,
> Together with my practice, made familiar
> To me and to my aid the blest infusions
> That dwells in vegetives, in metals, stones;
> And can speak of the disturbances that

Nature works, and of her cures; which doth give me
A more content in course of true delight
Than to be thirsty after tottering honour,
Or tie my treasure up in silken bags,
To please the fool and death.   (III.ii.26-42)

While it is improbable that a physician in real life would
explain himself like Friar Laurence or Cerimon, the fact
that Friar Laurence is cast as a friar in the first place lends
some cover and pretext to his unlikely exposition of the
healer's art. In the case of Cerimon, not even this small
gesture toward naturalism is offered. Virtually everything
we learn about Cerimon is there to establish his moral
bearings within the design of the play: "Your honour has
through Ephesus pour'd forth / Your charity, and hun-
dreds call themselves / Your creatures, who by you have
been restor'd." (III.ii.43-5) His powers of "restoration"
recall the purpose of the tale itself as Gower had stated it
in the prologue. His charity aligns him with Pericles, whose
gift of corn to Tharsus had brought "them life whom hun-
ger starv'd half dead" (I.iv.96), as well as with the good
fishermen of Pentapolis, who restored Pericles' sea-rusted
armor to him. As a rich man, Cerimon's rejection of wealth
and worldly glory contrasts with the antisocial "rich
miser" of the fishermen's parable and with the shaky glory
of Tharsus and its king and queen. His long monologue
has, of course, numerous precedents in the medieval drama,
among them the ending of *Everyman*, where Good-Deeds
alone accompanies the protagonist to the grave. When
Thaisa's coffin is washed ashore and he applies his restorative art to her "entranced" corpse, the audience would have

known exactly what to expect. For the scene also has its medieval precedents; it is analogous to the raising of the Queen of Marcylle, apparently dead after childbirth, and of Lazarus in the Digby *Mary Magdalene*, and Cerimon himself to the Christ of the miracle play. "The heavens through you, increase our wonder," marvels the trusty first gentleman whose choric role in the scene mirrors Gower's in the play as a whole, "And set up your fame forever." (iii.ii.98-9) It is worth noting that "wonder," the emotion so often appealed to in *Pericles* and the romances, is produced quite differently from "surprise," the more sophisticated effect that plays like those of Beaumont and Fletcher have on us. Surprise depends upon the frustration of our expectation, wonder on the fulfillment of them. In a play like *Pericles* we feel wonder when we finally see come true what we have all along taken on faith—in both St. Paul's sense of the evidence of things unseen and Coleridge's sense of willed belief in the dramatic illusion before us, incredible as it may be as an imitation of life.

If the fishermen do not talk like fishermen, nor Cerimon like a physician, the inmates of the brothel at Mytilene bear little resemblance to the more lifelike panders and bawds of *Measure for Measure* with whom they are often compared. The earlier scene with the fishermen had presented regenerate men, whose Biblical simplicity raised them above the social evils and human infirmities they discussed in parables. The brothel scenes by contrast present human nature at its most degenerate and infirm (as in *Measure for Measure*) but even the panders and bawds of this play make a habit of stepping outside their roles and commenting on them from the moral perspective of the play as a whole—not at all as in *Measure for Measure*. "The sore terms we stand upon with the gods," says the Pander to the Bawd, "will be strong with us for giving o'er." (IV.ii.32-3) Boult reports that their clientele listened to his advertisements of Marina "as they would have hearken'd to their father's testament." (IV.ii.96-7) Their profession is "no calling." (IV.ii.36) Their profane argot constantly reminds us of the religious authority they violate, and I venture to say that this is not the idiom of real or realistic prostitutes.

Nor is what follows. When Marina prays to Diana to preserve her virginity, the Bawd exclaims, "What have we to do with Diana?" (IV.iii.48) But Marina, as the human embodiment of Diana's divine grace, will reform the stews of Mytilene. "Did you ever hear the like?" one patron, taking over the moralistic function of the Chorus, asks his companion:

2. Gentleman. No, nor never shall do in such a place as this, she being once gone.

1. Gentleman. But to have divinity preach'd there! Did you ever dream of such a thing?

2. Gentleman. No, no. Come, I am for no more bawdy-houses.

Shall's go hear the vestals sing?   (IV.v.2-7)

The Bawd says "she would make a puritan of the devil" (IV.vi.9), and Boult, unable even to ravish her, confesses that "She makes our profession as it were to stink afore the face of the gods" (IV.vi.135-6), ingenuously echoing his father's testament (cf. 2 *Cor.*2:14). This "Piece of virtue," in short, converts her would-be corruptors to a man. In *Measure for Measure*, the lust of the flesh had been seen as endemic to human nature, and the best that the Duke could manage was to sacramentalize it. In *Pericles*, nature becomes redeemable, for grace, personified in Marina, abounds even to the worst of sinners, just as it had in countless miracle and morality plays before *Pericles*. Marina culminates a long and popular tradition of incorruptibly virtuous heroines going back to the saint's legend of St. Agnes. The pre-Shakespearean drama teemed with such maidens (Susanna, Virginia, Patient Grissil) who seem to have evoked nothing but admiration in contemporary audiences, and whose outlines are still visible in Desdemona and Cordelia. Shakespeare's audience, which retained much of the medieval delight in didacticism, had often "heard the like" and apparently enjoyed hearing it again.

In turning from a relatively naturalistic to a parabolic drama at this point in his career, in exchanging a Pompey for a Boult and a Lucio for a Lysimachus, Shakespeare does not so much repudiate verisimilitude as exchange one kind of verisimilitude for another. T. S. Eliot owlishly remarks that the characters of the last romances are "the work of a writer who has finally seen through the dramatic action of men into a spiritual action which transcends it" and that Shakespeare "makes us feel not so much that his characters are creatures like ourselves, as that we are creatures like his characters, taking part like them in no common action of which we are for the most part unaware."[10] It is not necessary to see *Pericles* as a Catholic drama to realize that it is a catholic one, and that the sense of universality it so powerfully conveys has much to do with its consistent adoption of the methods, if not the dogma, of an older dramatic tradition. Consider, for example, the first of its justly acclaimed recognition scenes. By this time in his career Shakespeare had made the recognition scene, as it is handed down from new comedy with its unmaskings and reunions, fully his own. Yet in three of his late recognitions—those of Lear and Cordelia, Pericles and Marina, and Leontes and Hermione—we may fairly detect something superadded to the conventions of new comedy and to the situations presented in his immediate sources, something which crystallizes the experience of a lifetime into a moment, which turns the theater into the great globe itself, and which reaches out from the situation on stage to implicate our own situation and our own roles of father or husband, daughter or wife. It seems to me that behind the immediate conventions and materials of each of these scenes lies another set of conventions and kind of material that works to endow them with their peculiar power and universality.

Perhaps the best way I can suggest the ultimate sources that Shakespeare imaginatively reworks in these scenes, particularly that of *Pericles*, and the nature of the verisimilitude attained in them is to summarize, at the risk of sounding like Gower, a song that old was sung: the legend of the Roman general Placidus who became St. Eustace.

[10] Quoted from an unpublished lecture of Eliot's by Kenneth Muir, *Shakespeare as Collaborator* (London, 1960), p. 83.

Placidus was converted while hunting by a vision of Christ
and proceeded to have himself, his wife, and two sons bap-
tized. Christ warns him that he will be so sorely tried,
tempted, and humbled as to become "another Job," and
Placidus asks only for patience to endure whatever comes.
His household is afflicted by pestilence, persecution, and
robbers. When he and his family embark for Egypt, his
wife is threatened with rape, and he is thrown overboard
with his two sons. His sons are carried off by a wolf and
a lion, but are rescued without Placidus' knowledge by
herdsmen, just as his wife is also spared from the assault
of the shipman. Fifteen years pass, in which Placidus,
stripped of all he once had and more humbled than Job,
tends the fields in a certain village. The Emperor sends
two knights to find Placidus, whom they recognize by a
scar on his head, and restore him to his generalship to put
down marauding barbarians. His sons are sent up from
their village. The battle won, his troops rest in a town
where his wife keeps an inn. She overhears her sons recounting their infancy and goes to the general:

> She saw in him signs, and knew by them that he was her
> husband, and then she might no longer forbear, but fell
> down at his feet and said to him: "Sir, I pray thee to
> tell of thy first estate, for I ween that thou art Placidus,
> master of the knights, which otherwise art called Eu-
> stace, whom the Saviour of the world hath converted,
> and hast suffered such temptation and such, and I that
> am thy wife was taken from thee in the sea, which
> nevertheless have been kept from all corruption, and
> haddest of me two sons Agapitus and Theospitus." And

Eustace hearing this, and diligently considered and beheld her, anon knew that she was his wife, and wept for joy and kissed her. . . . And she said: "Let us give thankings to God, for I suppose that like as God hath given to us grace each to find other, so shall he give us grace to recover our sons." And he said: "I have told thee that they be devoured of wild beasts"; and she then said: "I sat yesterday in a garden and heard two younglings thus and thus expounding their infancy, and I believe that they be our sons, demand them and they shall tell to thee the truth. Then Eustace called them, and heard their infancy and knew that they were his sons. Then he embraced them and the mother also, and kissed them also.[11]

The family is subsequently martyred by Hadrian for their refusal to do sacrifice to pagan idols. The legend of St. Eustace was the subject of a lost miracle play recorded under the whimsical title, "Placy Dacy, alias St. Eustacy," and performed at Braintree, Essex in 1534.[12]

It would be an error of misplaced concreteness to say that Shakespeare saw this story acted in a later production, or even that he was familiar with the career of St. Eustace.

[11] *The Golden Legend or Lives of the Saints as Englished by William Caxton* (London, 1900), VI, 91-3.

[12] See John M. Manly, "The Miracle Play in Mediaeval England," *Transactions of the Royal Society of Literature*, New Series, Vol. III, ed. Margaret L. Woods (London, 1927), p. 147. Although he does not have *Pericles* or the final romances specifically in mind, Manly persuasively roots the Elizabethan romantic drama in miracle plays like that of St. Eustace. See also Hardin Craig, *English Religious Drama of the Middle Ages* (Oxford, 1960), pp. 320-53, and R. G. Hunter, *Shakespeare and the Comedy of Forgiveness* (New York, 1965), pp. 130-41.

Neither can we say with much assurance what form such a story would have taken on the stage. We can only speculate, from the remains of the English miracle play which are extant, that such a play would have been episodic in structure from the nature of its subject matter and ceremonious and spectacular in treatment from the nature of its auspices and occasion. In sum, it would probably have made the sort of play of which *Pericles*, as I have tried to show, keeps reminding us. If Shakespeare was not familiar with the miracle play of St. Eustace, there can be little doubt that he was familiar with miracle plays which enacted similar romantic stories in similar ways, and I think it may fairly be said that his familiarity with this kind of drama directly affected the use he made of more immediate sources like Gower and Twine in *Pericles* and Greene in *The Winter's Tale*. The moment of recognition between Eustace and his wife lends itself to treatment as the kind of dramatic tableau we see in the figures of Cordelia and the kneeling Lear. As Eustace's wife recounts the story of their conversion and suffering and he weeps for joy, we can see how easily Shakespeare might have recast such a scene into that of Pericles' reunion with his daughter:

> Tell thy story:
> If thine considered prove the thousandth part
> Of my endurance, thou art a man, and I
> Have suffer'd like a girl; yet thou dost look
> Like Patience gazing on kings' graves, and smiling
> Extremity out of act.   (v.i.134-9)

Pericles asks if she is "flesh and blood . . . and are no fairy," for she looks "Modest as Justice" and seems "a palace /

For the crown'd Truth to dwell in" (v.i.120-22), just as Cordelia appears to her reviving father in their comparable scene as "a soul in bliss." Surely these references of Pericles and Lear to angels and allegorical figures are the fossils of similar scenes in an earlier drama, where Justice, Truth, Patience, and ministering angels did appear onstage bringing reunion and reconciliation, an earlier drama that, in Theseus' words, "if it would but apprehend some joy, / It comprehends some bringer of that joy."

As Christ's prediction of Job-like trials and suffering to Placidus suggests, his whole story exists in a very special sense for the sake of its recognition scene. For the miracle play presents an exemplary, if not explicitly allegorical, action which is in its very nature analogous to the experience of every good Christian as well as that of Christ himself. In *Pericles*, Gower similarly serves to connect our experience of the play with the experience the play presents. Just as Pericles' family is restored and he is redeemed from his almost purgatorial suffering, so the tale is conceived as a "restorative" to its audience. The "patience" that Pericles is said at several points in the play by several characters to lack Gower exhorts us to have, to bear with him as Pericles must learn to bear with misfortune. His impatient outcry upon the loss of Thaisa—"O you gods! / Why do you make us love your goodly gifts, / And snatch them straight away?" (iii.i.22-4)—is answered in the final act, as Diana appears to him in a vision, his daughter and wife are restored, and he hears the music of the spheres. He has been "sacred" to the gods in both senses of that primal word, both "cursed" and "blessed," as every man is in the Christian scheme of things, and the extremity of his suffering is recompensed in the sublimity of his exaltation. His recognition scene begins with our apprehension of a purgatorial figure dressed in sackcloth, fourteen years unshaven, fasting and virtually dead to the world and ends with a beatific vision, or rather audition, of the music of the spheres. "Come hither," he says to Marina, "Thou that beget'st him that did thee beget" (v.i.194-5), reversing the incest of the first scene into its opposite: the redemptive love of father and child at the center of the Christian mystery and paralleled in this play. The opening scene had suggested the fall; the closing ones the redemption. The "present kindness" of the gods, says Pericles at Diana's shrine at Ephesus, "Makes my past miseries sports" (v.iii.40-41), a paradox which recalls the *Exultet* of the Easter service when man's fall is said to be a happy fall, and which enforces the parallel between Pericles' experience and that of Christian history. When he asks "who to thank, / Besides the gods, for this great miracle" (v.iii.57-8), Pericles explicitly calls attention to the dramatic antecedents of his play, for what we call "miracle plays" were in their own time called simply "miracles." Pericles' beatific audition corresponds, with a difference, to the conventional ending of the miracle play in which the saint or the enlightened is translated to heaven to the accompaniment of angelic choirs.

The difference is that even though Pericles hears that music he does not die a martyr's death. He is not St. Pericles, nor was meant to be. He is revived by Marina's "sacred physic," just as Thaisa is revived by that of Cerimon, "through whom the gods have shown their power." (v.iii.60) Both of them are "saved" from death in a romantic but not in an explicitly Christian sense. The Christian story is a romance, but not all romances are Christian. Shakespeare takes pains to make clear that we are in a realm of analogy rather than identity. Marina has been "god*like* perfect, the heir of kingdoms, / And another life to Pericles thy father" (v.i.206-7), and as for Cerimon, "The gods can have no mortal officer / More *like* a god than you." (v.iii.62-3) Although Shakespeare is straining to its limit the analogy between the action and actors of this "great miracle" and those of the miracle play proper, it remains an analogy. Neptune and Diana, who preside over the action, are the conventional deities of classical romance rather than stand-ins for the high God of Christianity.[13] *Pericles* diverges from its medieval antecedents in ending not with the assumption of its hero into heaven but with his return to Tyre to carry on as prince. Although sympathetic critics of the play are sometimes carried away themselves by its heavenly music and liken the action of *Pericles* to that of *The Divine Comedy*, Pericles' career is actually closer to that of Spenser's Red Cross Knight, *alias* St. George, who after a painful ordeal of self-mortification, glimpses from afar the New Jerusalem, wants to go there

[13] The Act of Abuses of 1606 had technically forbidden dramatists from writing "God" or "Christ" into their plays but was often ignored in practice. *Henry VIII*, for example, repeatedly names God with impunity and leaves no doubt as to the nature of its presiding deity. By employing pagan deities from conventional romance in *Pericles*, and by surrounding them with Christian-providential associations, Shakespeare has the best of both worlds: a timeless romantic action with unmistakably Christian relevance. Similarly, the various settings of the play are at once classical and Biblical. Even if Shakespeare was heeding the Act of Abuses, it is merely another instance of the way the art of his necessities makes vile things precious.

directly, but has to return to this world to complete his mission in it. Like Mankind in *The Castle of Perseverance*, both Pericles and Thaisa withdraw from the pain and vicissitudes of the Earthly City (already represented in the brittle glory of Tharsus) into a decidedly medieval asceticism. But Shakespeare's way with them is that of Marina, Cerimon, and Gower: to restore them to the ranks of humanity. The perception of braver, newer, or better worlds, for Shakespeare as for Spenser, is never an end in itself but simply the means of modifying the way we look on this one.

The religious drama of the Middle Ages and early Renaissance was predicated on the belief in an unchanging reality superior to the world of appearances in which we live. The characters of Shakespeare's earlier plays, pre-eminently Hamlet, live and die knowing only "seems." Kent says "it is the stars that govern our conditions," while Cassius insists that "the fault . . . is not in our stars but in ourselves." Macbeth comes to believe that life is "a tale told by an idiot," and Edgar that "ripeness is all." Gloucester thinks at one point that the gods "kill us for their sport," while Hamlet, approaching the mood of the last plays in his final scenes, affirms that there is "a special providence in the fall of a sparrow" and "a divinity that shapes our ends"—though their existence remains questionable to the end. The very absence of a single theory of reality in these plays is a precondition for their more or less naturalistic technique, which, paradoxically, represents things only as they seem. Existence can be rendered naturalistically; essence cannot. When a poet attempts to represent the essential reality which lies behind the surface of things, as the dramatists of the Middle Ages did, as Spenser later does in *The Faerie Queene* and Milton does in *Paradise Lost*, he must resort to dark conceits or liken "spiritual to corporal forms, / As may express them best." (*P.L.*v.573-4) When Shakespeare turned to the romantic legend of Apollonius of Tyre, he may well have seen in it a paradigm of the moral life of man, for in its "pattern of painful adventures" all he had previously done in tragedy and comedy was summarized in "a tempest, / A birth and death." (v.iii.33-4) The titlepage of Twine's version of the story speaks of "The Patterne of painefull Adventures: Containing the most excellent, pleasant and variable Historie of the strange accidents that befell unto Prince Apollonius, the Lady Lucina his wife, and Tharsia his daughter. Wherein the uncertaintie of this world, and the fickle state of mans life are lively described." Shakespeare, while he plays down the "accidental" and plays up the providential aspect of the story, remains true to its essential pattern. The problem was how to represent such an action dramatically while faithfully conveying its exemplary nature.

The medieval drama had two invaluable assets which enabled it to project its Christian vision on the stage: an audience which already accepted its vision of life as the revealed truth and a readily available set of "corporal forms," also familiar to its audience—an anthropomorphic God, a whole bevy of saints, angels and devils incarnate, personified virtues and sins. Shakespeare capitalizes in Pericles on the response of an audience already familiar with an exemplary or allegorical kind of drama. For the coexistence of allegorical-religious and naturalistic-secular drama in Shakespeare's age implies the coexistence of two potential responses in Shakespeare's audience. The dramatic poet who earlier in his career had jibed satirically at a moribund dramatic tradition (it out-herods Herod) was to revert to that tradition for the first of his last plays. The gnomic, end-stopped, fitfully rhymed verse of the first acts of *Pericles*, it has been remarked, seems earlier than the earliest Shakespeare we know. It is clear from the plays-within-a-play of *Love's Labour's Lost*, *A Midsummer Night's Dream* and *Hamlet* that he was perfectly capable of resurrecting a more primitive verse style for his own purposes. In those plays the archaic style serves to differentiate the plays-within-a-play from the plays themselves, in fact, to make them *seem like plays* and the remarks of Berowne, Theseus, Hippolyta, Hamlet, and Gertrude which frame and interrupt them seem like life. In *Pericles* the deliberate archaism of the first act serves to tell his audience, already forewarned by the figure and speech of Gower, not to respond as they would to a naturalistic play, but to call up that other response still potential in their minds, the response appropriate to parabolic drama. Shakespeare seems to be saying through Gower's appeals and apologies and the archaic verse of the play itself what Theseus says to still Hippolyta's impatience with Bottom's play: "The best in this kind are but shadows; and the worst are no worse, if imagination amend them."

The significance of *Pericles* for our study of the final romances, for our understanding of Shakespeare's work as a whole, is not that it reveals Shakespeare undergoing (like one of his own romantic characters) a religious conversion or that it reflects the senility or serenity of his old age. Nor is it to be sought, as I for one believe, on the level of technical experimentation justified only by its fruits in *The Winter's Tale* and *The Tempest*. Anticipations of the romances to come are numerous and tantalizing—one thinks of the double recognition scene to be reenacted in *The Winter's Tale*; of Pericles' decision to forego the less rare action of vengeance on Cleon as prefiguring Prospero's; of Marina as a Proserpine figure snatched away by the pirate Valdes to the underworld of Mytilene, where she becomes its queen and brings renewal, like Perdita after her. Such features no doubt reveal a good deal about the romance poetics and mythic substructure common to all the last plays. Perhaps more importantly, however, *Pericles* reveals Shakespeare reassessing the premises on which his art had always been based, wholeheartedly returning to that kind of drama which to a great extent had helped shape his own, and attempting to recover the inclusiveness of old tales like those which, in Sidney's words, "holdeth children from play, and old men from the chimney corner."[14]

For like Marina's own art as described by Gower, the art Shakespeare employs in *Pericles* exerts its appeal on the naive and sophisticated alike and is itself naive and sophisticated at once:

> She sings like one immortal, and she dances
> As goddess-like to her admired lays.
> Deep clerks she dumbs, and with her needle composes
> Nature's own shape, of bud, bird, branch, or berry,

[14] *An Apology for Poetry*, ed. Geoffrey Shepherd (London, 1965), p. 113.

That even her art sisters the natural roses;
Her inkle, silk, twin with the rubied cherry.

(v.Chorus,3-8)

It matters less that her art prefigures that of Julio Romano
in *The Winter's Tale* than that both stand as a paradigm
of Shakespeare's own latest art, whose artifice is so complete as not only to bear the stamp of nature but to lay
claim to her recreative power. It is this kind of "prosperous
and artificial feat" (v.i.72) that Marina employs to revive
her wasted father, and that Shakespeare employs in the play
as a whole to revive a moribund dramatic mode, whose
romantic materials and didactic methods were inseparable
and harmonious, and which, though as crude and capti-
vating as the old tales Sidney mentions, also in Sidney's
words, "doth intend the winning of the mind from wickedness to virtue."[15] The peculiar power and universality
of *Pericles* and the subsequent romances, it seems to me,
has less to do with their "conventional" or "mythic" or
"archetypal" dimension than with their medieval dimension. Or perhaps the two are finally inseparable and the
same, to the extent that the apparent crudeness and naiveté
of such plays is the condition of their power and universality. Because virtually everything in such plays is subordi-
nated to a didactic purpose: they begin not in the middle
of an action but at the beginning and proceed linearly to
the end; they frankly announce and reiterate their designs
on the audience; and their characters are simplified types
rather than complex personalities. They may strike us as
technically crude, yet there is an important sense in which

[15] *Ibid.*

they hold the mirror up to nature as faithfully as the most sophisticated of plays, which we mistakenly equate with naturalistic.

If there is any truth in these contentions, they may help to explain why *Pericles* should have been among the most popular of Shakespeare's plays in its early years and among the least popular of them thereafter, as well as why it has very recently begun to regain a place for itself in contemporary repertories. The impulse to make what takes place on the stage an illusion of life—an impulse which one already feels in Jonson, which gains strength in Restoration and eighteenth-century comedy, and which culminates in Ibsen and Shaw—has been the dominant force in the English theater since the Renaissance. Such an orientation is, as I have tried to show, basically incompatible with the medieval dimension of *Pericles*, and to a lesser degree, of the subsequent romances. This basic incompatibility was sensed by Lamb when he remarked that he cared nothing for the "painted trees and caverns, which we know to be painted" in the elaborate stagings of *The Tempest* in his own time, for "spirits and fairies cannot be represented, they cannot even be painted—they can only be believed."[16] It also underlies Shaw's fine perception that *Cymbeline* "can be done delightfully in a village schoolroom, and can't be done at the Lyceum at all, on any terms."[17] Such remarks apply even more pointedly to *Pericles*. But the contemporary theater is entering a new phase. Beginning

[16] "On the Tragedies of Shakspeare," *The Complete Correspondence and Works of Charles Lamb*, ed. Thomas Purnell (London, 1870), III, 106.

[17] *Shaw on Shakespeare*, ed. Edwin Wilson (New York, 1961), p. 44.

perhaps with Brecht, whose notion of a didactic "epic theater" is profoundly anti-illusionist in principle, the plays which now hold the boards are conceived as anything but naturalistic imitations of life, and the stage has adapted itself to them. As long as it does so we will have a theater in which it is also possible to bring *Pericles* to life once again.

CHAPTER 6

Tragical-Comical-Historical-Pastoral:
Cymbeline and Henry VIII

This riddling tale, to what does it belong?
Is't history? vision? or an idle song?
—Coleridge

IT IS ALMOST as if *Cymbeline* and *Henry VIII* are conceived in reaction to the romances that precede them. For all the complexity of its action *Cymbeline* actually begins *in medias res*, enabling Shakespeare to dispense with the long time-lapse and choric links of *Pericles* and to return, at least partially, to the conventions of dramatic illusionism. If *Cymbeline* is less episodic in structure than *Pericles*, it is also less archaic in verse and less didactic in manner and tone. Then too, *Cymbeline* is a historical play, and it is possible to imagine Shakespeare attempting to bring the far-flung action of romance somewhat closer to home by assimilating it into the historical form, which for the Elizabethans functioned as a glass reflecting the present in the past. *Henry VIII* would seem to bear a similar relation to *The Tempest*. Although *The Tempest* goes about as far as romance can go in the direction of dramatic illusionism, its world remains essentially fabulous. It might be, in fact, has been, said that to ballast the insubstantiality of his last pageant faded, Shakespeare turns from the non-existent Mediterranean island of *The Tempest* to the real island of Britain, and from that play's "dark backward and abysm of time" to recent Tudor history.[1] The alternative title of *Henry VIII*, *All Is True*, would seem to support such a theory of its genesis. But whatever the value of these speculations, the facts remain that *Cymbeline* and *Henry VIII* are distinctive among the last plays for being histories and that neither has been considered an unqualified success. It may be that these facts are related and that *Cymbeline* and *Henry VIII*, taken together, illustrate some of the problems that arise when history is conflated with romance.

If there is one point on which most of the past criticism on *Cymbeline* is in agreement, it is that the play offers an astounding amount of internal incongruity. Samuel Johnson remarked on "the folly of the fiction, the absurdity of the conduct, the confusion of the names, and manners of different times, and the impossibility of the events in any system of life."[2] More sympathetic critics have since attempted to resolve its incongruities of time, place, and action into imaginative unity by approaching it as a national play, a Christian allegory, or a fashionable adventure into tragicomic romance. But as long as *Cymbeline* is viewed under one or another of these rubrics, it will remain an untidy potboiler. Critics from Samuel Johnson onward have looked for unity of action in a play where there is only the most extraordinary unity of design, the design that

---

[1] See R. A. Foakes, ed., *King Henry VIII* (New Arden Shakespeare, Cambridge, Mass., 1957), pp. xli-xlii.

[2] *Samuel Johnson on Shakespeare*, ed. W. K. Wimsatt, Jr. (New York, 1960), p. 108.

Elizabethan romance, Christian history and the Tudor myth of the British past all share, and that Shakespeare interweaves into the fabric of this play. Rather than an incongruous recasting of incompatible materials, *Cymbeline* is probably the most unified (which is not to say the best) romance that Shakespeare wrote.

The action of *Cymbeline* occurs on three distinct levels. There is the sexual or "romance" plot proper in which the marriage of Imogen and Posthumus has been challenged by Cymbeline and his Queen as the play opens and is later threatened by the sexual machinations of Iachimo and Cloten. On the familial and dynastic level, Cymbeline's sons and heirs, Arviragus and Guiderius, have been kidnapped from the court by Belarius and raised in a cave in the Welsh hills. At the level of international politics, friendly relations between Rome and Britain have been disrupted by Cymbeline's refusal, at the instigation of the Queen and Cloten, to render unto Caesar that which is Caesar's, with the consequences of a Roman invasion and a war of independence. Each of these actions is partially under way when the play opens: Imogen has already married Posthumus against her father's wishes, Belarius has kidnapped the princes twenty years before, and Britain has been paying tribute to Rome ever since the time of Julius Caesar. The fortunes of Britain pass from an insecure isolation through a crisis of hostilities to a new sense of security and identity—the cycle followed by the fortunes of Imogen and Posthumus, and by those of Belarius and Cymbeline's lost sons also. The fact that the play thus opens *in medias res*, at or near the lowest point in the

fortunes of all the principals should make us think twice
before charging Shakespeare with carelessness in deploy-
ing his materials, as critics were once quick to do.

It is strongly hinted that a rarer action is taking place
offstage behind the several actions of *Cymbeline*. Its title
would probably have been enough to remind its original
audience of the privileged setting the play occupies within
Christian history. Perhaps the only fact on which the
chroniclers of his reign were agreed was that Cymbeline
was king of Britain at the time of the incarnation. "Little
other mention is made of his doings," writes Holinshed,
"except that during his reign the Saviour of the world, our
Lord Jesus Christ the only Son of God, was borne of a
virgin about the twenty-third year of the reign of this
Cymbeline."[3] Spenser makes much of this fact (it is all he
does make much of in his reign) in the British chronicle
included in *The Faerie Queene*:

> *Caesar* got the victory . . . .
> Thenceforth this land was tributarie made
> T'ambitious *Rome*, and did their rule obey
> Till *Arthur* all that reckoning defrayd;
> Yet oft the Briton kings against them strongly swayd.
>
> Next him Tenantius raigned, then *Kimbeline*,
> What time th'eternal Lord in fleshly slime
> Enwombed was, from wretched Adam's line
> To purge away the guilt of sinfull crime:
> O joyous memorie of happy time,
> That heavenly grace so plenteously displayd;

---

[3] *Shakespeare's Holinshed*, ed. Richard Hosley (New York, 1968),
p. 4.

(O too high ditty for my simple rime.)
Soone after this the *Romanes* him warrayed;
For that their tribute he refused to let be payd.

(II.x.49-50)

Just before his victory over Antony, Octavius Caesar had prophesied that "the time of universal peace is near. / Prove this a prosp'rous day, the three-nook'd world / Shall bear the olive freely." (*A&C*, IV,vi.5-7) He is looking forward to the *Pax Romana*, his reign settled upon the world prior to the coming of Christ, while Cleopatra's dream of a universal emperor, though cast as a loving glorification of Antony, also suggests the king of kings whose reign they die too soon to see. Posthumus' "curiously oracular gaoler," as Northrop Frye terms him,[4] also envisions a time when we will be "all of one mind, and one mind good," when there will be "desolation of gaolers and gallowses" (v.iv.209-11); in sum, to a momentous change for the better in the fortunes of the entire human community.

This rarer action, although it takes place offstage and is only hinted at within the play, nevertheless lends its shape to the onstage action of *Cymbeline*. The incarnation represents a turning point within Christian history from the eras of nature and law to a new era of grace. The former are characterized by wrath and justice, motives associated with tragical history; the latter by love and mercy, motives associated with romantic comedy. Just such a movement occurs within *Cymbeline*, whose first four acts are a fabric of coercive and vindictive actions and reactions: Cym-

---

[4] *A Natural Perspective* (New York, 1965), p. 66.

beline's attempted coercion of Imogen into marrying Cloten, his banishment of Posthumus, Cloten's repeated assaults on Imogen's virtue, Rome's enforcement of her tribute on Britain, Britain's defiance of Rome, and so on. The Welsh setting may seem a virtuous refuge from the pressurized world of Roman politics and courtly intrigue, what Cloten, speaking of Britain calls "a world / By itself." (III.i.12-13) This is certainly how Belarius tries to represent it, but it actually represents a false refuge and a fugitive virtue. Belarius' flight to Wales with the princes was an act of retaliation in the first place; he keeps them there against their wills and in ignorance of their birth; and he himself lives in dread of a day of reckoning (a day which seems imminent once Guiderius slays Cloten). The entry of Cloten, a graceless figure spluttering threats and abuse, into the pastoral world reveals its inherent vulnerability to the world of history outside it, while his peremptory slaying at Guiderius' hands shows the latter to be, despite his idyllic upbringing, his father's son in more than a biological sense. When the ensuing Roman war threatens to turn the Welsh hills into a bloodbath, it looks as if the world of tragical history will engulf the world of pastoral romance altogether, making the green world red.

In fact, just the opposite happens. For as the principals act out their vindictive wills, they find themselves boxed into tighter and tighter corners (literally, in the cases of Belarius in his mountain cave and Posthumus in his prison-cell) and their freedom of action sharply contracted. The rhetoric of the later acts conveys a growing sense of human helplessness as the principals recognize that only some higher power can, in the jailer's words, quit them of the contradictions they have gotten themselves into. After learning the probable consequences of his brother's slaying of Cloten, Arviragus resigns himself to "Let ordinance / Come as the gods foresay it." (iv.ii.145-6) Pisanio, the reluctant agent of Posthumus' revenge on Imogen, is "Perplex'd in all" and reconciled that "The heavens still must work." (iv.ii.41-2) Posthumus himself, who seems to have gone completely limp by the time he realizes his folly, leaves it to the gods to "do your best wills / And make me blest to obey." (v.i.16-17) All this sounds very like stoicism, that fashionable Renaissance doctrine of apathy, whose danger, as Milton repeatedly warns, lies precisely in its being so near to Christian faith, and yet so very far from it. But the play brings its characters beyond stoicism, the locus of which occurs in the dirge sung over Fidele's "corpse." Its litany of "fear no more" may be appropriate to the pagan and pastoral setting within which it is spoken, but both song and setting are left behind by the movement of the play. For the tribulations transcended in the beautiful dirge— "the frown o' th' great," "the tyrant's stroke," "slander," "censure rash," even "the lightning flash / And th'all-dreaded thunder-stone" (iv.ii.258-71)—all are to be faced and feared again in the final scene when their agents (Cymbeline, Iachimo, Posthumus, and Jupiter himself) appear, and by the girl supposedly free from them. If *Cymbeline* were a strictly pre-Christian play, governed by the "thunder-bearer" of Posthumus' dream, who behaves as imperiously toward those unlaid ghosts as Cymbeline does toward his court, stoicism might be wisdom. But it is superseded in the course of the play along with Jupiter himself. For Jupiter is a divine lame-duck whose term of office is about to expire, and the ending of the play has more to do with the doctrine of another deity whose reign is about to begin.

In the final recognition scene, stoicism gives way to Christianity and tragical history gives way to romance. The old order does not die easily, however, and Cymbeline, whose apparently limitless capacity for royal anger has already come close to losing him his sons, his daughter, and his kingdom, is ready to reenact yet again his past errors. "We will die all three" (v.v.310) Belarius announces before revealing their true identities to him. Guiderius, for killing Cloten, "must / Endure our law: thou'rt dead" (v.v.298-9), and Belarius is sentenced to death twice by a still intransigent Cymbeline: first for speaking "too far" in Guiderius' defense and then again for admitting who he really is. As for Lucius and the Roman prisoners, Cymbeline has decreed that "nothing but our lives / May be call'd ransom" (v.v.79-80), until he learns "freeness of a son-in-law" and spares them. *Cymbeline* repeatedly brings its characters to the point of stoically accepting death as an escape from the miseries of life (the attitude voiced by Posthumus in prison and by Cymbeline's sons in their dirge for Fidele) only to awaken them to a resurrected life, not unlike that promised by Pauline Christianity, in which the old man dies that the new may be born. Imogen has already taken a potion which the Queen misrepresents as having "the king / Five times redeem'd from death." (i.vi.62-3) When asked at the conclusion whether she took the concoction, she replies: "Most like I did, for I was dead." (v.v.259) Belarius has already asked, upon seeing her among the Roman prisoners, "Is not this boy reviv'd from death?" (v.v.120) Posthumus, whose name refers both to the unusual circumstances of his birth and to the second life he is granted after contrition and imprisonment, has been condemned to death as a Roman. The most moving line Posthumus utters, "Hang there like fruit, my soul, / Till the tree die" (v.v.263-4), a line that brought tears to Tennyson's eyes, is a resonant echo of both the fall and the atonement. Even Iachimo is caught up in the new spirit of the final scene and undergoes an otherwise unmotivated, morality-like reformation. He is granted a second life by Posthumus, who tells him to "Live, / And deal with others better" (v.v.419-20)—a phrase that echoes the cardinal tenet of Christian mercy. At the end of *Cymbeline*, the characters are capable, by virtue of its setting in time, of new possibilities of redeeming themselves through their own actions. They suffer guilt and contrition, freely confess their crimes, and exercise forgiveness well beyond their capabilities at the beginning, where, as a choric gentleman had put it in the opening line of the play, "Our bloods / No more obey the heavens than our courtiers / Still seem as does the King's." The rarer action taking place offstage enables Cymbeline to say at the end, "Does the world go round? / If this be so the gods do mean to strike me / To death with mortal joy." (v.v.232-5) The world has indeed gone round, and Shakespeare exploits its revolution. The Roman gives place to the Christian not only within the action as a whole but within each character, and tragical history gives way to romance.

The only characters in the play who do in fact die are Cloten and the Queen, the latter of sheer despair and the former by decapitation at the hands of Guiderius. Guiderius says that he has "sent Cloten's clotpoll down the stream, / In embassy to his mother" (iv.ii.184-5), and he imagines it floating out to sea where it will "tell the fishes he's the queen's son, Cloten." (iv.ii.153) The descent of Cloten's head to the submarine world sorts well with the brutal nature he has exemplified throughout, but it is also a curious parody of the death of Orpheus, whose gory visage was also sent down a stream and out to sea. Cloten has already perverted the function of music by addressing an aubade to a married woman with the intention of seducing, or as he obscenely puts it, of "penetrating" her, and on the erotic level he is conceived as a kind of anti-Orpheus figure, who works in vain to untune the marital harmony of Imogen and Posthumus. The death of Cloten, dressed as he is in the clothes of Posthumus, is also figuratively the death of the Posthumus who would make a bet on his wife's chastity in the first place, arrange for his antagonist to have a go at it, believe the worst of her, generalize her imaginary promiscuity into that of all womankind, and leap to avenge it. In his refinishing of the play the testily anti-romantic Bernard Shaw has Imogen express at length her just indignation over Posthumus' conduct. If Shaw scores a point for psychological verisimilitude, he also throws the romantic resolution off balance. There is more than a touch of Cloten's sexual brutality and Iachimo's dirty-mindedness about Posthumus until both are finally purged by his ordeal of repentance, and in the peculiar logic of romance, his reformation is reflected in that of Iachimo, who has spent a night in Imogen's bedroom and wears her ring. Prospero will also purge by a similar kind of symbolic substitution whatever taint of Calibanism resides in Ferdinand by making him perform Caliban's role of log-bearer. The point is not that the ageing Shakespeare has grown puritanical, as is sometimes said, but that love is what binds the universe of romance together and faith is what makes it live, and the romancer who understands the form must come down hard on all perversions of love and betrayals of faith. In *Pericles* these perversions take the form of incest and prostitution; *Cymbeline* and *The Winter's Tale* present that sexual unhealthiness and immaturity which sees only adultery and betrayal in the most unwavering faith.

When we turn from the romance plot to the historical plot, we find that Cloten and his mother, also an Atè figure, perform a similar function there. They are the spokesmen for a militant and isolationist nationalism, which, it should be stressed, in any other Elizabethan history play than this one would be equated with virtue. But in *Cymbeline* the values of history are ultimately determined by the values of romance. The patriotic values of *virtus*, militarism, and sovereignty give way in the course of the play to virtue, peacemaking, and international alliance, and the exponents of the former, who have held Cymbeline's ear, fade away. Thus it is that Cymbeline, though free to break with Rome at the end after his military victory, chooses instead to follow the dictates of a yet undreamed of Geneva conference or United Nations by sparing the Roman prisoners and paying the Roman tribute. The historical action too is shaped by the rarer action taking place offstage and issues in the *Pax Romana* that precedes Christ's birth, the "gracious season" (v.v.402) Cymbeline proclaims at the end.

If *Cymbeline* dispenses with the cultivated archaism of *Pericles*, it nonetheless bears a strong resemblance in its romantic plot structure to several of the dramatic romances of the 1580's. Those early romances, plays that make Polonius' odd composite labels for the repertory of the "tragedians of the city" seem not entirely fanciful, often include a prominent historical element that proves, as with *Cymbeline*, not at all incompatible with their form of pastoral romance. At the conclusion of Peele's *Arraignment of Paris*, the various goddesses unanimously agree to resign their several powers to Queen Elizabeth, "The noble phoenix of our age." Clotho gives up her distaff, Lachesis her spindle, and Atropos her "fatal knife," while Diana, Juno, and Venus hand over the golden apple to the "peerless" Queen. Similarly at the end of *Mucedorus* Envy and Comedy resolve their argument over which of them is stronger by bowing together to the superior power of the Queen over human affairs. In the edition of that play published in 1610 the concluding compliment to James I is still more hyperbolic:

Comedy. But see, O see, the weary Sunne for rest
    Hath laine his golden compasse to the West,
    Where he perpetuall bide and ever shine,
    As Davids of-spring, in his happy Clime.
    Stoop, Envie, stoope, bow to the Earth with mee,
    Lets begge our Pardons on our bended knee.
                       [They kneele]

Envy. My Power has lost her Might; Envies date's
    expired,
    Yon splendant Maiestie hath feld my sting,
    And I amazed am.   *[Fall down and quake]*
Comedy. Glorious and wise Arch-Caesar on this earth,
    At whose appearance, Envie's stroken dumbe,
    And all bad things cease operation:
    Vouchsafe to pardon our unwilling errour . . . .
Envy. Amen.
    To Fame and Honour we commend your rest;
    Live still more happie, every houre more blest.[5]

To call any monarch, and particularly James I, "David's
offspring" and "Arch-Caesar on this earth," while it may
strike us as the most obsequious flattery, was not only so-
cially decorous but historically justified to his English subjects. The dedication to the King James Bible refers to the
deceased Elizabeth as "that bright *Occidental Star*," and to
England as "Our Sion." Cranmer's prophecy ex post facto
on the birth of Elizabeth at the end of *Henry VIII* is written in the same spirit and celebrates in Biblical imagery the
prosperity of her reign and that of her successor, who shall
rise Phoenix-like from her ashes. "The words I utter," he
says, "Let none think flattery, for they'll find 'em truth."
(v.v.16-17) These gestures in fact suggest an important
point of contact between the structure of romance and
the Tudor myth of the English past.

    The identifications that Peele and the anonymous author
and reviser of *Mucedorus* make between Elizabeth or

[5] Epilogue, 59-72. *The Shakespeare Apocrypha*, ed. C. F. Tucker
Brooke (Oxford, 1908), p. 126.

James and benevolent demigods who safeguard the peace and prosperity of England actually have less to do with historical truth than with that Tudor myth, whose chief features it might be useful to review briefly here. Geoffrey of Monmouth had forged the historical Arthur into a legendary figure, the deathless ruler of a united Britain, who, it was prophesied, would someday reappear and regain the British throne. Henry VII claimed this symbolic role, tracing his Welsh descent from Cadwallader, the last king of the unified island, and naming his eldest son Arthur. The Tudor chroniclers presented the accession of that House as the restoration of Britain to her former Arthurian glory after a long interlude of civil war and dissension. Thus it is that Greene has Friar Bacon prophesy at the end of his comical-historical-pastoral drama

> That here where Brute did built his Troynovant,
> From forth the royal garden of a king
> Shall flourish out so rich and fair a bud
> Whose brightness shall deface proud Phoebus' flower,
> And over-shadow Albion with her leaves.
> Till then the stormy threats of wars shall cease.
> The horse shall stamp as careless of the pike;
> Drums shall be turn'd to timbrels of delight;
> With wealthy favors plenty shall enrich
> The strond that gladded wand'ring Brute to see,
> And peace from heaven shall harbor in these leaves
> That gorgeous beautifies this matchless flower.[6]

The matchless flower is of course the Tudor rose, and the stormy threats of war begin with the deposition of Richard

[6] *Friar Bacon and Friar Bungay*, ed. Daniel Seltzer (Lincoln, Nebraska, 1963), p. 96.

II, materialize in the Wars of the Roses, and culminate
in the tyranny of Richard III. The landing of the Earl
of Richmond at Milford Haven and his defeat of Richard
at Bosworth Field were hailed in the chronicles as the long
deferred return of the once and future king. His son,
Henry VIII, succeeded in freeing England from papal
bondage, and his granddaughter, Elizabeth, established
domestic stability and secured the Protestant line. James
was Henry VII's great-grandson, and by his accession England, Scotland, and Wales were at last peacefully reunited
under a single monarch.

By the beginning of the seventeenth century English
history was commonly seen as what amounts to a romantic
comedy enacted under the watchful eye of God, whose
action spanned several centuries and whose final act was
the emergence of the House of Tudor:

> Wherein is to be observed the unscrutable providence
> of the Almighty, who, when it so pleaseth him, even
> from the most bad causes produceth most good effects.
> For had not this tyrant [Richard III] (though far off
> from conceiting any such happy event to the weal-pub-
> lic) made riddance of so many of the then factious fami-
> lies that might, and no doubt in their turns would, have
> been competitors of the sovereignty, wherethrough aptly
> survived an indubitate heir male of the one house [the
> Lancastrian Earl of Richmond] and an indubitate heir
> female of the other [Elizabeth of York], either of them
> marriageable and neither of them married; and had he
> not reigned so odiously that the two factious houses,
> sundering in all things else, of necessity concurred to
> suppress him their common enemy; the so bloody and

long-continued civil wars had still lived an Hydra, where-
unto the then studied union by this opportune marriage,
plotted and afterwards effected, was thenceforth (and
for ever may it be so) an Hercules.[7]

The historical imagination which reshaped the English
past so as to justify the divine right of the Tudors to men
closely followed the structural precedent of the Bible; and
like its Biblical model, English history takes on the formal
pattern of romantic comedy as it passes from the spiritual
captivity of Rome to Protestant freedom, from civil war-
fare to peace and prosperity, and from tyranny to justice.

In maintaining the symbolic role of Arthur established
by his great-grandfather, James corresponds in history to
the figure of Eros in comedy, while the opponent role of
Atè is ascribed to Richard III. Richard, in fact, becomes in
the hands of Shakespeare and his chronicle sources a devil
incarnate, the Vice of his own play. Richard is cast in
Satan's role not only for his alleged personal wickedness, but for the way his attempt to subvert God's historical
plan backfires upon himself, just as Satan's does in Milton's
retelling of the Christian myth. James, by contrast, was
styled in his own day "the Peacemaker" and was frequently
compared to Solomon, who "was a figure of Christ in that
he was a king of peace."[8] We recall that James is called

---

[7] "An Epitome of the Whole History of England," appended to
the 1602 edn. of William Warner's *Albion's England*. Quoted in E.M.W.
Tillyard, *Myth and the English Mind* (New York, 1962), pp. 50-51.

[8] The words are James's own. Quoted in Emrys Jones, "Stuart *Cymbeline*," *Essays in Criticism*, Vol. XI, No. 1 (Jan., 1961), 84-99. See
also J. P. Brockbank, "History and Histrionics in *Cymbeline*," *Shakespeare Survey 11* (1958), pp. 42-9. I am deeply indebted to both
articles for first directing my attention to the historical dimension of
Cymbeline.

at the end of the revised *Mucedorus* "Arch-Caesar on this earth," and in Dekker's *Magnificent Entertainment* his imperial character is inscribed in gold over a triumphal arch: "Tu Regere Imperio populos Iacobe memento, / Hae tibi erunt Artes, Pacique imponere morem, / Parcere Subiectis, et debellare Superbos."[9] These lines conjure up still another romantic story, that of the founding of another Troynovant by Aeneas, grandfather of Brute, modeled as they are on Anchises' prophecy of the coming of Augustus Caesar, another pacific emperor, during his vision of the future of Rome in the *Aeneid*. Merlin's prophecies of the second coming of Arthur, Anchises' of the coming of Augustus, and the Old Testament prophecies of the coming of a King of Peace all figuratively converge in the accession of James I to the English throne.

The proper and place names of *Cymbeline* compose a tissue of allusion that links its romantic world with this Tudor myth of British history, much as the proper and place names of *Pericles* (Antiochus, Tharsus, Ephesus) link the world of classical romance with those of the Bible and the miracle play. The name of the Roman general Lucius suggests that of the first Christian king of Britain, "good Lucius, / That first received Christianitie" (*FQ.* II.x.53), while the assumed names of Cymbeline's sons, Cadwal and Polydore, suggest, aside from their pastoral

---

[9] *The Dramatic Works of Thomas Dekker*, ed. Fredson Bowers (Cambridge, 1955), II, 262. Quoted by Emrys Jones, p. 92. Dekker borrows the inscription verbatim from *Aeneid*, VI,851-3, substituting "Jacobe" for Virgil's "Romane" and effectively merging the figure of James with that of Augustus Caesar. "Remember, James, to govern well the lands under your rule, to impose the customs of peace, to spare the beaten and beat down the proud—these will be your arts." (Trans. mine.)

value, the great Cadwallader as well as Polydore Vergil, the sixteenth-century historian who chronicled those shadowy kings, however skeptically, and linked them with the House of Tudor. Imogen, who moves on and connects every level of action in *Cymbeline* may well have been originally named Innogen after the legendary wife of Brute, a name which would also have more significance in the romance plot. In any case, the action and setting of *Cymbeline* would probably have been associated in the minds of its first audience with both the Brutan past and the Tudor and Stuart present. The place name "Milford Haven," used over and over again in the play, would have suggested the landing of Henry VII, the heir of Arthur and Cadwallader, who brought peace and national unity after years of war and division. The founding of Britain by Brute after domestic dissension in Rome displaces westward the civilization and empire founded at Rome by Aeneas out of the ashes of Troy. The reign of Cymbeline was seen as a pinnacle of national prosperity since the landing of Brute, with which it was intimately connected in British prehistory. Both Virgil's epic and Shakespeare's romance are, as J. P. Brockbank phrases it, "about a golden world delivered from a brazen by the agency of a miraculous providence."[10] The ending of *Cymbeline*, with its emphasis on peace, pardon, and harmony, bears implicit reference not only to Christian but to British history. James I, Henry's great-grandson, was repeatedly called a western monarch, established the union of all Britain, and was seen as a peacemaking King who envisioned the unification of European Christendom, the vision of the soothsayer Philharmonus of the "princely eagle, / Th'imperial Caesar"

[10] J. P. Brockbank, p. 42.

with "the radiant Cymbeline, / Which shines here in the west." (v.v.474-7)

The historical dimension of *Cymbeline* might seem, at first glance anyway, to close the gap between the golden world and the brazen world which is the peril of romance forms. Probably its historical action did have a certain topical relevance for Jacobean audiences and may even have enabled the play to be "Well likte by the kinge"[11] as late as 1633. But in the last analysis, the gap between romance and reality cannot be bridged by topical reference, no matter how skillful or subtle. For the Tudor myth, though it joins beautifully with Elizabethan romance and Christian history to form the romantic structure of *Cymbeline*, is very much of an age and not for all time. Even if the play's early audiences felt the golden world of Cymbeline's Britain was a faithful reflection of James's, later audiences would not. It is significant that D'Urfey's adaptation of the play after the Restoration changes its historical names to those of pure romance and thereby sacrifices its historical and topical dimensions altogether.[12] By then the Tudor myth had given way to what might be called the Stuart myth of a restored monarchy bestowing glorious order

[11] From Sir Henry Herbert's office book, reprinted in E. K. Chambers, *William Shakespeare* (Oxford, 1930), II, 352.

[12] It is worth noting in this connection that Colley Cibber's version of *Richard III* similarly omits the background of the Tudor myth in the scenes before Bosworth. See Clifford Leech, "Shakespeare, Cibber, and the Tudor Myth," *Shakespearean Essays*, edd. Alwin Thaler and Norman Sanders (Knoxville, 1964). On the erosion of the Tudor myth out from under D'Urfey's and other Restoration adaptations of *Cymbeline*, see Bernard Harris, " 'What's past is prologue': 'Cymbeline' and 'Henry VIII,' " *Stratford-upon-Avon Studies 8* (London, 1966), pp. 219-20.

after the libertarian convulsions of the Civil War—the myth that informs Dryden's *Astraea Redux* and that is as lifeless today as its Tudor counterpart was then. The historical names of *Cymbeline* no longer held the same magic for later Stuart audiences that they had for earlier ones. Nor have they anything like magic today, but at best a certain antiquarian interest. Such is the fate of topical reference and historical myths. By presenting a privileged moment in history *Cymbeline* ignores or betrays the principle of history, the reality principle of a brazen world. By conforming its historical action to the pattern of romance, that historical action loses all value as critique and corrective to a romance world all too easily dismissed as too good to be true. This is not to diminish the virtuosity and unity of a play in which Elizabethan romance, Christian history, and British history are skillfully interwoven into one romantic design. But romantic design is not all. The very greatest drama, romantic drama no less than other kinds, displays *mimesis* as well as *poesis*, correspondence to the outside world as well as internal coherence. *Cymbeline* is finally the victim of its own romantic unity, a unity of design so tight that it effectively seals off the play from the world we know. The play itself becomes what Cloten calls Britain, "a world / By itself," a stunning example of the insularity and insulation into which romance is always in danger of withdrawing. The same will not be true of *The Winter's Tale* and *The Tempest*.

Many of these strictures, however, do extend to *Henry VIII*. Like *Cymbeline*, this history play exploits the Tudor myth, albeit the other end of it, its resplendent fulfillment rather than its shadowy beginnings. The action of *Henry VIII* also moves toward a privileged moment in time, also the birth of a royal child whose reign will inaugurate a new order of things. Based like *Cymbeline* on the Tudor myth, *Henry VIII* also has a pervasive providential cast, to which its characters repeatedly draw attention with the almost choric refrain of "Heaven's above all yet" (iii.i. 100) and "The will of heaven be done." (i.i.209) In *Henry VIII* too, we are presented with an historical action shaped by romance, not as in *Cymbeline* one of several parallel romantic actions, but one to which the entire play is given over. For our purposes, this is the main source of the play's interest and failure.

To regard *Henry VIII*, in its use of the Tudor myth, as an interesting failure may help to illuminate the play and account for its historical reception. Such a view, however, does need some immediate qualification. After all, the first and second tetralogies rely on the Tudor myth without any apparent handicap. Both tetralogies, in fact, are shaped as romantic tragicomedies issuing in the accession of a Lancastrian sun-king whose reign brings in a new era of peace and prosperity. How is it that Shakespeare can employ the same romantic myth in his earlier histories with impunity but not in this his terminal history? The answer, I would suggest, lies in the way that myth is handled and the effect to which it is employed at these widely separated stages of his career. The happy ending of the first tetralogy (the landing of the Earl of Richmond and the establishment of the House of Tudor) is built upon the ruins of one tragic fall after another: those of Talbot, Henry VI, the Duke of York, and finally the tremendous downfall of Richard III, to name only the principal examples. Its romantic outcome is ballasted by the sheer weight of prior tragic experience. Even in the second tetralogy, where only *Richard II* is a tragical history proper, the romantic worlds of the three Henry plays are seriously darkened by such counterromantic phenomena as the death of Hotspur; the growing emphasis on age and disease; the gallows-humor, rejection, and death of Falstaff; and the asperity of Henry V's campaign in France. Henry V, both a de facto and de jure monarch, as well as an attractive man, has often been called Shakespeare's ideal king. But in these earlier histories there is no place for the ideal or the idyllic, except as a critical touchstone revealing by contrast the real state of England (John of Gaunt on his deathbed) or as an escapist daydream (Henry VI on his molehill). Henry V is actually presented as a man under considerable strain, and even though he regains "the world's best garden" of France and his play ends romantically with a wedding, the order he achieves is bought at a stiff price of self-discipline and turns out, as the final chorus stresses, to be soon overthrown. Neither tetralogy, though each employs a providential myth of history that is romantic in shape, can properly be called romantic history.

It might seem that *Henry VIII*, with its series of falls, contains enough in the way of tragical history to qualify its happy ending and avert any charge of romantic escapism. Yet the falls of *Henry VIII* are fundamentally unlike those of *Richard III*. When Hastings falls in *Richard III*, for example, he moralizes *de casibus virorum* in neo-Senecan imagery appropriate to the tragic context:

> O momentary grace of mortal men,
> Which we more hunt for than the grace of God!
> Who builds his hope in air of your good looks,
> Lives like a drunken sailor on a mast;
> Ready with every nod to tumble down
> Into the fatal bowels of the deep.
>
> (III.iv.96-101)

Later in the play, Buckingham moralizes in the same vein before his execution on All Souls' Day—one of the grim ironies of history that Shakespeare, following Halle and Holinshed, makes the most of:

> This, this All-Souls' day to my fearful soul
> Is the determin'd respite of my wrongs.
> That high All-Seer which I dallied with
> Hath turn'd my feigned prayer on my head,
> And given in earnest what I begg'd in jest.
>
> (v.i.18-22)

These are the conventional falls of the *de casibus* tradition beginning with Boccaccio and culminating in *A Mirror for Magistrates*. The emphasis is on the grand *éclat* of the fall itself (how the mighty are fallen!) and its divine justice. Sin and retribution are in one-to-one correspondence, while the sobering *exempla* of one fall after another illustrate the wages of political wrongdoing.

Although *Henry VIII* is related to the *de casibus* tradition (Wolsey was one of its favorite figures), the falls it presents are not conceived according to the conventional tragic formula.[13] The first of them, that of Buckingham,

---

[13] *Pace* Frank Kermode: "His [Wolsey's] fall is basically as simple as the simplest and most orthodox falls in the *Mirror*, for Wolsey's

199

is a paradigm for all the rest. His only "sin" is an excess of righteous anger against Wolsey, but his tone begins to change upon his arrest, and keeps changing thereafter:

> The law I bear no malice for my death,
> 'T has done upon the premises but justice;
> But those that sought it I could wish more Christian:
> Be what they will, I heartily forgiv'em;
> Yet let 'em look they glory not in mischief,
> Nor build their evils on the graves of great men,
> For then my guiltless blood must cry against 'em.
>
> (II.i.61-8)

> Sir Thomas Lovell, I as free forgive you
> As I would be forgiven: I forgive all . . . .
>   Nay, Sir Nicholas,
> Let it alone; my state now will but mock me.
> When I came hither I was Lord High Constable
> And Duke of Buckingham: now poor Edward Bohun;
> Yet I am richer than by base accusers.
>
> (II.i.82-104)

Unlike his father (whose fate he remembers) in *Richard III*, Buckingham does more than moralize on the poetic justice of his downfall. He expresses an entirely new sense

---

acts of conspiracy and treachery are directly responsible for his tragedy. . . . This, then, is the completely orthodox fall in accordance with contemporary Christian moral philosophy, and in a sense all the others are variants of it." "What is Shakespeare's *Henry VIII* About?" *Durham University Journal*, New Series, IX (March, 1948), 53. Although Wolsey's fall is the consequence of his sins and in that sense conventional, the same cannot be said of those of Buckingham and Katherine, which occur, not because of their vice, but in spite of their virtue.

of self in the language of Christian conversion. His loss of
secular wealth and station are more than compensated by
his gain of new spiritual wealth and station. Katherine similarly exchanges one kind of royalty for another as a result
of her fall. If she loses her earthly crown, she gains a heavenly garland in the beatific vision of angels that precedes
her death—a scene that contrasts pointedly with the pageant of Anne's secular coronation just before it.

Even Wolsey's becomes in Shakespeare's hands a fortunate fall, for in this play grace abounds even to the worst
of sinners:

> I have ventur'd
> Like little wanton boys that swim on bladders,
> This many summers in a sea of glory,
> But far beyond my depth: my high-blown pride
> At length broke under me, and now has left me
> Weary and old with service, to the mercy
> Of a rude stream that must forever hide me. . . .
> I feel my heart new open'd.   (iii.ii.358-68)

> Never so truly happy, my good Cromwell;
> I know myself now, and I feel within me
> A peace above all earthly dignities,
> A still and quiet conscience.   (iii.ii.377-80)

If the phrase "wanton boys" recalls another Shakespearean
context, the nature of the deity involved has changed considerably. Wolsey had compared himself to Lucifer,
"Never to hope again" (iii.ii.372), but the grace denied to
Lucifer extends to Wolsey, who exchanges, like Buckingham and Katherine, one kind of power and glory for a
better. In *Henry VIII*, the fall itself engages only part of

Shakespeare's poetic interest and energy, most of which
are devoted to presenting the spiritual rise that follows.
Each of the principals, in the phrase used of Buckingham
at his trial, *"fell* to *himself* again." (II.i.35) The falls of
Buckingham, Katherine, and Wolsey are all romantically,
rather than tragically, conceived.

If the falls of Hastings and Buckingham in *Richard III*
or Hotspur and Falstaff in *Henry IV* are good things from
the viewpoint of English history, those of Buckingham,
Katherine, and Wolsey are fortunate from their own viewpoint. Of course they are also fortunate from the perspective of English history, particularly the fall of Wolsey.
Under Wolsey's sway, England is portrayed as a land of
illusory splendor and concord, typified in the opening description of the Field of the Cloth of Gold:

> To-day the French
> All clinquant all in gold, like heathen gods
> Shone down the English; and to-morrow they
> Made Britain India: every man that stood
> Show'd like a mine. Their dwarfish pages were
> As cherubins, all gilt: the madams too,
> Not us'd to toil, did almost sweat to bear
> The pride upon them, that their very labour
> Was to them as a painting.   (I.i.18-26)

The precious diction and rhetorical excess suggest the artificiality of the Field and the vanity of its architect, Wolsey.
"Dwarfish pages" and "cherubins" are violently and ludi-
crously yoked together, while the comparisons of the
French to "heathen gods" and Britain to India are clearly
invidious: "Wherefore shall the heathen say: where is

nowe their God?" asks the Psalm, "Their idoles are silver and golde: even the worke of mens hands. . . . But thou house of Israel, trust thou in the Lord."[14] Though fallen on evil days, England will pass out from under the figure of idolatrous India (equated with the secular misrule and spiritual bondage of Wolsey's regime) and fulfill, like Israel, her chosen destiny (equated with the rule of God's deputies, Henry and Cranmer). The false pageantry of the Field and the dire tempest and "general prophecy" of breakdown that follow give way by the end of the play to the true pageantry of Elizabeth's christening and Cranmer's prophecy of national prosperity extending through two reigns. Cranmer's speech is based on several Biblical passages and celebrates in lush agricultural (if not quite pastoral) imagery the emergence of England as a promised land. Just as Buckingham, Katherine, and even Wolsey achieve, like Adam in *Paradise Lost*, a paradise within as a result of their falls, so the golden age of Elizabeth and James prophesied by Cranmer is seen as a paradise without. The Reformation of England reflects on a public and national level the hard-won personal reformations that precede it.

This recurrent pattern of secular fall and spiritual reformation suggests a close relation between the world of *Henry VIII* and that of the morality drama. In fact, the morality-world lies just beneath the surface of the play and often shows through it, as when Surrey calls Wolsey "Thou scarlet sin" (iii.ii.255) or Wolsey identifies himself with Lucifer. Once fallen, Wolsey's role shifts from

<hr />

[14] Psalms, cxv. 4-8. Quoted from a 1609 edn. of the *Book of Common Prayer*.

that of the Vice of the play to that of an Everyman figure, who repents and reforms prior to his death. Buckingham corresponds to the plain-spoken good counselor in the morality scheme, who is undone by the machinations of the Vice, and Katherine, said to love Henry "with that excellence / That angels love good men with" (ii.ii.33-4), to the good angel whose remonstrances are disastrously ignored. Henry stands at the center of the play's morality scheme and bears a strong family resemblance to a long line of wavering or misguided kings: Rex Vivus, Rex Humanitas, Magnificence, King Johan, James IV, and so on. With the falling away of his worser genius Wolsey, Henry assumes his full royal stature. It is a reformed Henry who singlehandedly prevents Cranmer's trial from turning into yet another undeserved, if fortunate, fall. "God and your majesty," petitions Cranmer, "Protect mine innocence, or I fall into / The trap is laid for me." (v.i.140-42) Cranmer's invocation of God and God's vicar on earth recalls and redresses Wolsey's presumptuous "*Ego et Rex meus*" (iii.ii.314) and establishes him as Henry's better genius. His remark also prefigures Henry's comment outside his trial, " 'Tis well there's one above 'em yet" (v.ii.26), where the ambiguous reference (Henry or God?) manages a partial identification of the two. As Henry audits the trial from the upper stage and enters like a *deus ex machina* to deliver Cranmer from his accusers and effect mutual forgiveness, he takes on a role similar to that of God's Nemesis in the pro-Catholic morality *Respublica* (1553), who delivers the commonwealth from the Vices that afflict her and restores her to "tholde goode eastate."[15] Perhaps an even closer morality counterpart to Henry is the figure of Imperial Majesty in the anti-Catholic *King Johan* (1530-36), called at one point "Of the Christian fayth . . . the true defender" and the champion of the struggle against Rome begun by John. The Interpreter who introduces the second part of the play expounds the allegory:

> This noble Kynge Johan, as a faythfull Moyses,
> Withstode proude Pharo for hys poore Israel,
> Myndynge to brynge yt owt of the lande of darkenesse,
> But the Egyptyanes did agaynst hym so rebell
> That hys poore people ded styll in the desart dwell,
> Tyll that duke Josue, whych was our late Kynge Henrye,
> Clerely brought us in-to the lande of mylke and honye.[16]

Like these early political moralities, *Henry VIII* holds up a mirror not really to history but to a partisan myth of history, a "chosen truth" (Prologue, 18) that is romantic in shape. The play may begin in the brazen world of history as we know it but it certainly ends in the golden world of romance as we like it: a promised land, a land of milk and honey, a brave new world.

It is the almost undisguised presence in *Henry VIII* of the forms and figures of the political morality that dis-

---

[15] *Respublica*, ed. W. W. Greg (Early English Text Society, London, 1952), line 1922, p. 66.

[16] *King Johan*, ll. 1106-1112. *Specimens of the Pre-Shaksperean Drama*, ed. J. M. Manly (Boston, 1897), I, 563.

tinguishes it from Shakespeare's earlier histories and links it with his final romances. Just as *Pericles* and *Cymbeline* seem closer in certain respects to the pre-Shakespearean romantic drama than to his own romantic comedies, so *Henry VIII* seems closer to plays like *Respublica, King Johan,* and *Magnificence* than to his own *Richard III* or *Henry IV.* It is for this reason that attempts to discuss *Henry VIII* in terms derived from the earlier histories are bound to come to grief. Although we are told that *Henry VIII* "is as political in its concerns as any of Shakespeare's English histories, and the importance of each major character depends (as usual in the histories) on the relation between that character and the King,"[17] anyone looking for a complex study of politics here will be disappointed. The relation of subject to king, the fascinations and responsibilities of power, the evolving definition of a just, but hardly ideal, commonwealth—these are the concerns of the histories. The histories deal in the art of the possible; *Henry VIII*, in the art of the impossible. The histories explore a world of means; *Henry VIII* presents a world of ends. When morality survivals occur in the naturalistic context of the earlier histories (Prince Hal's program of reform in his first soliloquy is a good example) they tend to create problems by appearing causeless and unmotivated in a world dominated by causality and motivation. When Henry VIII says in an early aside—

> I may perceive
> These cardinals trifle with me. I abhor

[17] Paul Bertram, "Henry VIII: The Conscience of the King," *In Defense of Reading*, edd. Reuben A. Brower and Richard Poirier (New York, 1962), pp. 156-57.

This dilatory sloth and tricks of Rome.
My learned and well-beloved servant Cranmer,
Prithee return. With thy approach I know
My comfort comes along   (II.iv.233-8)

there is no problem, because virtually the entire play works
at the level of Prince Hal's soliloquy. How he perceives
Wolsey's tricks, why he remains under Wolsey's influence
for yet another act are less important than the fact that
Henry is beginning to see what everyone else knows already, the *données* of the play. Similarly, *Henry VIII*
does not focus on the conflicts of motive and interest that
precipitate its falls nor on the psychology of its conversions
but on the facts of fall and conversion. The process by
which things come about in this play, quite literally, only
God knows. Whereas the earlier histories are political
dramas overseen by God, *Henry VIII* is a providential
drama witnessed by men.

If *Henry VIII* has less in common with the histories
than meets the eye, it has more in common with the romances. Its movement from a fallen to a reformed kingdom is virtually an orthodox translation of the heterodox
actions of the romances. The pagan deities who preside over
Pericles, Cymbeline, and *The Winter's Tale* are superseded
by the Christian God. Classical allusion is largely replaced
with scriptural allusion. Cerimon and Prospero, who assume their demi-godlike control over the actions of *Pericles* and *The Tempest* through the art of magic, give place
to Henry, who assumes his demi-godlike control over the
action of *Henry VIII* through the Erastian organization
of the English Church and the Tudor and Stuart doctrine

of divine right. The trials and tribulations of romance, by which character is tested and out of which good ultimately comes, become in this play the actual trials of Henry's reign—of which history offers no shortage. Concomitantly and more importantly, the leading motif of the tempest yields to that of the fall. In all of the romances except *Cymbeline*, the tempest is, like Shelley's west wind, destroyer and preserver at once, the means of separation and reunion, punishment and purgation. Most of the tempest-tossed characters of the romances can finally say with Ferdinand, "Though the seas threaten, they are merciful. / I have curs'd them without cause." (*Tem.*, v.i.178-9) In Marvell's phrase, they are literally "shipwrackt into health." In *Henry VIII*, the motif of the blessed tempest, though persisting in the form of a ubiquitous imagery of sea, storm, and shipwreck, gives way to another romantic paradox, the Christian motif of the fortunate fall. Each of its falling principals leaves his trial, mounts the scaffold, or faces ignominy and death with a new "fortitude of soul." (III.ii.388)

The explicitly Christian and historical world of *Henry VIII* may have seemed closer to home to an audience that still cherished Henry's memory than the far-fetched and anachronistic realms of the romances; but to us it must seem further from home. If the play started out as a return from a fabulous to a factual world, it winds up as an escape into a world even more fabulous than those of the romances: the mythic realm of a Tudor golden age. *Cymbeline* had exploited the same myth as a point of contact between the historical present and a prehistoric golden age. *Cymbeline* has about the same claim to truth as the broadside ballads of Autolycus in *The Winter's Tale*. The "gracious season" it proclaims represents the amoral fantasy of pure wish-dream, in so far as its golden age is created out of nothing and bears no moral or mimetic relation to any reality we know. *Cymbeline* is at least aware that the first requirement for any golden age is that it be long past or not yet come. Unlike *Cymbeline*, however, *Henry VIII* does not exist outside history, and the golden age it proclaims has even less claim to truth (despite the play's subtitle) than the ballads of Autolycus. Its golden age represents not creation out of nothing but the distortion of something, a gilded age passed off as a golden, and as such is hardly more than glorified propaganda.

The "chosen truth" of this play is so much more "chosen" than "true" as to be quite incredible. Too much is censored out or glossed over: Henry's ill-starred daughter, Mary, who was in her adolescence during most of its action; the bloody fates soon to overtake Anne, Cromwell, and Chancellor Thomas More (to restrict the list only to characters who appear in the play); Henry's kaleidoscopic array of wives, two of whom (including Anne) were to go to the block after trials as rigged as that of Buckingham. Shakespeare's exclusion of the nastier aspects of a reign littered with corpses and haunted by ghosts, his all too orthodox whitewashing of Henry himself, and that wishful prophecy of glory under James I simply will not abide our questions—questions that the history form fairly demands that we ask. For history, the mode in which the reality principle commands its fullest recognition, and romance, the mode in which it receives its freest treatment, are the poles of Shakespeare's imaginative universe and are irreconcilably opposed. The Orpheus of the song sung to Katherine may have been able to make "trees, / And the mountain tops that freeze, / Bow themselves when he did sing" (iii.i.3-5), but not even Shakespeare can bend the brute facts of Henry's reign into a triumphant romantic pattern. Even the greatest romancer has limits on his power. Whereas John of Gaunt eulogized England as an "other Eden, demi-paradise" in a history play that made clear he was voicing a wish rather than a fact, *Henry VIII* tries to present the thing itself and confuses the wish and the fact. It ends where the two previous romances do not: at the point where we leave pastoral Bohemia and Prospero's island to return to an older and less brave world where death and mutability are facts of life. At the end of *The Winter's Tale* Mamillius and Antigonus remain dead, and not quite everyone is redeemed at the end of *The Tempest*. That we are pointedly reminded in those plays of such things is one measure of their ultimate fidelity to the world we know. In *Henry VIII*, the circle of redemption is too all-inclusive to be true. *Et in Arcadia, Ego.*

CHAPTER 7

Our Carver's Excellence:
The Winter's Tale

In that which the Poet speakes or reports of another
mans tale or doings . . . he is as the painter or kerver
that worke by imitation and representation in a forrein
subject; in that he speakes figuratively, or argues sub-
tillie, or perswades copiously and vehemently, he doth
as the cunning gardiner that using nature as a coadinator,
furders her conclusions and many times makes her ef-
fectes more absolute and straunge. But for that in our
maker or Poet, which restes onely in devise and issues
from an excellent sharp and quick invention, holpen
by a cleare and bright phantasie and imagination, he
is not as the painter . . . nor as the gardiner . . . but
even as nature her selfe working by her owne peculiar
vertue and proper instinct and not by example or
meditation or exercise as all other artificers do, is then
most admired when he is most natural and least arti-
ficiall.
                                        —George Puttenham

In *The Winter's Tale* we are confronted with an imaginative unity of a different order of magnitude from that of
Cymbeline. If this play too presents the emergence of
pattern out of the flux and diversity of human life, it associates that pattern much less closely than *Pericles* and
Cymbeline with the workings of the gods. Apollo presides
over the world of this play in principle rather than in
person as the "blessed, breeding sun" (*Timon*, iv.iii.1)
which sustains the life of nature through photosynthesis

and as the patron deity of the arts. Man now assumes sole responsibility for the shaping (and misshaping) of his affairs, for the possibility of failure is real and great. The wicked are not reassuringly punished early, as they were in *Pericles*, but the innocent are struck down—as far as we then know, struck dead. Nor does the audience have that assurance offered by the title and setting of *Cymbeline* that the action will issue in a "gracious season" until the scene shifts to pastoral Bohemia in the fourth act, and even then the outcome remains in doubt—the title, after all, could mean either "a sad tale" (as Mamillius suggests) or a fairy tale (as Ben Jonson insists). Like the two earlier romances, *The Winter's Tale* encompasses both a personal and a communal action, but rather than independent or parallel, they are one and the same. For the Sicilian court conducts itself with the intimacy of a large family, and as the oracle makes clear, Leontes' fate as husband and father is intertwined with the fate of the realm. Like *Pericles* and *Cymbeline*, this play also cultivates the naiveté of an older drama with its sprawling action and Chorus of Time and constantly reminds us that we are watching an old tale. But unlike the earlier romances, whose self-consistency I have tried to show, *The Winter's Tale* is also self-explanatory in the way the greatest art always is and requires no special or prior awareness on the part of the audience for its world to live and its action to work.

No play of Shakespeare's (I venture to say not even *Hamlet* or *Lear*) creates a world of greater amplitude and variety. The peculiarly Shakespearean ability to create in a mere three thousand lines an imaginative environment so fully realized that we take it, like Hermione's "statue," for life itself and its creatures for fellow human beings is nowhere more in evidence than in *The Winter's Tale*. An early performance of the play seems to have had just such an effect upon Simon Forman:

> Observe ther howe Lyontes the kinge of Cicillia was overcom w^t Jelosy of his wife with the kinge of Bohemia his frind that came to see him. and howe he Contrived his death and wold have had his cup berer to have poisoned. . . . Remember also the Rog that came in all tottered like coll pixci /. and howe he feyned him sicke & to have bin Robbed of all that he had and howe he cosoned the por man of all his money. and after cam to the shep sher with a pedlers packe & ther cosoned them Again of all their money And howe he changed apparrell w^t the kinge of bomia his sonn. and then howe he turned Courtiar &c / beware of trusting feined beggars or fawninge fellouss.[1]

By the time Forman is done with his almost hypnotic recitation of the events of the play, whatever frail distinction may have existed in his mind between art and life has broken down altogether: "beware of trusting feined beggars or fawninge fellouss." But even so tough-minded a verisimilitude man as Samuel Johnson, while by no means happy with the "absurdities" of the play, remarks that "The character of Autolycus is very naturally conceived and strongly represented." And of Leontes' self-recrimi-

---

[1] Forman's manuscript account of the Globe performance of May 15, 1611 occurs in his *Booke of Plaies* at the Bodleian Library (*Ashmole*, 208). Reprinted in *The Winter's Tale*, ed. by J.H.P. Pafford (New Arden Shakespeare, Cambridge, Mass., 1963), pp. xxi-xxii.

nations in the third act: "This vehement retraction . . .
accompanied with the confession of more crimes than he
was suspected of, is agreeable to our daily experience of
the vicissitudes of violent tempers and the eruptions of
minds oppressed with guilt."[2] On the much vexed matter
of Leontes' jealousy, often invidiously compared with that
of Othello, it was Coleridge who shrewdly observed that
"the natural effects and concomitants of this passion" are
more, not less, truly represented in the later than in the
earlier play.[3] For if Leontes' suspicions seem sudden and
unaccountable, it is the nature of jealousy that it has neither
rational cause nor adequate motivation, that its fantasies
are created out of nothing; otherwise it is not jealousy.
Hazlitt too was profoundly moved by Kemble's recreation
of "the growing jealousy of the King"; by Mrs. Siddons'
acting of "the painted statue to the life"; and by Ban-
nister's Autolycus—"we shall never see these parts so acted
again."[4] Such acting is of course only possible when the
characterization itself is lifelike enough to sustain it.
Shakespeare's earlier idealized heroines (Desdemona and

[2] *Samuel Johnson on Shakespeare*, ed. W. K. Wimsatt, Jr. (New
York, 1960), p. 80.

[3] *Shakespearean Criticism*, ed. Thomas Middleton Raysor (Everyman's Library, New York, 1960), I, 110-12. Coleridge may take his
cue from the worldly wisdom of Emilia, who observes that "jealous
souls . . . are not ever jealous for the cause / But jealous for they're
jealous." (*Othello*, III.iv.158-60)

[4] *The Complete Works of William Hazlitt*, ed. P. P. Howe (London,
1934), V, 376-77. Interestingly enough, *The Winter's Tale* alone among
the romances managed to thrive under the remorseless illusionism of the
nineteenth-century stage, albeit in a slightly altered form. See the
stage history included by J.H.P. Pafford in his New Arden edition, pp.
175-81.

Cordelia) are superb portraits of faith-in-love, but which of them has the working pulse, the flesh-and-blood vitality of Hermione? Which of them can we even imagine conceiving and bearing a child? If the superhuman patience they exemplify is hard to bring to life on stage because it is hard for an actress to justify psychologically (why does Cordelia not explain herself in the opening scene of *Lear* or Desdemona defend herself in the brothel scene of *Othello?*), Hermione presents no such problem, since she finely expresses her sense of wrong. If you believe that the representation of character, the ability to touch all the stops of human passion, is Shakespeare's greatest gift as a dramatist, then *The Winter's Tale*, as Inspector Bucket would say, is the play for you.

But what makes the lifelike characterization all the more remarkable is the fact that it is in the service of "an old tale still." Because we do not normally expect three-dimensional characterization or scenic verisimilitude from romance, the temptation is to write off these aspects of *The Winter's Tale* at the outset and concentrate instead on its fictiveness or conventionality.[5] This seems to me a serious

---

[5] Northrop Frye, for example, remarks in his seminal essay on the play that "the principle of 'all's well that ends well' holds in comedy, however great nonsense it may be in life" and that "the kind of art manifested by the play itself is in some respects closer to [Autolycus'] 'trumpery' ballads than to the sophisticated idealism and realism of Polixenes and Romano." "Recognition in *The Winter's Tale*," *Fables of Identity* (New York, 1963), pp. 107, 114. Similarly, Norman Rabkin regards Leontes' jealousy, among other things, as "the kind of thing that happens in fairy tale; but it happens here in a hitherto realistic court." *Shakespeare and the Common Understanding* (New York, 1967), p. 217. A rare attempt to establish the careful verisimilitude of the play is that of J.H.P. Pafford in his introduction to the New

mistake, for it is precisely in its combination of romantic design with mimetic fidelity to life as we know it that this play transcends *Pericles* and *Cymbeline* and takes its place among the very greatest of Shakespeare's works. Although he once again draws freely upon moldy old tales and musty old plays, their forms and figures are now wholly naturalized. If the jealousy of Leontes mirrors that passion as it exists in living men more faithfully than that of Othello, it also comes literally out of the blue—the kind of heaven-sent, or rather hell-sent, madness with which Atè, Tisiphone, and Envy conventionally afflict the protagonists of the dramatic romances of three decades earlier. (It is worth recalling that Shakespeare deliberately omits the ready-made motives for Leontes' jealousy that Greene had provided in *Pandosto*.) The point is that it is both psychologically convincing that Leontes' jealousy is sudden and inexplicable (do we really understand any better than the Elizabethans the *causes* of destructive behavior?) and structurally necessary to the play's romantic form that he be suddenly and disastrously jealous? If Hermione is endowed with a psychic life and past which enable her to remember the kindness of her father, "The Emperor of Russia," during her trial, she also functions in that scene, in the play as a whole, much as a long line of personified virtues had functioned in theirs—something to which she actually draws our attention:

Arden edition, though he repeatedly falls back on the momentum and engagement assumed to exist in the theater as the means of suspending our disbelief. Although his argument begs the question—how does the play insure our theatrical engagement?—his basic claim seems to me essentially valid.

> If powers divine
> Behold our human actions (as they do),
> I doubt not then but Innocence shall make
> False Accusation blush, and Tyranny
> Tremble at Patience. You, my lord, best know
> (Who least will seem to do so) my past life
> Hath been as continent, as chaste, as true,
> As I am now unhappy; which is more
> Than history can pattern, though devis'd
> And played to take spectators.   (iii.ii.28-36)

I have capitalized her terms (some editors wisely do so anyway) to make this point, but a Jacobean audience would have recognized them immediately as the personifications of an older dramatic tradition. If it is tempting to talk about Falstaff as if he were a real person rather than a dramatic character, then Shakespeare's next most tempting rogue in this way is Autolycus. Yet he, life Falstaff, is also that "reverend Vice," the hardiest survivor of the religious drama and, in a phrase used of the Vice figure in Middleton's greatest play, "a wondrous necessary man" in the action of romance. Autolycus may be more sophisticated in every way than Conditions in *Common Conditions* or Shift in *Clyomon and Clamydes*, but he performs the same essential function within his romantic play that they do in theirs: by sowing confusion in pursuit of self-interest he ultimately promotes the interest and felicity of the principals. "Here come those I have done good to against my will," says Autolycus virtually summing up his role, "and already appearing in the blossoms of their fortune." (v.ii.124-26) As Vice, Autolycus often addresses the audience directly to let us in on his schemes, much as Iago does in *Othello* and Edmund in *Lear*. But unlike the passed-over ensign and bastard son of those plays, this Vice is cast as a rogue pure and simple; he tells us it is his inherited and chosen vocation. As a result, there is no conflict or tension between what is mimetically natural for him to say or do at any given moment and what the design of the play requires him to say or do, as there sometimes is with Iago and Edmund.[6]

The question inevitably arises, how does Shakespeare manage to vivify these conventional figures out of an older drama? One answer is suggested by the detail of Hermione's recollection of her father during her trial. Shakespeare often endows his major characters with a life that extends beyond the confines of the immediate action, and of which we catch fleeting glimpses as they speak or are spoken of by others. Shylock's mention of the ring he had in his bachelorhood of Leah momentarily flashes forth a life of the emotions we would all too readily have denied him. Cassius' recollections of Caesar sick and Caesar drowning open up a dimension of human frailty in a character who would like to think of himself and have others think of him as superhuman. Lady Macbeth's remark about having "given suck," aside from giving critics an occasion to speculate on how many children she had, adds a layer of irony to the fate which enfolds her, just as the resemblance she notes between Duncan and "my father as he slept"

---

[6] A good example in the case of Edmund is his motiveless reformation at the point of death. For a definitive treatment of the numerous contradictions within the characterization of Iago, see Bernard Spivack, *Shakespeare and the Allegory of Evil* (New York, 1958).

adds another. There must be a hundred such moments in Shakespeare. It is a striking feature of *The Winter's Tale* that it reveals much more of the vital information concerning the principals than is, strictly speaking, required by the plot or usual even in a Shakespearean play. Aside from Hermione's mention of her father, there is Leontes' sudden recollection of his childhood: "Looking on the lines / Of my boy's face, methoughts I did recoil / Twenty-three years, and saw myself unbreech'd / In my green velvet coat." (1.ii.153-56) Polixenes similarly recounts, at Hermione's bidding, the "unfledg'd days" when he and Leontes "were as twinn'd lambs that did frisk i' the sun, / And bleat the one at th' other." (1.ii.67-8) Leontes volunteers a brief account of his courtship of Hermione, how "Three crabbed months had sour'd themselves to death, / Ere I could make thee open thy white hand, / And clap thyself my love." (1.ii.102-4) At a more mundane and quotidian level, it is revealed that Leontes cannot sleep: "Nor night, nor day, no rest" (ii.iii.i); "Madam, he hath not slept to-night." (ii.iii.31) Nor are these revelations of the characters' past or offstage lives confined to the tragic *mimesis* of the first three acts. At the sheepshearing festival, the Old Shepherd recounts at some length his deceased wife's activities on similar occasions in the past. The world of this play is populated with characters who were young once, had fathers, courted, married, need sleep and are irritable when they do not get it, and who bear an extraordinary resemblance in all these things to the men and women we know in the real world.

Whatever the truth of this point, there can be no doubt that *The Winter's Tale* marks an important breakthrough in Shakespeare's romantic art and that this breakthrough has much to do with its unprecedented romantic verisimilitude. In *Pericles* certain essential moments in the life of every man (the loss of youthful innocence, a betrothal feast, "a tempest, / A birth and death") form a series of archetypal scenes. Whatever claims of verisimilitude we may make for that play take off from its presentation, like that of the medieval religious drama, of an overview of human life in its typical and recurrent aspect rather than in its existential particularity. *The Winter's Tale* also presents the archetypal aspect of human experience, but it does so by making the part suggest the whole, the personal suggest the universal, the momentary self-revelation of a character evoke a complete offstage existence. Whereas Pericles' "fall" into the knowledge of good and evil had formed a highly ritualistic scene unto itself, Leontes' comparable initiation into sexual awareness and corruption is cast as a passing reminiscence of childhood innocence. Whereas Marina's birth at sea and in storm was portrayed as the entry of the child into the fallen natural order, that of Perdita in prison, whatever its symbolic associations, is first and foremost a biological event—right down to the clinical details of its being a premature birth precipitated by the nervous strain on Hermione. Even when the symbolic associations of Perdita's birth are most stressed (when the Clown meets "with things dying" and his father "with things new-born" [III.iii.112-13]) the Old Shepherd's language, in its homeliness and rusticity, underscores this baby's flesh-and-blood humanity. If Marina was Infans, Perdita is a "barne" as well as Infans. Similarly, the feast of Simonides, where Pericles wins Thaisa, is divided in

The Winter's Tale between Leontes' reminiscence of his courtship of Hermione in the first act and the sheepshearing festival of the fourth. In *Pericles* that scene had been presented as what Macbeth terms "life's feast," from which Pericles, like Macbeth, is first alienated and into which he, unlike Macbeth, is eventually reintegrated. Though just as central to the structure and imagery of *The Winter's Tale*, the feast is no longer primarily a symbolic or archetypal feast of life. If the sheepshearing festival of the fourth act is an annual folk ritual celebrating the rebirth of nature, it is also a particular event with a strong realistic flavor. If the imagery of eating and drinking that dominates the early scenes of the play suggest the vital rhythms of human life (which in Leontes' case are now tainted with poison), it also arises naturally out of the concrete situation of extended hospitality. Nothing in the dramatic world of *The Winter's Tale* exists purely or simply for its archetypal dimension. The play does not allow us to forget that symbols and archetypes are first of all the things themselves, that without the dancer there would be no dance.

In moving from *Pericles* to *Cymbeline*, one can already detect on Shakespeare's part a new effort to meet the needs of theatrical illusionism at least half-way. This is not simply a matter of characterization but of language and dramaturgy as well. *Cymbeline* begins not only *in medias res* but in mid-dialogue, the language of which is much closer to what we think of as common speech than the archaic verse of the chorus and opening scene of *Pericles*. It is almost as if Shakespeare had set out after *Pericles* to ballast his subsequent romances with a prevailing idiom as much of this world as their fantastic and far-fetched subject matter is of another. But if *Cymbeline* goes half-way with the canons of verisimilitude, *The Winter's Tale* goes even further, especially with respect to decorum in language. For like the characters who speak it, the language of this play is at once wholly of this world and at the same time dipped in another. Not only in such special effects as the tortured cadences and coarse diction of Leontes' jealousy or the rustic dialect of the Shepherd and Clown but in the conversational norm of the play from the first scene onward we are never very far from common speech.

The play opens, in fact, in the midst of a dialogue as casual and apparently undirected as life itself. Archidamus and Camillo discuss a projected visit to Bohemia "this coming summer," the relative "magnificence" of their kingdoms' hospitality, and the long-standing friendship of their kings: "there is not in the world either malice or matter to alter it." The topic of conversation shifts to the "comfort" and "promise" of prince Mamillius, how he "physics the subject, makes old hearts fresh," and how "they that went on crutches ere he was born desire yet their life to see him a man." In a skillful piece of exposition Camillo describes the past friendship of the kings (the counterpart to the speech on Posthumus's past in *Cymbeline*, "I cannot delve him to the root" [1.i.28ff]), but still further naturalized:

> They were trained together in their childhoods, and there rooted betwixt them then such an affection which cannot choose but branch now. Since their more mature dignities and royal necessities made separation of their

society, their encounters, though not personal, have been
royally attorneyed with interchange of gifts, letters,
loving embassies, that they have seemed to be together,
though absent; shook hands, as over a vast; and embraced, as it were, from the ends of opposed winds.
                                                    (i.i.21-31)

Given the courtly setting, the idiom of Camillo and
Archidamus, with its mildly euphuistic balance, witty turns
of phrase, and frequent figures of speech, is perfectly colloquial. But to the extent that their figures of speech play
on the impossible and conjure up the miraculous, their
language is simultaneously an oracular language, reflective
of the romantic nature of the play as a whole. If the re-
ciprocal visit to Bohemia is never to take place, Camillo
will nonetheless sample Bohemian hospitality in another
sense and see the "great difference" Archidamus speaks of.
If Mamillius's comfort and promise die with him, his
capacity to make old hearts fresh will be fulfilled through
his alter-ego Florizel and his sister Perdita. If there is indeed malice and matter to alter the kings' friendship, at
least in the diseased fantasy-world of Leontes' mind, they
will nevertheless shake hands over a vast "gap of time"
(v.iii.154) and embrace from the ends of opposed winds
by the end of the play. For in the romantic design of *The
Winter's Tale*, death and disease will be transcended, time
and space telescoped almost at will, and impossibilities
made to seem unexceptionable. The reunion later envisioned and engineered by Camillo, though it strikes Florizel as "almost a miracle" (iv.iv.535), turns out to be in
the very nature of things, entirely within man's power
and of man's making.

The language of the opening scene is natural too, not only in the sense that it is lifelike or colloquial, but also in the sense that it constantly refers to biological and physical nature: "there rooted betwixt them then such an affection which cannot choose but branch now." The words "rooted" and "branch" are of course buried metaphors, so much a part of common speech we hardly think of them as such—the most inconspicuous and least noticeably artificial kind of metaphor, the kind most frequent in this play and, I suspect, more frequent here than in any other play of Shakespeare's. The characters of *The Winter's Tale* can scarcely say anything at all without casting it in a natural metaphor in both senses of "natural." Polixenes is anxious to return home because of what may "breed" there in his absence; the word "breed," along with its companion "issue," suggest at once the healthy renewal of life through offspring and (to Leontes' tainted mind) the copulation of the animals. Hermione, on whose ribald banter Leontes seizes as proof of his suspicions, makes the innocent mistake of asking him to "cram's with praise, and make's / As fat as tame things" (i.ii.91-2), comparing herself in her pregnant state to the domestic animals that support human life but also breed promiscuously. Leontes picks up this strain of imagery later on when he calls Mamillius his "bawcock," his "wanton calf," as well as "this kernel," and "this squash." (i.ii.121-6,159-60) Hermione refers to Mamillius as the "first-fruits of my body" (iii.ii.97), and Antigonus leaves the "blossom" Perdita on the Bohemian coast, where he prays her character and fortune may "breed" her. Paulina describes Leontes' jealousy as fancies "too green and idle for girls of nine" (III.ii.181-2), though he has already denied to Camillo that he would accuse his queen "Without ripe moving to 't." (I.ii.332) At the sheepshearing festival, Perdita lacks flowers appropriate for those fanciful girls of more than nine, Mopsa and Dorcas, to "wear upon your virgin branches yet / Your maidenheads growing" (IV.iv.115-16) —a charitable assumption on Perdita's part. In Camillo's plan that the lovers make for Sicilia, Florizel finds "some sap." In *The Winter's Tale* ripeness, and the whole process of birth, growth, death, and rebirth that it implies, really is all.

Whether or not this pervasive imagery of natural process expresses Shakespeare's reawakened love for the Warwickshire countryside, as used to be said, it is obviously central to the experience and effect of the play. For one thing, it works to establish a vital counterpoint between the rhythms of external nature and the rhythms of human life. When Camillo says of Leontes' jealousy that "you may as well / Forbid the sea for to obey the moon" (I.ii.432-3) as try to reason him out of it, and Paulina characterizes it as "dangerous unsafe lunes" (II.ii.30), the destructive forces at work in the play are linked with the phases of the moon. Similarly, when Leontes bids Perdita welcome to Sicilia "As is the spring to th' earth" (V.i.151), its rising action is made to coincide with the renewal of nature. Such moments (there are too many of them to enumerate) work cumulatively to endow the action of the play with something of the inevitability of natural process itself.

This use of imagery takes on special importance because *The Winter's Tale* is a romance. For the highly
artificial ups and downs of romance—to which Camillo
calls attention when he moralizes in the conventional
terminology of the form that "Prosperity's the very bond
of love, / Whose fresh complexion and whose heart together / Affliction alters" (iv.iv.574-6)—need all the authority and authentication that nature can confer on them.
As the play's romantic form moves miraculously from birth
through death to rebirth, so too does the natural world
every day, month, and year. It is, of course, a convention
of pastoral romance as ancient as *Daphnis and Chloe* that
the fortunes of its principals follow closely upon the natural cycle of the changing seasons. But Shakespeare characteristically deepens that convention by reminding us of
winter death even in the midst of vernal renewal. (Right
at the outset he transposes the settings of *Pandosto* and
places the winter's tale proper in traditionally pastoral
Sicily.) In Perdita's exquisite speech at the Bohemian
sheepshearing it is the wintry "winds of March" (iv.iv.120)
that daffodils take with beauty, and she receives Camillo's
compliment that he could live simply by gazing at her
with the unromantic reminder that he would be "so lean
that blasts of January / Would blow you through and
through." (iv.iv.111-12) Although Shakespearean comedy and romance from *Love's Labour's Lost* through *The
Tempest* often includes a song celebrating the return of
symbolic spring or summer, and within those songs a reminder of the wind and the rain past and to come; nowhere else are the depredations of winter so powerfully

realized and insistently recalled, as when Polixenes breaks up the Bohemian idyll with blasts of rage as wintry as Leontes' or Paulina plans to depart after the closing reunion for "some wither'd bough" (v.iii.133) to lament her lost Antigonus.

The play's appeal to the natural cycles of birth, death, and rebirth as a compelling precedent, for its own romantic action gains much of its persuasiveness from the fact that those cycles are existentially realized on stage: the natural one through the expanded time-scheme and setting, and the human one through a procession of characters representing all the ages of man from the infant Perdita through the boy Mamillius, the youthful Florizel, the middle-aged kings to the Old Shepherd fast approaching senility and second childhood. When we hear in the opening scene of a projected visit to Bohemia "this coming summer," and see the action shift to that place and season with the fourth act, we learn that the seasons change in the world of this play just as they do in the real world. If this seems like no great revelation, of how many plays (even Shakespearean plays) can it be said? When Camillo says that Leontes' grief is such that "sixteen winters cannot blow away, / So many summers dry" (v.iii.50-51), what seems merely a figurative way of saying sixteen years (and would be in another play) is also a statement of literal fact in a play whose years are shown to consist of winters and summers.

The imagery faithfully reflects not only the world outside the play but the world inside the play as well. The idyllic landscape of Leontes' boyhood, where he and Polixenes used to "frisk i' the sun" like "lambs," turns out to have an objective existence in the world of the play when we see Florizel at the Bohemian pastoral. When Camillo refers to "they that went on crutches ere he [Mamillius] was born" in the opening dialogue, he might almost have been thinking of the Old Shepherd himself, later described as a "weather-bitten conduit of many kings' reigns." (v.ii.56-7) In disclosing his suspicions to an incredulous Camillo, Leontes calls him "a fool, / That seest a game play'd home, the rich stake drawn, / And tak'st it all for jest." (1.ii.247-9) His image later materializes in the figure of the Clown, who sees Antigonus savaged and his ship destroyed (what he calls the "land service" and the "sea service"), and takes both calamities for something very like a jest. Similarly, when Leontes says that his wife "deserves a name / As rank as any flax-wench that puts to / Before her troth-plight" (1.ii.276-8), his image finds its objective correlative in those flax-wenches of dubious morals, Mopsa and Dorcas, who in the Clown's words "wear their plackets where they should bear their faces." (iv.iv.245) And when Camillo confides that behind his plan for the lovers' deliverance lies his own "woman's longing" (iv.iv.667) to revisit his native Sicilia, his expression reflects not only the real world, in which we know that pregnant women have strong and impulsive yearnings, but the play world, in which a pregnant woman is one of the major characters. The world of *The Winter's Tale* is so inclusive that virtually anything its characters may happen to mention has an objective existence somewhere within it. The play thus creates the illusion, I myself believe more than any other play of Shakespeare's, of being a perfect model of the great globe itself. The world of this romance is so completely and minutely imagined that, paradoxically, it leaves very little to our imagination —even its notorious geographical "blunders" like the seacoast of Bohemia and the island of Delphos are not passing spatial anachronisms but fully realized settings within the play. This is not to endorse the Romantic fallacy, discussed in the appendix, that imaginative coherence within the work is all, but to suggest that in *The Winter's Tale* imaginative coherence within the work and mimetic correspondence to the world outside are never really at odds. *Mimesis* and *poesis* are here one and the same.

Perhaps the best example of the romantic verisimilitude I have been struggling to describe is the Chorus of Time. Though few students of the play would now deny Shakespeare's authorship of the Chorus, the view of it as a crude makeshift, to which he was forced by the unwieldiness of his romantic materials, still persists. But the art of Shakespeare's necessities is strange and can make vile things precious. For the point that cries out to be made after so much fuss about the handling of time in the play is that time is made to behave in *The Winter's Tale* not less but more like it does in life than in any previous Shakespearean play. In defending Shakespeare against the rigors of neoclassical doctrine, Samuel Johnson might have had *The Winter's Tale* in mind when he says that "Time is, of all modes of existence, most obsequious to the imagination: a lapse of years is as easily conceived as a passage of hours."[7] We are used to thinking of time as an austere reality-principle that tyrannizes over human life and frustrates human desire, and this is, generally speaking, how it is

[7] *Samuel Johnson on Shakespeare*, p. 39.

presented in Shakespearean tragedy. But as Johnson reminds us, time in the real world may be as much the slave of human consciousness as its master, and it is this aspect of time that Shakespeare exploits in his comedies and romances.

Leontes in fact illustrates Johnson's principle of temporal obsequiousness in the first act when he tells us that "Looking on the lines / Of my boy's face, methoughts I did recoil / Twenty-three years." (1.ii.153-5) So does Polixenes a few lines later when he remarks on his own son's capacity to make "a July's day short as December." (1.ii.169) All the argument over extending Polixenes' visit turns on the fact that nine months have seemed a very short time to Leontes and Hermione and a very long time to Polixenes, who is worried about the state of his realm. "Time travels in divers paces with divers persons," Rosalind had observed in the Forest of Arden, and she illustrated her point with the case of the impatient lover, for whom "If the interim be but a se'nnight, Time's pace is so hard that it seems the length of seven year." (*A.Y.L.*, III.ii.304-13) Leontes' own case during his courtship of Hermione is an example of this: "Three crabbed months had sour'd themselves to death" (1.ii.102) before Hermione finally accepted him. To the penitent Leontes of the last act, his sixteen years of "saint-like sorrow" have seemed millennial, like the "Ten thousand years together" (III.ii.211) of self-mortification Paulina had ordained for him after the trial. The Chorus of Time, with all the obsequiousness of a servant, asks us to regard the passage of time within the play with the same imaginative elasticity with which we regard its passage in life. And in the characteristic way of *The Winter's Tale*, the mental faculty by which we do so is built into the world of the play.

But by soliciting our imaginative cooperation in the dramatic process, however easy it may be for us to give it, the Chorus of Time also works to make us aware of the play as a play. Like Gower in *Pericles*, Time mediates between the worlds of life and art and plays upon our sense of their separateness and their continuity, their dissimilarity and their resemblance. He reminds us, that is, that his powers of destruction and recreation (his speech is the apotheosis of the play's imagery of natural process) extend beyond the play world into the real world, and that the principals are subject to the same laws as we. Time "tries all" (iv.i.1) of us just as he tries Hermione and Leontes: "so shall I do / To th' freshest things now reigning, and make stale / The glistering of this present, as my tale / Now seems to it." (iv.i.12-14) Perdita and her fortunes will be "brought forth" as an actress is brought forth onto the stage, but also as a child is brought forth into the world: "By law and process of great nature" (ii.ii.60), as Perdita was brought forth earlier. In enforcing this analogy between the stage and the world, Time is of course only making explicit what has been implicit all along. When Hermione compared herself to the exemplary heroines of an older dramatic tradition, she had conceived of herself as more unhappy than "history can pattern," as playing a role that had been played many times before in life as well as art. When Leontes tells his son "Thy mother plays, and I / Play too; but so disgrac'd a part" (i.ii.187-8), he casts himself as the stock figure of the cuckold in a typical comedy of affliction. But he goes on to suggest that life imitates art:

> There have been,
> (Or I am much deceiv'd) cuckolds ere now,
> And many a man there is (even at this present,
> Now, while I speak this) holds his wife by th' arm,
> That little thinks she has been sluic'd in 's absence.
>
> (1.ii.190-94)

The stage is all the world, or at least one-tenth the world, by Leontes' calculations. The effect of these moments is not very different from those in Shakespeare's earlier plays when characters draw attention to their plays as plays.

When Macbeth compares his life to "a poor player / That struts and frets his hour upon the stage" or Cleopatra imagines herself watching "Some squeaking Cleopatra boy my greatness," they point up the skillful illusionism of the plays in which they appear by contrasting them with the crude or bad or unconvincing art in which they might have appeared. Similarly, in such theatrically self-conscious plays as *A Midsummer Night's Dream* and *Hamlet*, the productions of Bottom and Hamlet make Shakespeare's seem realistic by contrast. For Shakespearean artifice achieves its unparalleled verisimilitude by being not merely self-conscious of its own artificiality but self-critical of it. This is no less true of *The Winter's Tale* and *The Tempest* than of the preceding tragedies; if anything, it is more true of them. Because their romance form potentially enjoys the freest license with respect to reality, it also stands in need of the severest internal qualification.

The Bohemian pastoral functions within *The Winter's*

Tale much like those earlier plays-within-the-play, that is, as the locus of imaginative self-consciousness and self-criticism within the play. Certain misapprehensions about Bohemian innocence are still widespread; the detritus, I suspect, of the Victorian spiritual biography of Shakespeare, with its stress on the rusticated idealism of his last years, and of the Romantic myth of the noble savage, with its glorification of the primitive and the natural. Obviously Bohemia is a more innocent setting than Sicilia in so far as it exists in closer touch with external nature and at a lower level of conspicuous consumption. But the naturalness of Bohemia is no more to be equated with virtue than the sophistication of Sicilia is with vice. (If earlier Renaissance pastoral literature, Italian and English, tends to make or imply such identifications, the fact that Shakespeare has shrewdly transposed the settings of *Pandosto* should alert us to his freedom in handling sources.) The fact is that at the Sicilian court Leontes alone is guilty of intrigue and suspicion, and even though he projects these vices onto those around him, the rest of the court is convinced of Hermione's innocence and speaks out in her behalf. It is in Bohemia where what Hamlet suggestively terms "country matters" greet us at every turn. There the Old Shepherd believes that the babe he finds must be the product of "some stair-work, some trunk-work, some behind-door-work" (III.iii.73-75)—the bastard Leontes supposes her to be—and that "between ten and three-and-twenty" there is nothing but hooliganism and "getting wenches with child." (II.iii.59-62) The tittering of Mopsa and Dorcas at the sheepshearing would seem to confirm his suspicions. Autolycus ushers in the "sweet o' th' year" with a song about whoring and thieving, while his presence at the Bohemian idyll makes it more like a Newgate pastoral than an image of the golden age, and links it not only with the innocent fishermen of Pentapolis in *Pericles* but with its underworld of Mytilene as well. The real difference between Sicilia and Bohemia has to do with the uses and status of the imagination in each. Leontes' mad delusion had been presented as a perversion of the imagination, as a blasphemous imitation of God's own creative activity. But if Leontes creates dangerously and disastrously out of nothing, Autolycus creates the nothing that is trumpery-art, and therein lies the difference.

For the imaginative activity of Bohemia, because it is entirely natural, is also amoral. Much of the subject matter of Leontes' insane dreams is actually reworked by Autolycus and rendered into harmless fantasy. One of his ballads transmutes a potential tragedy of unrequited love into the comic extravagance of a monstrous "cold fish." Another deals mirthfully with a love-triangle and betrayal of faith. And a third relates "how a usurer's wife was brought to bed of twenty money-bags at a burden, and how she longed to eat adders' heads and toads carbonadoed." (iv.iv.263-6) When Mopsa asks if it is "true," Autolycus produces "the midwife's name to 't, one Mistress Taleporter, and five or six honest wives that were present." The subject of the ballad recalls the earlier childbirth which was all too true, while the "five or six honest wives" who allegedly verify it recall Leontes' wife, whose "honesty" was viciously doubted. Harsh reality has been transmuted into harmless fantasy. Autolycus does the same sort of thing in his account of the imaginary horrors which await the Clown, "who shall be flayed alive, then 'nointed over with honey, set on the head of a wasps' nest, then stand till he be three quarters and a dram dead; then recovered again with aqua-vitae or some other hot infusion; then, raw as he is, and in the hottest day prognostication proclaims, shall he be set against a brick wall, the sun looking with a southward eye upon him, where he is to behold him, with flies blown to death." (iv.iv.785-93) Here in a comically exaggerated form we have the deadly swoon of Hermione, the attempts to revive her, and her eventual resurrection. Autolycus is not the only one present whose imaginative efforts work in this way. Perdita's reply to Florizel's remark about strewing his corpse with flowers—"not to be buried, / But quick, and in mine arms" (iv.iv.131-2)—redeems not only a grim turn in their romantic conversation, but also on another imaginative level, the fate of her own brother and Florizel's alter ego. Florizel himself likes to create mythologies that are manifestly more beautiful than true, calling the sheepshearing festival "a meeting of the petty gods" and Perdita "no shepherdess, but Flora / Peering in April's front." (iv.iv.2-4) Even the notorious bear, the embodiment of the darker and more wintry side of Bohemian nature is a morally neutral, because wholly natural, version of Leontes (the association suggests itself through his name) who is really responsible for Antigonus' death. The whole scene exists at two imaginative removes from life.

The imaginative fecundity of Bohemia is certainly a refreshing change from the insane and destructive illusion which had tyrannized over Sicilia, but not really much more than that. It is as easy to sentimentalize the folk ritual and popular art of the rustics' sheepshearing festival into something profound and "authentic" as it is to romanticize Caliban's apprehension of "sounds and sweet airs" into the inherent musicality of the noble savage. The Old Shepherd praises Perdita's natural skill at dancing; there are the twelve herdsmen dressed as satyrs, whom Polixenes welcomes as "those that refresh us" (iv.iv.335) and whose dance, it is announced, "will please plentifully" (iv.iv.332); and above all there is the virtuoso performance of Autolycus. The dance of the satyrs offers the pleasant entertainment of pure spectacle, while the cheap artifacts Autolycus peddles, as well as his fantastic broadsides, are by his own admission "trumpery" and anticipate the "trumpery" with which Prospero distracts the drunken conspirators of *The Tempest*. Both Autolycus' and Prospero's trumpery-art are intended by their practitioners as mere distractions; both subserve the higher artistic design of the play itself even as they are a parody of it. "No hearing, no feeling, but my sir's song," says Autolycus, "and admiring the nothing of it." (iv.iv.613-15) While the rustics admire the nothing of it, Autolycus is able to practice his true vocation, the art of conycatching. If his ballads do not measure up, as pure fantasy, to Bacon's or Jonson's canons of mimetic empiricism, they do create a self-contained world sanctioned by the mimetic idealism of Sidney. (Sidney himself, though scornful of untutored folk art, was surprised at his own capacity to be moved by the old ballad of Chevy Chase.) And the responses of Mopsa and Dorcas—"Bless me from marrying a usurer";

"Is it true, think you"—are close in their naive confusion of art and life to that of Simon Forman to *The Winter's Tale* itself and to that of the Simon Forman who exists at some level in the most sophisticated of us. But that is the most one can say for Autolycus' ballads. For if the dreams of Leontes corrupt and pervert the reality of the Sicilian court and the truth of his own marriage—"You had a bastard by Polixenes, / And I but dream'd it!" (III.ii.83-4)—the satyrs' dance and Autolycus' fantastic ballads bear little mimetic relation to any outside reality whatever. Whereas Leontes' imaginative constructs are positively immoral, those of Autolycus are wholly amoral, despite the fact that Dorcas draws a moral on the inadvisability of marrying usurers and to that extent the imaginative life of Bohemia may be seen as an improvement upon, certainly a relief from, that of Sicilia. But Autolycus' art, in that it never leads us back to life, is really a low parody of the high art of the play itself. It frightens, fears, and flees nature in the way that Ben Jonson wrongly accused *The Winter's Tale* itself of doing, but which romance forms may all too easily do.

Shakespeare's last two romances are built upon a quite different principle, the principle enunciated by Polixenes in his debate with Perdita on cross-breeding:

> Nature is made better by no mean
> But nature makes that mean: so, over that art,
> Which you say adds to nature, is an art
> That nature makes. You see, sweet maid, we marry
> A gentler scion to the wildest stock,
> And make conceive a bark of baser kind

By bud of nobler race. This is an art
Which does mend nature—change it rather—but
The art itself is nature.   (iv.iv.89-97)

Perdita, in her transcendent naturalness, resists or misses
the point. She mistrusts artifice of any kind, from the art
of painting one's face to the art of hybridization, which
she ironically equates with bastardization. She is even uneasy in her roles of mistress of the feast and of queening
it as the prince's betrothed: "Methinks I play as I have
seen them do / In Whitsun pastorals: sure this robe of
mine / Does change my disposition." (iv.iv.133-5) Her
remark reminds us that still another kind of art operates
in Bohemia, the art of play acting.[8] Not only Perdita but
virtually everyone present at the sheepshearing is playing
a role and appears in disguise: Autolycus as peddler, Florizel as "humble swain," Polixenes and Camillo as country
gentlemen. Given the nature of the Bohemian setting,
these roles are a far cry from the "disgrac'd" parts of
hobby-horse and cuckold in which Leontes had miscast
his wife and himself, even though Polixenes will soon
belie his own argument for marrying gentle scions with
wild stocks by reenacting the insane rage of Leontes. But
the very fact that Polixenes does break up the Bohemian
festival suggests the fragility of this pastoral world, its
fugitive and cloistered virtue. The breaking-up of the

[8] On theatrical self-consciousness in *The Winter's Tale,* see Ann
Righter, *Shakespeare and the Idea of the Play* (Baltimore, 1967), pp.
172-86, and *Shakespeare and the Common Understanding,* pp. 192-233.
On nature and art, see Frye, *Fables of Identity,* pp. 107-18; Frank
Kermode, ed., *The Winter's Tale* (Signet Shakespeare, New York,
1963), pp. xxi-xxxv; and Edward William Tayler, *Nature and Art
in Renaissance Literature* (New York, 1964).

feast corresponds to the breaking-up of Prospero's betrothal masque in *The Tempest* and to the destruction of Pastorella's kingdom in *The Faerie Queene* (vi.x), for the good pastoral romancer is aware of the limits and temptations of the pastoral vision, its potential truancy and untruth.

It is left to Camillo to pick up the pieces after the destructive conduct of first Leontes and then Polixenes and to shape the ensuing events. In so doing, Camillo takes on the role of stage manager of the subsequent action and unwittingly follows the principle set forth in Polixenes' speech. "Methinks I see," says Camillo,

> Leontes opening his free arms and weeping
> His welcomes forth; asks thee there 'Son,
>   forgiveness!'
> As 'twere i' th' father's person; kisses the hands
> Of your fresh princess; o'er and o'er divides him
> 'Twixt his unkindness and his kindness; th' one
> He chides to hell, and bids the other grow
> Faster than thought or time.   (iv.iv.548-55)

It is only appropriate that Florizel should find "some sap in this," not merely because the scenario Camillo imagines does come prophetically true in the next scene, but because this exercise of the imagination works with and for human nature and is directed toward mending the broken natural bond between father and son and healing that all but ruined piece of nature, Leontes. Camillo has been characterized throughout as "priest-like" (i.ii.237), "clerk-like experienced" (i.ii.392), "the medicine of our house" (iv.iv.588), as spiritual and physical healer to both troubled kings, while his kind of art is both moral and recreative in a way which the earlier versions of art in the play are not. His art forces the anti-artificial Perdita to take on still another disguise as a princess which is really no disguise at all—"the art itself is nature"—and makes use of the lower artistic services of Autolycus: "We'll make an instrument of this; omit / Nothing may give us aid." (iv.iv.626-7) The reunion in Sicilia that Camillo designs and engineers turns out to be the perfect collaboration of art and nature described by Polixenes: its instruments are the Clown and Autolycus, the former literally a "natural" who, as Autolycus puts it, "wants but something to be a reasonable man" (iv.iv.606-7), and the latter a kind of Jacobean Artful Dodger.

In his presentation of the outcome of Camillo's art, the first recognition scene, Shakespeare has the choric gentlemen who recount the reunion to us insist on its likeness to an old tale, but only to repudiate that likeness and establish the reality of what has happened. "Such a deal of wonder is broken out within this hour, that ballad-makers cannot be able to express it." (v.ii.23-5) What has occurred, that is, is all the more miraculous in its effect than anything art in the usual sense could produce for being life itself: "Most true, if ever truth were pregnant by circumstance: that which you hear you'll swear you see, there is such unity in the proofs." (v.ii.31-3) Art is repudiated even as life is asserted. Gower had done something similar in disclaiming the power of his crude choric artifice compared with the scenes themselves, and Prospero will abjure the rough magic which produces dazzling illusions in favor of life itself. Even the highest artifice included in *The Winter's Tale*, that of Julio Romano, is finally renounced

although it comes closest to the art which the play en-
dorses and illustrates. Julio's art is described as a realism
so transcendent that "had he himself eternity and could
put breath into his work, [he] would beguile Nature of
her custom, so perfectly is he her ape." (v.ii.96-9) It fulfills the conditions of Jonson's mimetic empiricism and
Sidney's mimetic idealism at once; it is perfectly faithful
to nature even as it brings forth a second nature; it fills
us with the admiration and delight of pure romance while
it simultaneously instructs us in the ways of nature, for
Julio's "excellence" consists in his ability to carve the passage of time into his work, to accommodate the realities
of imperfection and flux even as he transcends them in
marble. But we learn that Julio never did a statue of
Hermione, and the hyperboles of Renaissance art criticism
applied to his work dissolve at a touch into the humane
moral artifice of Paulina, as the fantastical histrionics of
Autolycus had been absorbed into the beneficent design
of Camillo, and as the marble statue of Hermione melts
into her living form.

The fact is that even Julio's artifice (precisely because
of its alleged transcendence) is dangerously close to losing
touch with life and must be repudiated by the artist who
is to remain faithful to life. The value of the imagination
for such an artist exists not in and for itself but in its body-
ing forth of the ideal into human life, in its holding out,
and holding out for, brave new worlds which this world
must make an effort to reach. The imaginative settings of
the Welsh hills in *Cymbeline*, pastoral Bohemia in *The
Winter's Tale*, and Prospero's island in *The Tempest* embody in an all but impossible purity the values finally

incorporated into the societies which leave those idealized landscapes for a more livable reality. For a few rarefied moments the creative and recreative power of the imagination is literally made flesh in the statue scene and the impossible comes true. Paulina's art literally recreates (in both senses) Leontes' shattered life. The pain of his earlier madness is redeemed by "the pleasure of [this] madness" (v.iii.72-3) and "this affliction has a taste as sweet / As any cordial comfort." (v.iii.76-7) Earlier he had compared himself to one whose vital functions of eating, drinking, and sleeping had been poisoned by spiders in his cup and tails of wasps in his bed. "If this be magic," he says when Paulina disclaims all magic, "let it be an art / Lawful as eating" (v.iii.110-11), an art as natural as the means by which life and health are sustained. That art, as Paulina makes clear, requires that "You do awake your faith" (v.iii.94-5); the faith which now revives Hermione as its absence had previously "killed" her, but also the imaginative faith by which the entire scene works on the stage (no one who has seen the play well performed will doubt that it does work) by which we "credit [this] relation," in Pericles' phrase, "to points that seem impossible" even as we realize that there is no statue, that the art itself is nature, and that all can be rationally explained.

No play of Shakespeare's (perhaps not even *The Tempest*) so perfectly fulfills the conventions of romance while testing them so rigorously against the touchstone of brazen reality. In *The Winter's Tale* Shakespeare has solved what might be termed the problem of Job's daughters, the central problem of romance, as he never had before.

How do you manage to redeem all sorrow and repair all loss, as the romance form requires, while simultaneously bringing home the abiding sense of sorrow and loss, as they would certainly linger on in life? This is the problem that Julio would have overcome, had he carved Hermione's statue, by the brilliant touch of a wrinkled face. This is one of the chief problems of the problem comedies, where the principals do not change sufficiently for us to believe in the formal resolution of their problems. Even in *Pericles* and *Cymbeline*, because death is presented more as a symbol than a natural fact, the resurrections and restorations of those plays tend to remain merely symbolic also. In *The Winter's Tale* death is presented with the force of reality itself, perhaps because for most of the play we, as well as the characters, are forced to accept it as reality: "there is such unity in the proofs." And if Hermione is restored, Mamillius and Antigonus are not. That she and Perdita should be, says Paulina, is after all

> as monstrous to our human reason
> As my Antigonus to break his grave
> And come again to me; who, on my life,
> Did perish with the infant.　　　(v.i.41-4)

In the last act Leontes' responsibility for his family's death is not glossed over or ignored, but repeatedly insisted on in the true but tactless remarks of those around him as well as in his own self-recriminations. When Hermione is restored, when the romance form asserts its prerogatives like the force, in Dylan Thomas's words, that through the green fuse drives the flower, these realities are not wishfully denied. Rather the play asserts that such an outcome, so unforeseen and "monstrous" to all we have seen and known of reality, really is a miracle. The ending is as miraculous as that which it overcomes is felt to be real. Mamillius and Antigonus *are* restored in the figures of Florizel and Camillo; yet the latter do not fully replace the former but are some compensation for their loss. The art of the play, like that of Julio, is romantic and realistic at once: the art itself is nature.

This paradox is at the heart of the play (it is expounded by Polixenes and exemplified by Julio) and is also at the heart of the romance form. As the mode in which the imagination enjoys its freest exercise, romance is able to get in more of life (in that sense it is truer to life than any other literary mode), but by its very inclusiveness creates more problems for the artist in making its world mimetically convincing. In *The Winter's Tale* Shakespeare again turns to old tales—not only to Greene's *Pandosto* but the dramatic romances that held the boards before his career began—and this time vivifies them as Paulina does Hermione's "statue" and Leontes himself, frees their conventions of stiffness and charges them with life. For just as life is redeemed by art in the world and action of the play, so too the romance form is now redeemed by life. This play illustrates no cold-blooded interest in dramatic craftsmanship, or weariness of life, or absorption in playmaking for its own sake. The motto for *The Winter's Tale* and *The Tempest* is not art for art's sake (the climax of both plays is the repudiation of art) but art for life's sake. In a play in which nearly every line is a comment on every other line, Shakespeare creates not only a glittering artifact but one of his most successful representations of this world.

Perhaps the most acute comment on *The Winter's Tale* is the marginal gloss Herman Melville scrawled beneath Polixenes' speech on the identity of nature and art. He wrote: "A world here."[9] For our final impression of the play is of a world where time and death, though they exist for certain, are purged of their terror, and whose inhabitants, though they cannot frisk forever in the sun, are nevertheless hard at play.

[9] Melville's copy of Shakespeare is in the Houghton Library at Harvard. *The Dramatic Works of William Shakespeare* (Boston, 1837), III, 65. I am grateful to Harry Levin for bringing it to my attention.

CHAPTER 8

Undream'd Shores:
The Tempest

> They do play two games not unlike chess. . . . In the
> latter is exhibited very cleverly, to begin with, both the
> strife of the vices with one another and their concerted
> opposition to the virtues; then, what vices are opposed
> to what virtues, by what forces they assail them openly,
> by what stratagems they attack them indirectly, by what
> safeguards the virtues check the power of the vices, by
> what arts they frustrate their designs, and finally, by
> what means the one side gains the victory.
>
> —Thomas More

WHEN Gonzalo in the second act of *The Tempest* con-
founds ancient Carthage in modern Tunis, Antonio compares the old man's lapse of memory to the poet Amphion's
"miraculous harp," at whose sound stones took their places
within the wall of Thebes. "What impossible matter,"
Antonio jibes, "will he make easy next?" (ii.i.85) It is
easy to imagine Ben Jonson, who had jibed at Shakespeare
for giving Bohemia a seacoast in *The Winter's Tale*,[1] ask-

---

[1] Jonson thought the joke was on Shakespeare when he said that
"Shakespear, in a play, brought in a number of men saying they had
suffered shipwrack in Bohemia, wher ther is no sea near by some 100
miles." "Conversations of Ben Jonson and William Drummond of
Hawthornden" (1619), *Critical Essays of the Seventeenth Century*,
ed. Joel E. Spingarn (Oxford, 1908), I, 213. Aside from the fact that

ing the same question on his way to see *The Tempest* for the first time. For if Gonzalo is comically unlike Amphion, the Shakespeare of the last romances, and of *The Tempest* in particular, is not. By a similar poetic magic, Shakespeare contains an action that stretches from "the dark backward and abysm of time" to the dramatic present, from a lost Golden Age to a future Apocalypse, and that spans the Mediterranean from Italy to North Africa, and the Atlantic from the Old World to the New, to a single afternoon and a single place, an island brought forth from the sea by the kind of spontaneous generation Antonio goes on to ridicule. The raw material of the three earlier romances now takes its place within the neoclassical architecture of *The Tempest* like the stones of the wall of Thebes. Not only does Shakespeare "make easy" his impossible matter, but he departs from his usual practice and makes it up. The absence of a literary source for *The Tempest* only reinforces the already strong sense, arising from the fantastic nature of its island setting and of its native inhabitants, of creation out of nothing. If the Shakespeare of *The Winter's Tale* is like Julio Romano, the painstaking carver whose art is indistinguishable from nature itself, the Shakespeare of *The Tempest* is more like Amphion, the poet-magician who calls into being a second nature, like and unlike nature, at the touch of a miraculous harp.

It is the very self-consistency of the world of *The Tem-*

Jonson seems to have confused in his memory *Twelfth Night* and *The Winter's Tale*, the joke about the seacoast was almost certainly on him. See S. L. Bethell, *The Winter's Tale: A Study* (London, 1947), pp. 32-5.

pest that has rendered the play at once so impenetrable to criticism and so susceptible to allegorization. "The human and imaginary characters," writes Hazlitt, "the dramatic and the grotesque, are blended together with the greatest art, and without any appearance of it. . . . As the preternatural part has the air of reality, and almost haunts the imagination with a sense of truth, the real characters and events partake of the wildness of a dream."[2] The "undream'd shores" (*W.T.*, iv.iv.568) of the island, the purely imaginary characters of Ariel and Caliban, and the otherworldly art of Prospero himself, though they condition the remarkable unity of *The Tempest*, work also to seal off the play from life as we know it and to provoke the mind to seek correspondences to life as we know it. Add to these internal features its strategic position in Shakespeare's working life and the absence of a literary source, and the brood of allegorizations it has spawned becomes practically inevitable. Allegory, in its modern usage, presupposes self-consistency and self-containment. Many nineteenth-century and some twentieth-century interpreters have conversely assumed that a self-consistency and self-containment of this order must presuppose allegory. And so we have Shakespeare (Prospero) bequeathing his Art (Miranda) to John Fletcher (Ferdinand); Shakespeare (Prospero) emancipating his Imagination (Ariel) and retiring to Stratford (Milan); God (Prospero) guiding Erring Man (Alonso and the rest) through the World (the island) to Salvation (homecoming); the Renaissance

[2] William Hazlitt, *Characters of Shakespeare's Plays*, ed. Ernest Rhys (Everyman's Library, London, 1906), p. 89.

(Prospero) releasing Poetry (Ariel) from the bondage of Medieval Scholasticism (Sycorax); and so on.[3] (Ironically enough, it is only recently that *The Tempest* itself has begun to be freed from the bondage of scholastic "allegoresis.") It is not that attempts to allegorize the play are wrong (indeed any attempt to interpret a work of literature must to some degree allegorize it) but that the particular historical and theological meanings assigned to *The Tempest* have tended in their misplaced concreteness to eclipse rather than illuminate the play. To adapt a line of Shelley's to this most Shelleyan of Shakespeare's plays, the almost hermetic self-containment of *The Tempest* remains, its many allegorizations change and pass.

There is, however, an older and looser sense in which *The Tempest* is an allegory. If allegory signifies for us the kind of work in which everything stands in one-to-one relation to something outside it, allegory for the Elizabethans held a wide range of possible applications. They subsume so many kinds of literary expression under the term allegory, what we would variously call proverb, fable, parable, emblem, that one begins to suspect the allegories Elizabethans saw in literature lay as much in the eye of the beholder as in the design of the author.[4] Without unduly medievalizing the Renaissance, it may be said that most books, even those whose characters are preeminently human, could be read allegorically because the

[3] For an interesting account of allegorical interpretation of *The Tempest*, see A. D. Nuttall, *Two Concepts of Allegory* (London, 1967), pp. 1-14.

[4] See Joshua McClennen, *On the Meaning and Function of Allegory in the English Renaissance*, University of Michigan Contributions in Modern Philology, No. 6 (Ann Arbor, 1947).

book of nature could be also. Something of the typological awareness of medieval preachers and schoolmen survives when Marvell identifies the human soul in a drop of dew, when Milton recasts the succession of tyrannies that is human history into a providential scheme, and even (to turn from life to literature) when Hamlet images his own and every man's situation in the fall of a sparrow. For literature, like life, would repay in kind the fineness and power of perception brought to bear on it. It is easy to imagine an early audience of *The Tempest* seeing in it everything from an entertaining spectacle to a parable (a word used interchangeably with allegory) of the life of man. Nor is it hard to imagine its author, as much as the author of *The Faerie Queene*, deliberately casting his play as a "dark conceit"—the very difficulty of which forces its audience to work hard to understand it and puts them into a position analogous to that of the characters themselves, who also have to work hard for understanding. Those in the audience willing and able to labor in their minds, like Gonzalo and Alonso within the play, might win through to an understanding of its events, while others unwilling or unable, like Antonio and those archetypal groundlings, Stephano, Trinculo, and Caliban, might deny or miss its meaning. *The Tempest*, more than any other play of Shakespeare's, asks to be seen as glittering illusion or as essential reality, and its cast divides the possibilities of response among them.

If this most "allegorical" of Shakespeare's plays does not have a literary source in the usual sense, it does have historical sources: William Strachey's *A True Reportory of the Wreck and Redemption of Sir Thomas Gates, Knight* and Silvester Jourdain's *A Discovery of the Bermudas.* Although their titles promise a documentary fidelity to fact, the "Bermuda pamphlets" are anything but mundane reportage of contemporary history. Both accounts consistently allegorize the events they purport merely to describe:

> It pleased God out of His most gracious and merciful providence so to direct and guide our ship (being left to the mercy of the sea) for her most advantage . . . . Every man bustled up and gathered his strength and feeble spirits together to perform as much as their weak force would permit him; through which weak means it pleased God to work so strongly as the water was stayed for that little time . . . and the ship kept from present sinking . . . .
>
> And there neither did our ship sink, but, more fortunately in so great a misfortune, fell in between two rocks, where she was fast lodged and locked for further budging . . . . But our delivery was not more strange, in falling so opportunely and happily upon the land, as our feeding and preservation was beyond our hopes and all men's expectations most admirable.[5]

Both Strachey and Jourdain, in their readiness to see the miraculous at work, to moralize on the conduct of the crew, and to discern the hand of providence in every turn of events, take what may be called Gonzalo's view of their experience. That experience is cast as one of trial and de-

[5] Silvester Jourdain, *A Discovery of the Bermudas* (1610). Reprinted in *A Voyage to Virginia in 1609,* ed. Louis B. Wright (Charlottesville, 1964), pp. 106-08.

liverance under the watchful eye of God, in the course of which everyone's true nature is revealed and the best in some is brought out. Strachey frames his picture of the Bermudan wreck and redemption within the larger picture of the wreck and redemption of the Virginia colony itself:

> The ground of all those miseries, was the permissive Providence of God, Who in the fore-mentioned violent storm separated the head from the body, all the vital powers of regiment being exiled with Sir Thomas Gates in those infortunate (yet fortunate) islands. The broken remainder of those supplies made a greater shipwreck in the continent of Virginia by the tempest of dissension: every man, overvaluing his own worth, would be a commander; every man, underprizing another's value, denied to be commanded.[6]

Strachey is quoting from "a book called *A True Declaration of Virginia* . . . published by the Company," which describes in detail the wretched state of affairs the Bermudan survivors discovered upon their return to Virginia. But even that nightmarish interlude, which included mutiny, famine, and cannibalism, was providentially prescribed for the ultimate recovery of the colony: "*Quae videtur paena, est medicina,* that which we accompt a punishment against evill is but a medicine against evill."[7]

---

[6] William Strachey, *A True Reportory of the Wreck and Redemption of Sir Thomas Gates, Knight* (1610). Reprinted in *A Voyage to Virginia in 1609,* ed. Wright, pp. 95-96.

[7] From the volume Strachey refers to as *A True Declaration of Virginia.* Reprinted in *Tracts and Other Papers,* ed. Peter Force (Washington, 1844), III, 11. Its full title—"A True Declaration of the

The tempest, be it natural or social, that turns out for the best, functions in the narratives of these early voyagers in much the same way that the *felix culpa* functions within Christian history: as a kind of divinely staged *peripeteia* through which potential tragedy turns into tragicomedy. Phrases like "more fortunately in so great a misfortune" and "those infortunate (yet fortunate) islands" suggest that their authors might well have had that central paradox of Christian history in mind even as they shaped their own historical narratives.

It has often been remarked that the opening storm, insular setting, and providential design of *The Tempest* probably derive from the Bermuda pamphlets, but there is also an important sense in which the Bermuda pamphlets derive from romances like *The Tempest*. Aside from the implicit resemblances to the pattern of Christian history, Strachey and Jourdain model their accounts on romantic narratives as old as the *Odyssey* and as recent as the *Arcadia*, the actions of which often begin with a shipwreck on unknown shores, followed by a period of physical hardship and spiritual trial, and finally homecoming and reunion. (The first book of the *Aeneid*, which mirrors the large historical movement of the poem as a whole, follows just such a pattern.) The point is not that Strachey and Jourdain may have read these books, though it is probable they did, but that the Elizabethans conceived of their

---

Estate of the Colonie in Virginia, With a confutation of such scandalous reports as have tended to the disgrace of so worthy an enterprise"— indicates the promotional nature of the piece. But if its purpose is transparent, its terminology is revealing: "What is there in all this tragicall Comaedie that should discourage us with impossibilitie of the enterprise?" (p. 11).

voyages of exploration and colonization in terms of romance. The word "adventure" was applied both to the romances they devoured and the commercial enterprises they sponsored. Any gap between literature and life is closed in the very name of Sir George Summers' wrecked flagship, the *Sea Venture*, and the vessels built by the Bermudan castaways for their departure were named, with romantic decorum, the *Patience* and the *Deliverance*. When the anonymous author of *A True Declaration* speaks of "those infortunate (yet fortunate) islands," he almost certainly has in mind, not only Christian history, but the legendary Fortunate Isles, traditionally located, like Bermuda, far to the west. When the Bermudas were renamed the Summer Islands a few years earlier, it is hard not to believe those English voyagers had not only their admiral's name in mind but the faraway places of romance. Confronted with the unknown quantity of the New World, Renaissance voyagers repeatedly fall back on the romantic imagination of the Old to define and characterize it.

For to the minds of the early voyagers, the New World was as much a moral and mythological landscape as a physical and geographical one. In both its benign and sinister aspects it was described as if it existed outside of time and space, more like the settings of Dante and Spenser than anything on the known map of Europe. Columbus, as everyone knows, thought he had discovered the terrestrial paradise, and Amerigo Vespucci similarly described the South America he had almost certainly never seen, compiling his idealized account of the place, like many who had seen it, out of earlier literature. To Peter Martyr, the natives of Cuba "seem to live in the golden world, without toil, living in open gardens, not entrenched with dikes, divided with hedges, or defended with walls . . . without laws, without books, and without judges." Arthur Barlow characterizes the Indians of Virginia as a people "most gentle, loving, and faithful, void of all guile and treason and such as lived after the manner of the Golden Age," and their land as productive of "all things in abundance as in the first creation, without toil or labour."[8] The classical myth of a primordial Golden Age and the Christian myth of a lost paradise were repeatedly invoked to describe a contemporary reality. Michael Drayton, eulogizing the Virginia voyage of 1607, styles the English plantation "Earth's onely paradise" where "the golden age / Still natures law does give."[9] Such hyperbolic accounts of the New World of course invited parody, such as the description of Virginia in *Eastward Ho!*, where it is said that even the chamberpots of Virginia are made of pure gold—an instance of conspicuous consumption borrowed from More's *Utopia*. Nor did Renaissance travelogues invariably picture the Americas as the landscape of one's dreams. They also contained accounts of a dark and terrifying, but equally fantastical, nightmare world of "ravenous Harpies," "wild men . . . without any certaine

[8] *The Decades of the New World*, trans. Richard Eden (1555). Excerpted in *Renaissance Reader*, edd. J. B. Ross and Mary M. McLaughlin (New York, 1961), p. 151. Barlow's remark occurs in a letter to Sir Walter Raleigh published by Richard Hakluyt, *The Principall Navigations* (1589). Reprinted in *The Elizabethans' America*, ed. Louis B. Wright (Cambridge, Mass., 1965), p. 109.

[9] "To the Virginia Voyage," *Poems of Michael Drayton*, ed. John Buxton (Cambridge, Mass., 1933), I, 123-24.

language," and "a Monster of the Sea like a Man," of cannibals and devils.[10] Events in Virginia in 1609 showed how easily the American utopia eulogized by Drayton could turn into a scarifying dystopia; how its noble savages could become bloodthirsty adversaries; and how the English colony itself could fall into practices as beastly as the worst of the New World's benighted inhabitants. The darker and less hospitable aspects of the New World did not go unrecognized. The Bermudas were in fact called The Devil's Islands and avoided by mariners "as Scylla and Charybdis, or as they would shun the Devil himself"[11] before Strachey and Jourdain reported to the contrary. But even the grim reputation and hostile potential of the Bermudas turn out to be part of God's providential plan:

> True it is, that as Almighty God set the cherubims and the blade of a sword shaking in fearful manner to keep Adam from coming into Paradise, so by fearful tempests and terrible lightning and thunder God hath terrified and kept all people of the world from coming into these islands to inhabit them, as appeareth by divers signs of shipwreck in divers places about the islands . . . but now, since it hath pleased God to discover them

[10] From *The Decades of the New World*, quoted in *The Tempest*, ed. Frank Kermode (New Arden Shakespeare, Cambridge, Mass., 1954), p. xxxiii. On the background of Renaissance travel literature, Kermode's introduction is, as on most other matters relating to *The Tempest*, indispensable. See also R. R. Cawley, "Shakespeare's Use of the Voyagers," *PMLA*, XLI (1926), 688-726, and esp. Leo Marx, "Shakespeare's American Fable," *Massachusetts Review*, Vol. II, No. 1 (Autumn, 1960), 40-71.

[11] Jourdain, *A Voyage to Virginia*, ed. Wright, p. 108.

unto and to bestow them upon His people of England, here have been no such tempests nor danger, His holy and great name be therefore praised.[12]

Thus Lewis Hughes, minister of God and exorcist of witches, in 1615. All that is now required of Englishmen to regain this divinely ordained paradise, like the one reserved for Adam and Eve and all their children and grandchildren in Milton, is their own good efforts.

The Renaissance voyagers, particularly Strachey, Jourdain, and Hughes, in their casting about for classical and Christian analogues to their experience, in their eagerness to see the miraculous at work and the special providence of God in all that happens, to see hope in disaster and lessons in trials, remind us more than a little of Gonzalo. From his comments on the breakdown of shipboard discipline during the opening storm to his wishful celebration of everyone's self-recovery near the end, Gonzalo tries, like the Renaissance voyagers behind him, to see a providential design in the experience of the play, to moralize that experience into what the Renaissance would call an "allegory." In doing so, although he does not "mistake the truth totally," as Antonio claims, he does have to bend reality ever so slightly to the desires of his mind and to that extent falsify it; not quite everyone, for example, has found himself by the end of the play as Gonzalo would like to think. His allusions to Carthage and "widow Dido" do distort Virgil in the strenuous effort to hammer out the parallel, and are representative of his efforts at per-

[12] *A Letter Sent into England from the Summer Islands* (1615). Excerpted in *The Elizabethans' America*, p. 202.

ception throughout. One such effort is his benevolent vision of an island utopia:

Gonzalo. Had I plantation of this isle, my lord,—
Antonio. He'd sow't with nettle seed.
Sebastian.   Or docks, or mallows.
Gonzalo. And were the King on't, what would I do?
Sebastian. 'Scape being drunk for want of wine.
Gonzalo. I'th'commonwealth I would by contraries
　Execute all things; for no kind of traffic
　Would I admit; no name of magistrate;
　Letters should not be known; riches, poverty,
　And use of service, none; contract, succession,
　Bourn, bound of land, tilth, vineyard, none;
　No use of metal, corn, or wine, or oil;
　No occupation; all men idle, all;
　And women too, but innocent and pure;
　No sovereignty;—
Sebastian. Yet he would be King on't
Antonio. The latter end of his commonwealth forgets
　　　　the beginning.
Gonzalo. All things in common Nature should produce
　Without sweat or endeavor: treason, felony,
　Sword, pike, knife, gun, or need of any engine,
　Would I not have; but Nature should bring forth,
　Of it own kind, all foison, all abundance,
　To feed my innocent people.
Sebastian. No marrying 'mong his subjects?
Antonio. None, man; all idle; whores and knaves.
Gonzalo. I would with such perfection govern, sir,
　T'excel the Golden Age.　　　　　(ii.i.139-63)

Whether the island is in fact "lush and lusty" with grass, as Gonzalo earlier says, or "tawny . . . . With an eye of green in 't," as Antonio and Sebastian contend, is less important than the state of mind of the speaker, which the island, like a mirror, reflects. Just as the forest of Arden had seemed a more commodious place to Duke Senior than it had to Jaques and Touchstone, so Gonzalo sees a potential utopia where Antonio and Sebastian see only a wasteland. But the issues at stake have widened considerably since *As You Like It*. Whereas Duke Senior had found "tongues in trees, books in the running brooks, / Sermons in stones, / and good in everything," Gonzalo proceeds to imagine not simply a reformed microcosm of the court but a brave new world founded on revolutionary principles, one that not merely equals but actually excels the Golden Age.

The similarities between his daydream of an island utopia and the voyagers' dreams of the New World quoted above are obvious. Gonzalo's speech is in fact lifted in its entirety from the supposedly firsthand account of the New World which Montaigne reports in "Of the Cannibals." But if Montaigne glorifies pristine America mainly to indict degenerate Europe, his irony undergoes a seachange in Shakespeare's hands. Gonzalo's ideal commonwealth presupposes the benignity of nature and the instantaneous perfectibility of man, highly questionable assumptions in view of the natural disaster which has left them stranded on the island in the first place and the cynical banter of Antonio and Sebastian, whose capacity for redemption is still in doubt even at the end of the play and whose very presence to that extent invalidates Gonzalo's

ideal. The speech is not simply the fancy of an old innocent (Ferdinand and Miranda are the voices of real innocence within the play), for Gonzalo should know better.
His banishment of "treason" from his vision of the good
and natural life represents a spurious attempt to escape
from the burden of history into a timeless realm of romance, when he himself is at least implicated in the trea-
sons which drove Prospero from his dukedom twelve years
before and which are about to be reenacted, this time directed against Alonso. It is characteristic of Shakespearean
irony that the villains are permitted to express some telling
truths; recall the pedant Holofernes' just rebuke of the
nobles in *Love's Labour's Lost* for their reception of the
Worthies' Pageant ("This is not generous, not gentle, not
humble"), or Regan's remark that Lear "hath ever but
slenderly known himself," or the corrupt tribune Brutus'
remonstrance to Coriolanus ("You speak o' th' people, /
As if you were a god to punish, not / A man of their in-
firmity"). The jibes of Antonio and Sebastian that frame
Gonzalo's monologue no doubt damage their speakers
more than their target, but they also serve to remind us
that there is no escape from history, that Gonzalo envisions
a commonwealth not simply of "contraries" but of contradictions, and that life offers real resistance to the fiats of
the idealizing imagination.

The fact is that Gonzalo's "allegorical" reading of events
is repeatedly qualified by the events themselves in something of the same way that the neat *de casibus* pattern of
Gloucester's pseudo-tragedy had been qualified by the
authentic tragedy of Lear. Similarly, *The Tempest* itself
is not so much a straight reflection of earlier Renaissance

travel literature as an ironic commentary on it. Consider, for example, the scene in which Ariel and the other spirits present the starving courtiers with a banquet. Even the skepticism of Antonio and Sebastian breaks down, and they momentarily suspend their disbelief: "Now I will believe / That there are unicorns," says Sebastian, "that in Arabia / There is one tree, the phoenix' throne; one phoenix / At this hour reigning there." And Antonio echoes: "travellers ne'er did lie, / Though fools at home condemn 'em." (III.iii.21-7) Gonzalo characteristically goes even further in not only accepting the reality of these "strange shapes" but assuming their benevolence:

> If in Naples
> I should report this now, would they believe me?
> If I should say, I saw such islanders—
> For, certes, these are people of the island,—
> Who, though they are of monstrous shape, yet, note,
> Their manners are more gentle, kind, than of
> Our human generation you shall find
> Many, nay, almost any.   (III.iii.27-34)

The speech illustrates once again Gonzalo's readiness to find good in everything and, with its flattering contrast of native with European manners, reflects the reports of numerous Renaissance "soft primitivists," notably Montaigne.[13] But Gonzalo's generous sentiments once again prove misplaced as Ariel reenters "like a Harpy," claps his wings over the banquet which disappears, and pronounces

[13] See *The Essayes of Montaigne*, trans. John Florio (1603), ed. J.I.M. Stewart (New York, 1933), p. 164. On "soft" and "hard" primitivism, see A. O. Lovejoy and George Boas, *Primitivism and Related Ideas in Antiquity* (Baltimore, 1935), p. 10ff.

his sentence of "ling'ring perdition" on the three men of sin present. Of course Gonzalo's trust, as Prospero standing on the upper stage reminds us, is not ultimately misplaced, for the spirits are in his service and the play in which they appear does turn out after all to be a romance. But at this stage in the development of the play his instinctive goodwill is sentimental, untested and unconfirmed by experience.

Or consider the savage of *The Tempest*. Rather than the rough diamond of Renaissance pastoral romance or his counterpart in Renaissance travel literature, the noble savage of the New World, Caliban is, as Prospero never tires of insisting, "a born devil, on whose nature / Nurture can never stick." (iv.i.188-9) It is only too easy, in our post-Enlightenment bias toward the primitive and the natural, to sentimentalize Caliban, to point to his sensitivity to the sounds and "qualities" of the island, to his poignant dream-life, and to his harsh treatment at Prospero's hands. But it is wiser to take our cue from Prospero than from Gonzalo. For Prospero has himself tried the enlightened approached to Caliban, had presumed the educability of the creature and treated him kindly, with near-disastrous results. Caliban's romantic and idealized prototype may be the noble American Indian then on exhibit in England, where according to Trinculo, such a "monster would make a man" (ii.ii.31), but Caliban is a degraded version of this figure. As Trinculo's quibble implies, Caliban represents not human nature without nurture but subhuman nature incapable of receiving nurture. Just as Swift makes his Houyhnhnms horses to prevent our confusing them with men, so Shakespeare makes his Caliban half fish to prevent our mistaking him for a human being. His physical deformity is index of his moral status. Just as Richard III is incapable of kindness and love, which he says "be resident in men like one another, / And not in me," so Caliban is capable only of unkindness and lust. "Deformed persons are commonly even with nature," writes Bacon, "for as nature hath done ill by them, so do they by nature. But because there is in man an election touching the frame of his mind, and a necessity in the frame of his body, the stars of natural inclination are sometimes obscured by the sun of discipline and virtue."[14] As the monstrous offspring of his mother's demoniality, however, Caliban is congenitally vicious and incontinent. Even his dreams of music and riches are entirely of the senses. Language for him is no more than the means of cursing his teachers, and he repays Miranda's efforts to educate him with attempted rape. The "salvage and deformed slave" of the *dramatis personae* is the creation of a primitivism harder than Spenser's, whose Salvage Man treats the defenseless Serena with instinctive gentility, and much harder than Montaigne's, whose cannibals Caliban resembles in little else than his name. One aspect of the ironic tightening-up of romance conventions that occurs from *The Winter's Tale* to *The Tempest* is the way the unformed but docile "natural" of the former play, the Shepherd-Clown, gives place to the deformed and intractable "natural" (as Trinculo calls Caliban) of the latter—a difference that helps to account for Prospero's notorious harshness.

But if the hard line Prospero comes to adopt toward

[14] "Of Deformity," *Selected Writings of Francis Bacon*, ed. Hugh D. Dick (Modern Library, New York, 1955), p. 113.

Caliban is understandable, what are we to make of his similar treatment of Ferdinand? Prospero's management of the "romance" plot proper within *The Tempest* is, like his handling of everything else, curiously anti-romantic. After brainwashing Ferdinand through Ariel's dirge into accepting his father's death, Prospero further afflicts and humiliates him during the first strange and fatal interview with Miranda. Prospero's harshness cannot be written off as the parental tyranny of Shakespearean heavy fathers from old Capulet through Polixenes nor, as is sometimes said, as that nervous tension which accompanies the magician's role, for Prospero reveals himself fully conscious of what he is about. Lest their love "too light winning / Make the prize light" (I.ii.454-5), he tells us in one of several asides, Prospero embarks on a program for trying Ferdinand that includes subjection to Caliban's labors and a coarsened version of his diet: "Sea-water shalt thou drink; thy food shall be / The fresh-brook mussels, wither'd roots, and husks / Wherein the acorn cradled." (I.ii.463-6) Behind these lines lies not only the natural fare the Bermudan castaways had found so appetizing but the traditional menu of milk, honey, and acorns "wherewith licentious Poesie hath proudly imbellished the golden age."[15]

For Prospero's program stands on their heads not only the romantic diet but most of the other romantic myths and motifs of love in the Golden Age. Recall that Gonzalo, as well as abolishing all labor and decreeing hearty meals for everyone in his utopia, had also abolished marriage. Yet he would have everyone "innocent and

[15] *The Essayes of Montaigne*, p. 164.

pure," a society like that of the golden age celebrated in Tasso's *Aminta*, whose "golden laws" proclaim "That's lawful which doth please,"[16] but which is reduced in the corrupt mind of Antonio to a collection of "whores and knaves." Prospero, however, will have no part of golden-age sexual ethics, nor is his standard of innocence and purity in the least ambiguous:

> If thou dost break her virgin-knot before
> All sanctimonious ceremonies may
> With full and holy rite be minister'd,
> No sweet aspersion shall the heavens let fall
> To make this contract grow.   (iv.i.15-19)

Prospero also executes all things by contraries, but without contradiction. Behind Ferdinand's labor of love is the logic of Dante's *Purgatorio*. By subjection to Caliban's diet and drudgery, Ferdinand is to be purged of the Caliban within, of the impulse to bow down in idolatry at the first sight of Miranda (as Caliban does to Stephano, and Amerindians did to European voyagers), and of the memory of those ladies at the Neapolitan court, the harmony of whose "tongues hath into bondage / Brought my too diligent ear." (iii.i.41-2) In so far as Ferdinand regards his servitude as the condition of his freedom, however, it begins to resemble Ariel's labor more than Caliban's: that labor which Yeats calls "blossoming or dancing'" and which represents the fulfillment of human nature rather than its curse.

---

[16] "*S'ei piace, ei lice*," from *Aminta*, First Chorus ("*O Bella Età de l'Oro*"), trans. Samuel Daniel in "A Pastorall" (1592), *Complete Works of Samuel Daniel*, ed. A. B. Grosart (London, 1885), I, 261.

The bethrothal masque Prospero stages for the couple is a figuration on Gonzalo's utopia and enacts on a mythological level the human action of the play. Now it is Prospero's turn to try his hand at making allegories, and the product is more sophisticated in every sense than that of Gonzalo:

> Earth's increase, foison plenty,
> Barns and garners never empty;
> Vines with clust'ring bunches growing;
> Plants with goodly burthen bowing;
> Spring come to you at the farthest
> In the very end of harvest!
> Scarcity and want shall shun you;
> Ceres' blessing so is on you.
>
> (iv.i.110-17)

In what amounts to a revision of Gonzalo's earlier vision, Prospero has made some significant changes. Whereas Gonzalo had simply banished by fiat all the nastier aspects of civilization, Prospero's working principle in the masque is that of inclusion. The traditional golden motif of eternal spring has been added, and the bans on "tilth" and vineyards have been lifted. The "foison" of Gonzalo's speech stands, but it is now seen as the fruit of tilth, of labor, of agri*culture*. The blessing that Ceres comes "to estate / On the blest lovers" (iv.i.85-6) is not a piece of choice real estate like Hughes's Bermuda or Gonzalo's island plantation but an estate of the spirit; not the result of a pagan or primitivist subversion of European customs but of their fulfillment; not the spontaneous generation of nature but a collaboration of nature with nurture; not a paradise needless of moral and physical effort but one dependent on both. The "evils" of labor, vineyards, marriage are all present in a redeemed form. The dance of Nymphs and Reapers, which suddenly vanishes as Prospero remembers "the beast Caliban," represents a disciplined harmony analogous to that of Mount Acidale (*FQ*,vi.x), where Colin Clout pipes to his love amid a dance of naked Graces, and which also suddenly vanishes upon the intrusion of the as yet remiss and self-indulgent Sir Calidore. When Ferdinand remarks, "Let me live here ever; / So rare a wonder'd father and a wife / Makes this place Paradise," he is quickly silenced by Prospero. Ferdinand cannot live "ever" with his wife in the seeming paradise of their father's making, but like Spenser's Red Crosse and Calidore, Sidney's Pyrocles and Musidorus, Milton's Adam and Eve, and the Dante of the *Comedy*, must return from this ideal vision to historical reality, to the continuing labor of governing Naples and himself. The spirit Ariel may sport endlessly after summer in an ideal landscape at the end of the play, but its human beings may not.

For even though Prospero's vision is a more full and comprehensive model of the redeemed world than Gonzalo's, it too is based on some rather arbitrary exclusions: the enforced absence of Venus and Cupid, who thought "to have done / Some wanton charm upon this man and maid" (iv.i.94-5) being one. As its banishment of lust suggests, not even the masque of Ceres is to be taken at face value, so mistrustful is *The Tempest*, is this "ideal" drama,[17] of the endeavors of the idealizing imagination,

[17] Samuel Taylor Coleridge, *Shakespearean Criticism*, ed. Thomas Middleton Raysor (Everyman's Library, London, 1960), II, 130.

of Prospero's as well as Gonzalo's attempts to allegorize experience. While there are no cynical courtiers present to mock Prospero's vision of the good and natural life, as there were at Gonzalo's, there is a Caliban plotting at that very moment to destroy it. And Prospero is aware of his own limitations as a utopist, serves as his own severest critic. The masque of Ceres is framed by his own commentary on it as a "vanity of mine Art" (iv.i.41) and as an "insubstantial pageant faded." (iv.i.155) Prospero has good reason to be aware of the "vanity," the frivolousness and pride and self-indulgence, of artistic endeavor, for it was by overdoing his passion for the liberal arts that he lost his dukedom in the first place. By indulging his desire to luxuriate in the paradise of his books, a desire very close to Ferdinand's during the masque, and "neglecting worldly ends" (i.ii.89), Prospero created a power-vacuum in Milan into which Antonio stepped. In Prospero's description of the Milanese coup d'état, his passion for the contemplative life amounts to nothing less than a hedonist idyll—"my library / Was dukedom large enough." (i.ii. 109-10)—an escape from the public responsibilities of office into a private and insular world of art.

While Prospero studied an art wholly benign but completely out of this world, dedicated himself to "closeness and the bett'ring of my mind" (i.ii.90), Antonio was busily exercising an art altogether this-worldly: the Machiavellian art of the player-king:

> Being once perfected how to grant suits,
> How to deny them, who t'advance, and who
> To trash for over-topping, new created

The creatures that were mine, I say, or chang'd 'em,
Or else new form'd 'em; having both the key
Of officer and office, set all hearts i' th' state
To what tune pleas'd his ear . . . .

                        like one
Who having into truth, by telling of it,
Made such a sinner of his memory,
To credit his own lie, he did believe
He was indeed the duke; out o' th' substitution,
And executing th' outward face of royalty,
With all prerogative;—hence his ambition
    growing,—

. . .

To have no screen between this part he play'd
And him he play'd it for, he needs will be
Absolute Milan.   (I.ii.79-85, 99-109)

Musical and dramatic talent seems to run in the family, for Antonio apparently possesses the theatrical gifts of setting a score, creating character, managing plots, and playing roles that Prospero displays on the island, but all to perverted ends. We see in action Antonio's talent for envisioning and casting scenes when he tempts Sebastian to play the same part with respect to his brother Alonso that he himself had played toward his brother twelve years earlier: "My strong imagination sees a crown," he tells Sebastian, "Dropping upon thy head" (II.i.202-3)— a vision of royalty that aligns him with other visionaries and dreamers in the play, Prospero, Gonzalo, and as we shall see, Caliban. The episode of the Milanese coup illustrates, among other things, how easily that art which is uncontrolled by ethical and social concern collapses into egocentricity, at best the self-indulgence of a Prospero and at worse the self-aggrandizement of an Antonio. The two brothers divide the libertine potentialities of the imagination between them.

There is an important sense, then, in which Prospero himself stands in need of redemption at the outset of the play as much as the others, whose guilt is more blatant. And he does seem to have changed during his twelve-year exile, both in his attitude toward his dukedom and in his attitude toward his art. Whereas he had previously neglected the former as a result of his total absorption in the latter—"My library / Was dukedom large enough"—he now directs his art outward onto the world. The art that had been an end in itself is now the means, not only of recovering his dukedom, but of exercising his function as governor. The art of power and the power of art have become in Prospero's hands, not divided and distinguished worlds as they were before, but one and the same thing. The first requirement, in Renaissance terms, for the prince and the theurgist alike is self-discipline, and this Prospero would seem to have achieved. Having learned the hard way to discipline himself, to keep his own aesthetic passion in its proper place, he now bends his efforts to redressing the disorder of the Milanese court and the inward disorder of the individuals who compose it, that disorder revealed in the opening storm scene, where Antonio and Sebastian see the Boatswain's honest efforts to save them as an act of social insubordination worthy of hanging, while the real subversives are the courtiers themselves; or, closer to home, the spiritual anarchy within Caliban that causes him

to claim kingship of the island "by Sycorax my mother"
(I.ii.333) and just as rashly to resign his claim to the be-
sotted Stephano.

To restore spiritual and social order Prospero employs
his "so potent art." As Northrop Frye remarks: "Each
[group of characters] goes through a pursuit of illusions,
an ordeal, and a symbolic vision."[18] Ferdinand is led by
Ariel's music into love at first sight of Miranda, and after
his ordeal as log-bearer, both are treated to the vision of
the betrothal masque. Prospero has Ariel present the starving and exhausted courtiers, after their vain wandering in
search of Ferdinand, with a tantalizing banquet only to
have it vanish like a mirage and leave them tormented by
their own frustrated appetite. The banquet, whatever its
significance as an allegorical emblem,[19] works dramatically
to mirror their own grasping natures, as does the Harpy

[18] Introduction to *The Tempest* (Pelican Shakespeare, Baltimore,
1959), p. 15. Frye's view of the play as a mythic rendering of "the
great rising rhythms of life: marriage, springtime, harvest, dawn, and
rebirth" (p. 26), though it appears in many places, is crystallized here.
Although his is surely one of the most eloquent critical statements ever
written on the play, it seems to me to overlook the play's profoundly
anti-romantic elements. Those elements received equally eloquent, if
perhaps disproportionate, testimony in a lecture delivered by Harry
Berger, Jr. at Yale University in March 1968, and subsequently published under the title "More than the Miraculous Harp: An Iconolog-
ical Prelude to *The Tempest*," *Occasional Stiles V* (New Haven, 1968),
95-119. It is not to disavow my debts to the readings of Frye and
Berger when I submit that the truth about *The Tempest* lies in between,
that its romance movement is tested, qualified, and authenticated by its
anti-romantic countermovement.

[19] On the emblematic meaning of the disappearing banquet, see Kermode, p. 169, and R. G. Hunter, *Shakespeare and the Comedy of Forgiveness* (New York, 1965), pp. 233-35.

form in which Ariel appears to pronounce his sentence on the "men of sin" present. That sentence, with its language of surfeit and regurgitation, arises from the physical image of the banquet and reflects the almost cannibalistic appetite of men " 'mongst men unfit to live," men who in a phrase of Shelley's have "made the world their prey" and who are actually about to prey on one another. Prospero has Ariel lead Caliban and his drunken crew on a penal trek through the nastier spots on the island:

> I beat my tabor;
> At which, like unback'd colts, they prick'd their ears,
> Advanc'd their eyelids, lifted up their noses
> As they smelt music: so I charm'd their ears,
> That, calf-life, they my lowing follow'd, through
> Tooth'd briers, sharp furzes, pricking goss, and thorns,
> Which enter'd their frail shins: at last I left them
> I' th' filthy-mantled pool beyond your cell.
>
> (iv.i.175-82)

These men (and one not-quite-man) of more than average sensuality are misled and tormented by the mutiny of their own senses, which land them in the slimy element appropriate to their gross and brutal natures. Prospero then proceeds to deceive their eyes with illusory wealth in a kind of parody of Caliban's recurrent wish-dream of "riches / Ready to drop upon me." (iii.ii.139-40) When Trinculo and Stephano linger over the "trumpery" laid out to distract them from their scheme, "divers Spirits, in shape of dogs and hounds" (iv.i.254.S.D.) drive them off, the same spirits that appeared to the courtiers as a Harpy and "strange shapes" and to the lovers as goddesses and nymphs. To those who "received not the love of the truth," writes an earlier voyager to Italy, "God shall send them strong delusion."[20] The author of *A True Declaration* had moralized upon the mutinies in Virginia by quoting St. Augustine to the effect that "every inordinate soule becomes his own punishment."[21] In his capacity as master illusionist, and to that extent "god o' th' island" (i.ii.392), Prospero sends a rare vision or a maddening hallucination to each of the principals according to his ability and need, an idealized projection or a grotesque parody of the spiritual condition of each, their basest obsessions or highest aspirations made flesh.

Earlier in this study I tried to show how Shakespeare's tragedies could be seen as romance *manqué* and his romances as salvaged tragedy. This formulation applies particularly well, it seems to me, to *Hamlet* and *The Tempest*. For Prospero, like Hamlet, is faced with a world disjointed by a usurpation and (attempted) fratricide, and the two most intellectual of Shakespeare's heroes both have recourse to a kind of art in their attempts to set it right. Prospero, though half-tempted to follow Hamlet and pursue the wild justice of revenge, finally decides under Ariel's prompting to shape the conclusion of his play on the Christian and romantic motive of forgiveness rather than the Hebraic-Hellenic and tragic one of retribution:

> Though with their high wrongs I am struck to th'
> quick,
> Yet with my nobler reason 'gainst my fury
> Do I take part: the rarer action is

[20] 2 Thess. 2: 10, 11. Geneva trans.
[21] *Tracts and Other Papers*, ed. Force, III, 15.

In virtue than in vengeance: they being penitent,
The sole drift of my purpose doth extend
Not a frown further. So release them, Ariel:
My charms I'll break, their senses I'll restore,
And they shall be themselves.   (v.i.26-32)

Whereas Hamlet had staged his "Mousetrap" to catch the king's conscience only in the sense of ascertaining his guilt, Prospero employs his art to catch Alonso's conscience in a different sense: to exploit the purgative effect of dramatic illusion as the beginning of repentance and reformation—the process that Hamlet, in his wholly external view of Claudius as an irredeemable villain, could not see at work even in Claudius's lapsed, but not quite lost, soul. By holding the mirror of his art up to the courtiers, Prospero seeks to show them their corrupted natures and the way back to "their proper selves." (iii.iii.60) It is almost as if Prospero had seen *Hamlet* and were determined to do better than Hamlet had done, to close the gap between the liberal arts and life, between philosophy and action, that Hamlet had been unable to close, and thereby avoid the tragic outcome of the earlier play.

But as I have tried to show, *The Tempest* is finally intolerant of all attempts to allegorize or idealize experience, whether they be ours or those of the characters within the play. Prospero's scenario is a noble one to be sure, born of the loftiest ideals and aspirations of the Renaissance mind, and if he could successfully stage it, he would no doubt deserve the titles of god and superman, philosopher-king, and ideal Christian prince that critics have bestowed on him. But *The Tempest* is as much about the limitations of the idealizing imagination as it is about its power, and of this Prospero seems to grow increasingly aware. Why, for example, does Prospero persist in referring to his art as a "vanity" and a "rough magic"? Why does he feel that he has to abandon it at all? And finally, just how successful is his art in producing his stated objectives?

Something that Prospero seems to have missed in *Hamlet,* and that he has to learn for himself, is that any attempt to manipulate human life artistically, even in a good cause, has its attendant dangers. Hamlet's attempt to do so is at best an evasion of real action and at worst an expression of that self-righteous euphoria characteristic of stage "revengers." Not only in *Hamlet,* but throughout Shakespeare's work we find a healthy mistrust of characters who turn the world into a stage on which to mount their histrionic or directorial fancies, the "good" characters (Friar Lawrence, Henry IV, Duke Vincentio), as well as the "bad" (Richard III, Richard II, Iago). Only in *The Winter's Tale* is the power of art in human life seen as wholly positive, and there Shakespeare takes pains to establish that the art employed by Camillo and Paulina is "an art," as Polixenes unwittingly puts it, "Which does mend nature—change it rather—but / The art itself is nature." Paulina expressly disclaims all magical art in her unveiling of Hermione's "statue," and Leontes says then that "If this be magic, let it be an art / Lawful as eating," which of course it is, since she uses no art at all. The same cannot be said of Prospero's art. "This is no mortal business, nor no sound / That the earth owes" (1.ii.409-10):

> Full fadom five they father lies;
> Of his bones are coral made;

Those are pearls that were his eyes:
  Nothing of him that doth fade,
But doth suffer a sea-change
  Into something rich and strange.

(i.ii.399-404)

The exquisite dirge presages the spiritual transformation
Prospero's art does work on Alonso, but in so doing suggests the ambivalent moral status of that art. For the sea
change it describes (imagine a coral and pearl Alonso) is
unnatural and artificial in the extreme, quite unlike the
transformation of Hermione's "statue" in *The Winter's
Tale*, but very like the transformations of Autolycus's fantastic ballads. Ariel's song also conjures up the kind of
transformation that medieval and Renaissance alchemists,
highly suspect artificers, attempted to perform, the trans-
mutation of base substances into pure and precious ones.
(Prospero associates his art with alchemy in the opening
lines of the last act, and with astrology, a sister-science of
doubtful repute, during his exposition to Miranda in the
first.) My point is not that Prospero's art is downright
wicked (Shakespeare makes clear that it is theurgy or
"white-magic" he practices as opposed to the goety or
"black-magic" practiced by Sycorax) but that associations
of dark and prideful learning still cling to it, despite the
fact that it is now directed toward a good end. For in
Prospero's artistic manipulation of human life lies a danger
that besets the modern psychotherapist as much as the
Renaissance magician: the danger of playing God. Hamlet
casts off that theatrical role, with its attendant dangers of
pride and self-indulgence, only in the last act of his play,
and Duke Vincentio (as I for one believe) is never suf-

ficiently self-aware to cast it off. It is necessary, not so much to render the ending of *The Tempest* one of un-alloyed joy, for it is not that, but to dramatize Prospero's reform of himself, that he repudiate his art and return to the ranks of humanity. To do so is to renounce the total success of his "project," to make himself vulnerable again. But it is also to renounce once and for all that untrans-muted residue of self-dramatization and self-aggrandize-ment inherent in any effort to recreate the world after one's desires and in one's own image. So far as Prospero is concerned, his renunciation *is* his real triumph. When he resolves to "drown my book," he redeems the belated promise of an earlier magician of the Elizabethan stage to "burn my books." He redeems the Faustus in himself. The "mercy" he finally exercises and asks the audience to exercise on him is the mature and social equivalent of the adolescent and histrionic "magic" he had formerly in-dulged.

The "brave new world" that emerges in the final scene is neither so brave nor so new as Prospero himself could have wished, neither the paradise regained Ferdinand had seen in the betrothal masque nor the golden age restored of Gonzalo's fancy. Presented with the son he believed dead, Alonso questions whether this too is not merely one more "vision of the island." (v.i.176) But the vision of Ferdinand and Miranda at chess is made "of flesh and blood," like the man (as Alonso is amazed to discover) who made it possible. So too the "blessed crown" Gonzalo calls down in prayer on the couple is, or soon will be, literal fact, the reality of which Antonio's and Caliban's delusions of royalty and riches are mere parodies. Even

Sebastian exclaims: "A most high miracle!" (v.i.177) He is referring, as Pericles had done at the end of his play, to the working out of Providence and to the old plays in which that working out was portrayed. But the pattern of the miracle play fits only Alonso's family, despite the efforts of Gonzalo to squeeze everyone into it. In his last great monologue on the renunciation of his art, Prospero speaks scornfully of that art as "this rough magic," and it is rough indeed compared with the creative activity of God—the divinity who alone, as Hamlet says in his final act, "shapes our ends, / Rough-hew them how we will."

In his appropriation and secularization of the forms of the medieval religious drama for his final romances, Shakespeare reassigns the role once played by the grace of God to the art of man: the role of raising and reforming mere nature. In the romances art is still closely associated with grace. But just as the private imaginative visions of Gonzalo, Antonio, and Caliban all fade before Prospero's higher and more comprehensive vision, so too, it is strongly hinted, Prospero's own vision fades before that of God. There is a point at which artistic transformation ends and divine transubstantiation begins, as in the Mass or the Apocalypse, and *The Tempest* stops this side of it. Intimations of Apocalypse are at hand in Prospero's speech on the ending of the revels, in which cloud-capped towers, gorgeous palaces, solemn temples, and the great globe itself—man's noblest artifacts and the material world of which they are made—are condemned to demolition to make room, in the Christian scheme of things, for the eternal art and architecture of the New Jerusalem, suggested perhaps in Gonzalo's summarial speech by the "lasting pillars" (v.i.208) on which this marvelous episode of human history is to be set down in gold. That brave new world will be built on a firmer base and of a more substantial fabric than was Prospero's vision in the bethrothal masque and is "Too high a ditty" for Shakespeare's, as for Spenser's, "simple song." (*FQ*,i.x.55) Prospero's vision was dispelled because "the beast Caliban" had literally been forgotten in its making, that hunk of brute nature that Prospero has to "acknowledge" in the end but cannot reform. Also outside the magic circle of raised human nature at the end is Antonio, who willfully defies any art, however transcendent, to reform him. Both figures perhaps suggest in different ways the ultimate resistance that life throws up against being transmuted into art at all, and especially into romance; that renders any human art finally no better than the world it works with and on; and that makes Prospero's efforts at once so potent and so limited, so fully and so merely human.

But if Prospero is not God, to what extent or in what sense may we legitimately think of him as Shakespeare? They are clearly analogous figures up to a point, not simply because they share a talent for putting on shows and because the epilogue fits the stage manager and the magician alike, but because both are directly concerned with the creation of brave new worlds, or more precisely with transmuting old worlds into new, brazen into golden. *The Tempest* is a definition in action of the poetics of romance, a kind of commentary on the imagination that created it, for Prospero goes about his project in much the same way that Shakespeare goes about his. The author of

"Of the Cannibals," ever *divers et ondoyant*, sets forth the principle on which both Prospero and Shakespeare proceed. "Such an Idea of Policie," writes Montaigne, "or picture of government, were to be established in a new world; but we take a world already made and formed to certain customes: wee engender not the same as Pyrrha, nor beget it as Cadmus. By what means soever we have the privilege to re-erect and range the same anew, we can very hardly wrest it from the accustomed habit and fold it hath taken, except we breake all."[22] The creation of brave new worlds, whether in literature or in life, is achieved not by despising or ignoring the imperfections of this old one (as Gonzalo does in his vision of the island or Prospero had done before his deposition), but by repairing them. Wine is a grace of civilization which may be abused by a Stephano, Trinculo, or Caliban, but which finds a place in Prospero's vision of abundance. The "letters," which Gonzalo would prohibit along with wine, may be profaned by a Caliban or over-indulged by an immature Prospero, but it is the power conferred by his book that enables the Christian Platonist to reorder his society and redeem at least one guilty soul. Any brave new world is merely an old one rehabilitated. Our initial impression of *The Tempest* as the product of spontaneous generation, of Shakespeare's own magical imagination, is finally inadequate. Prospero and Shakespeare do not, as Gonzalo and Antonio do, create out of nothing or out of themselves. Just as Prospero attempts to build a new Milan out of the ruins of its original social structure, so Shakespeare builds the play itself out of imperfect literary structures—travelers' tales, moldy old

[22] "Of Vanitie," *Essayes*, p. 864.

morality plays, pastoral romances—some of it second hand and shabby stuff, but capable of renovation. Even a miraculous harp like Amphion's needs stones to work on.

But here the analogy between Prospero and Shakespeare breaks down, and Shakespeare becomes, in Joseph Warton's words, "a greater magician than his own Prospero."[23] For the vision of the play as a whole is greater than any single vision it contains, including that of Prospero. While Prospero labors, finally with only partial success, to create a brave new world, Shakespeare is creating his own, with complete success, in the form of the play itself. And Prospero's partial failure becomes the condition of Shakespeare's total triumph, for as we have seen, the ultimate validity of any romance world depends on an implicit recognition that romance is all but impossible to achieve while remaining faithful to life. To the extent that Gonzalo's word is more than the miraculous harp, that he can effortlessly bring forth utopian islands from the sea, he is an untrustworthy romancer; to the extent that Prospero's word is finally less than the miraculous harp, he is an unsuccessful one. Shakespeare's is the harp itself. For in the making of the play Shakespeare begins where Prospero ends: with the awareness that there is a fatal gap between the ideal world of romance and the real world of history, and that no act of magic can ever make them one.

At this point in our efforts toward demystification, it might be well to take our cue from Prospero and abjure magic, with its intimations of superhuman power, as a

---

[23] *The Adventurer*, No. 97 (Oct. 9, 1753). Quoted in Herbert Spencer Robinson, *English Shakespearian Criticism in the Eighteenth Century* (New York, 1932), p. 85.

metaphor for romance and romance-making in favor of
another of the play's images, namely that of chess, with
its suggestion of acquired skill. The game of chess, particularly the moralized version of it described in the epigraph to this chapter, is "not only a game in *Utopia*," as
Michael Holquist has pointed out, but "the game *of*
utopia" and "suggests the underlying structure of almost
all utopian fiction,"[24] including *The Tempest*. The important thing for our purposes about More's utopian chess,
and the morality plays in which he delighted and on which
he patterned it, is that the virtues always win out in the
end. *The Tempest* contains several such games, but their
outcomes are by no means so assured. Gonzalo plays a
game of utopia in which he thinks he has swept the vices
off the board, when he is actually surrounded and defeated
by them. Although Prospero's more formidable tactics
work according to plan until the very end, when he does
win at least two of his games, he is stalemated in at least
two others. By denying total victory to the virtues, Shakespeare has effectively widened play beyond the self-contained chessboard of utopia, where the virtues always win,
and onto the surrounding battleground of history, where
they sometimes do. The battleground of history is also
the world of the audience, where we worldlings and groundlings find ourselves striving for our moral lives with a master who has anticipated all possible defenses and counter-
attacks in a game we can win only if he does. This is the
game of *The Tempest*, and its closest analogue within the
play is the chess game between Ferdinand and Miranda.

[24] "How to play Utopia: Some brief notes on the distinctiveness of
utopian fiction," *Yale French Studies*, No. 41 (1968), 109.

There, all suspicion of deceit and fear of losing have passed into perfect trust, and Miranda's affirmation that "for a score of kingdoms you should wrangle, / And I would call it fair play" (v.i.174-5) is also ours.

The Shakespeare of *The Tempest* may be a greater master than Prospero, but the Shakespeare of the final romances as a group is not. Whereas Northrop Frye would have him "a master who wins them all by devices familiar to him, and gradually, with patient study, to us,"[25] my own patient study suggests a more fallible figure: a Shakespeare neglectful of the worldly ends of *mimesis* and verisimilitude in *Pericles,* and forgetful of the eternal conspiracy of history against romance in *Cymbeline* and *Henry VIII.* In the end, Shakespeare and Prospero resemble each other in nothing so much as their common capacity for triumph and failure, the former providing the touchstones by which we know the latter. In *The Tempest* Shakespeare reconciles the claims of history and romance by combining an historical action of a Milanese coup d'état spun out of pure fiction with a romantic action of shipwreck and deliverance grounded in recent history. When he tries in his last play to identify the real shores of his native Britain with the undreamed shores of his two previous romances, the result is a confusion of realms worthy of Gonzalo. With *The Tempest* Shakespeare leaves behind the realm of true romance, a realm, in the words of Eliot's *Marina* "more distant than stars and nearer than the eye," where victory issues from a holding action with defeat, or not at all, and total victory is always Pyrrhic.

[25] *A Natural Perspective* (New York, 1965), p. viii.

BIBLIOGRAPHICAL

APPENDIX

The Fortunes of Romance

What we have gotten by this revolution, you will say,
is a great deal of good sense. What we have lost, is a
world of fine fabling.

—Richard Hurd

THE EARLIEST allusions to Shakespeare's final romances
serve mainly to confirm their popularity. The play most
often mentioned then is, paradoxically, the one least often
discussed and performed now: *Pericles, Prince of Tyre*.
Within a year of its first performance at the Globe, *Pericles*
seems to have become a byword for box-office success:

Amazde I stood, to see a Crowd
Of *Civill Throats* stretched out so lowd;
(As at a *New-play*) all the Roomes
Did swarme with *Gentiles* mix'd with *Groomes*,
So that I truly thought all These
Came to see *Shore* or *Pericles*.[1]

The play was apparently still going strong five years later
when a certain Robert Tailor wrote in his prologue to
The Hog Hath Lost His Pearl (1614) that "if it prove so
happy as to please / We'll say 'tis fortunate, like *Pericles*."[2]

[1] From the anonymous pamphlet, *Pimlyco or Runne Red-cap* (1609),
sig. C. Reprinted in E. K. Chambers, *William Shakespeare* (Oxford,
1930), II, 217.

[2] *Dodsley's Old English Plays*, ed. W. Carew Hazlitt (London, 1875),
XI, 428.

It seems to have been just as successful with "gentles" as with "grooms." "In the kinges greate Chanber," writes Sir Gerrard Herbert of a performance at court in 1619, "they went to see the play of Pirrocles, Prince of Tyre which lasted till 2 aclocke. . . . The Imbassadour parted next morninge for France at 8 aclocke, full well pleased."[3] The advertisement of the "much admired Play, Called Pericles," which appears on the titlepage of its first quarto, was evidently no misrepresentation.

Not only *Pericles* but the subsequent romances as well seem to have been just as appealing to aristocratic as they were to popular audiences. *The Winter's Tale, The Tempest,* and (probably) *Henry VIII* were selected for performance during the nuptial festivities of James's daughter Elizabeth and Frederick, the Elector Palatine of Germany, in 1613. Both *Cymbeline* and *The Winter's Tale* were performed at the court of Charles I in January 1633; the former was "Well likte by the Kinge," and the latter, "likt."[4] All attempts—and there have been many—to account for the nature of the last romances in terms of Shakespeare's alleged intention of catering to either the popular or refined taste of his Jacobean audience are clearly invalidated by their contemporary reception. If the romances were written for the consumption of the "groundlings," the nobility apparently was not aware of it; if they

[3] From a letter to Sir Dudley Carleton, dated May 24, 1619. *Calendar of State Papers Domestic, James I,* Vol. 109, No. 46. Reprinted in Chambers, *William Shakespeare,* II, 346.

[4] From Sir Henry Herbert's office book. Reprinted in Chambers, II, 352.

were fashioned to the sophisticated taste of the private theatergoer, the masses did not stay away.[5]

The enjoyment of a French ambassador and two Stuart kings notwithstanding, Shakespeare's chief dramatic rival insisted that *Pericles* and the later romances are artless potboilers cooked up for the taste of the vulgar. In Ben Jonson's reiterated objections to plays more successful at the box office yet apparently less well made than his own, professional jealousy and neoclassical doctrine are present in equal measures. Wounded by the failure of *The New Inn*, Jonson took out his resentment on *Pericles*:

> No doubt some mouldy tale,
> Like *Pericles*; and stale
> As the Shrieve's crussts, and nasty as his fish-
>   scraps, out [of] every dish
> Throwne forth, and rak't into the common tub,
> May keepe up the *Play-club*;

[5] The thesis that Shakespeare accommodated his art to the style of the private theaters was first advanced by A. H. Thorndike, *The Influence of Beaumont and Fletcher on Shakespeare* (New York, 1901) and often restated early in this century. The most discriminating attempt to account for the nature of the romances in terms of theatrical auspices is that of G. E. Bentley, "Shakespeare and the Blackfriars Theatre," *Shakespeare Survey 1* (Cambridge, 1948), pp. 38-50. The last words on the matter belong to F. P. Wilson, *Elizabethan and Jacobean* (Oxford, 1945), pp. 126-8, and Alfred Harbage, *Shakespeare and the Rival Traditions* (New York, 1952), who argues convincingly that the romances are "popular in type" (p. 86). It is worth noting that both Ben Jonson and Bernard Shaw, the two most vehement critics of the romances attack them not on the grounds of over-refinement but of vulgarity.

There, sweepings do as well
As the best order'd meale.[6]

And he certainly had popular plays like *Pericles*, *The Winter's Tale*, and *The Tempest* (if not these specific plays) in mind when he praised his own artistic integrity:

[The author will not] purchase your delight at
    such a rate
As, for it, he himself must justly hate:
To make a child, now swaddled, to proceede
Man, and then shoote up, in one beard, and weede,
Past threescore years. . . .
He rather prayes, you will be pleas'd to see
One such, to-day as other playes should be;
Where neither *Chorus* wafts you ore the seas;
Nor creaking throne comes downe, the boys to
    please.

Thou wert never more fair in the way to be
cos'ned then in this Age in *Poetry*, especially in
Playes: wherein, now the concupiscence of Jigges
    and
Daunces so raigneth, as to runne away from Nature,
and be afraid of her, is the onely point of art that
tickles the Spectators.

If there bee never a *Servant-monster* i' the *Fayre*;
Who can helpe it? he [Jonson] sayes; nor a nest of
Antiques? He is loth to make Nature afraid in
    his playes,

---

[6] "Ode" appended to *The New Inn* (1630), *Ben Jonson*, edd. C. H. Herford, Percy and Evelyn Simpson (Oxford, 1938), VI, 492-93.

like those that beget *Tales, Tempests,* and such like
Drolleries.[7]

Within this mixture of abuse, snobbery, and bluster is a
fair summary of the defining features of Shakespearean
romance: its archaism, its spatial and temporal sprawl, its
fondness for music, dance, and spectacle, and especially,
its inclusion of nonnatural elements and reliance on non-
naturalistic techniques of presentation. Underlying Jonson's
animadversions on all these counts are the critical premises
and prejudices later to surface in most of the neoclassical
attacks on the romances from Dryden to Bernard Shaw.

The best neoclassical criticism in English has often
managed to transcend its own dogmas: one thinks of Sidney's readiness to appreciate a good "mouldy tale," however unclassical, when he finds one in the old ballad of
Chevy Chase, or of Samuel Johnson on the shifting of
scenes in *Antony* ("He that can take the stage at one time
for the palace of the Ptolemies may take it in half an hour
for the promontory of Actium"). With the romances, un-
acceptable a priori to the canons of neoclassical illusionism,
this has rarely happened. Dryden is a case in point:

Poetry was then [in the age of Elizabeth], if not in its
infancy among us, at least not arriv'd to its vigor and
maturity: witness the lameness of their plots: many of
which, especially those which they writ first (for even
that age refin'd itself in some measure), were made up

[7] Prologue to *Every Man in His Humour,* Ben Jonson, III, 303;
"Preface to *The Alchemist,*" *Critical Essays of the Seventeenth Century,*
ed. Joel E. Spingarn (Oxford, 1908), I, 16; and Induction to *Bartholomew Fair,* Ben Jonson, VI, 16.

of some ridiculous, incoherent story, which in one play
many times took up the business of an age. I suppose I
need not name *Pericles, Prince of Tyre*. . . . Besides . . .
*The Winter's Tale, Love's Labour Lost, Measure for
Measure.*[8]

Here Dryden has the heavy task of censuring his beloved
Shakespeare lightened for him by the convenient assumption of his time that *Pericles* was a very early play. But
in the case of *The Tempest* he is forced to some very uneasy shifts to square his admiration for the play with
critical premises that would limit that admiration:

> And Poets may be allowed the like liberty, for describ-
> ing things which really exist not, if they are founded
> on popular belief: of this nature are Fairies, Pigmies,
> and the extraordinary effects of Magick; and thus are
> Shakespeare's *Tempest*, his *Midsummer Night's Dream*
> . . . to be defended.[9]

By the same critical logic one would have to assume,
against all probability, that the audience of the *Odyssey*
believed the Cyclops really existed, and that Shakespeare's
contemporaries believed a Mediterranean Bermuda really
existed; or, in the case of *The Winter's Tale*, that Bohemia
was believed to have a seacoast. But Spenser himself does
not expect his audience to believe in the geographical
reality of Fairyland. Clearly we should retrace our steps.
Rather than depending upon the audience's prior belief

[8] *Essays of John Dryden*, ed. W. P. Ker (New York, 1961), I, 165.
[9] "The Author's Apology for Heroic Poetry and Poetic License,
Prefixed to *The State of Innocence, and the Fall of Man, an Opera*"
(1677), *ibid.*, I, 187.

in impossibilities, as Dryden would have it, do not the plays in question induce in their audience the requisite belief (if that is the right word) in fairies, magic, nonexistent islands and seacoasts? As Paulina, about to perform the apparently impossible task of bringing a statue to life, says to the court of Sicilia in *The Winter's Tale*: "It is required / You do awake your faith." (v.iii.94-5) In the romances Shakespeare asks his audience to do just that, to awaken its poetic faith in so far as it needs to be awakened and as much as it is required, which is much less than neoclassical doctrine commonly holds.

The Tempest is unique among the last plays not because it is the only one in which Shakespeare takes pains to sustain theatrical illusion, but because it is the only one in which he adheres closely to the unities, though their deployment in that play seems to me more an erudite joke than an essential condition of its effect. Yet their reassuring presence may well account for the fact that *The Tempest* has enjoyed a more stable reputation than *The Winter's Tale*. *The Tempest* is just as teeming with impossibilities as any of the other romances, but the fact that it alone seems to go half-way with the canons of neoclassical illusionism in presenting those impossibilities allows the neoclassical critic to go half-way also and accept them. Dryden, for example, is willing and able to come to terms with Caliban:

He [Shakespeare] seems to have created a person which was not in Nature, a boldness which at first sight would appear intolerable: for he makes him a Species of himself, begotten by an *Incubus* on a Witch; but this as I have elsewhere prov'd, is not wholly beyond the bounds of credibility, at least the vulgar stile still believe it. We have the separated notions of a spirit, and of a Witch . . . therefore as from the distinct apprehensions of a Horse, and of a Man, Imagination has form'd a *Centaur*, so from those of an *Incubus* and a *Sorceress*, *Shakespear* has produc'd his Monster. Whether or no his Generation can be defended, I leave to Philosophy; but of this I am certain, that the Poet has most judiciously furnished him with a person, a Language, and a character, which will suit him, both by Fathers and Mothers side. . . . His person is monstrous, as he is the product of unnatural lust; and his language is as hobgoblin as his person; in all things he is distinguish'd from other mortals.[10]

By stressing the decorum-within-impossibility of Caliban's language and characterization (if such a creature as Caliban really existed, this is how he would sound and what he would be like) Dryden manages to transform what to the hardnosed neoclassicism of Jonson had been a bugbear into a "beauty." Yet in adjusting his critical premises to accommodate the play, Dryden also distorts the play to accommodate his critical premises. As Samuel Johnson was soon to point out, Caliban's language is not really "hobgoblin" at all: "let any other being entertain the same thoughts, and he will find them easily issue in the same expressions."[11] Characters who do not exist in nature must nevertheless speak in a language that does; otherwise the

[10] Preface to *Troilus and Cressida*, *ibid.*, I, 219-20.
[11] *Samuel Johnson on Shakespeare*, ed. W. K. Wimsatt, Jr. (New York, 1960), p. 72.

play in which they appear becomes the real monster. The principles of neoclassical decorum will take us only so far toward justifying Caliban's presence in *The Tempest* before they break down altogether.

Despite the greater flexibility with which Johnson applied neoclassical doctrines to Shakespeare's work, his pronouncements on the last romances reflect the limitations of his century's reception of them. Once again it is *The Tempest* that comes closest to gaining critical approval:

> It is observed of *The Tempest* that its plan is regular. . . . But whatever might be Shakespeare's intention in forming or adapting the plot, he has made it instrumental to the production of many characters, diversified with boundless invention, and preserved with profound skill in nature, extensive knowledge of opinions, and accurate observation of life. In a single drama are here exhibited princes, courtiers, and sailors, all speaking in their real characters. There is the agency of airy spirits and of an earthly goblin. The operation of magic, the tumults of a storm, the adventures of a desert island, the native effusion of untaught affection, the punishment of guilt and the final happiness of the pair for whom our passions and reason are equally interested.[12]

Johnson is not quite clear on this point, but he seems to say that the regularity of the plan is the necessary precondition for presenting so diverse an assortment of characters and incidents. In the case of *Cymbeline* no such regularity exists to tame the comparably wild diversity of the play:

[12] *Ibid.*

This play has many just sentiments, some natural dialogues, and some pleasing scenes, but they are obtained at the expense of much incongruity.

To remark the folly of the fiction, the absurdity of the conduct, the confusion of the names and manners of different times, and the impossibility of the events in any system of life, were to waste criticism upon unresisting imbecility, upon faults too evident for detection, and too gross for aggravation.[13]

The Winter's Tale fares only somewhat better: "This play, as Dr. Warburton justly observes, is, with all its absurdities, very entertaining. The character of Autolycus is very naturally conceived and strongly represented."[14] *Pericles* was banished outright from Johnson's, as from most eighteenth-century, editions.[15]

Johnson's observations on the romances typify the fully

[13] *Ibid.*, p. 107.

[14] *Ibid.*, p. 80.

[15] The first, so far as I know, to presume mixed authorship in *Pericles* was George Lillo in the prologue to his adaptation of its last two acts, entitled *Marina* (1738).

> We dare not charge the whole unequal play
> Of Pericles on him; yet let us say,
> As gold though mix'd with baser matter shines,
> So do his bright inimitable lines
> Throughout those rude wild scenes distinguish'd stand,
> And shew he touch'd them with no sparing hand.

Malone included it, however, in his Supplement to Steevens' edition even though Steevens had written him: "I must acquit even the irregular and lawless Shakespeare of having constructed the fabrick of the drama, though he has certainly bestowed some decoration on its parts." Quoted in *Pericles*, ed. F. D. Hoeniger (New Arden Shakespeare, Cambridge, Mass., 1963), pp. lii and lxx.

blown neoclassical response to them. He finds it possible to salvage the "natural dialogues" of *Cymbeline* and the characterization of Autolycus in *The Winter's Tale* only after demolishing the larger embracing structure of these plays. Johnson's critical practice mirrors the theatrical practice of his age. Every one of the romances except *Cymbeline* (for a very brief period) was staged throughout the eighteenth century only in a revised and regularized form; and these "improved" versions invariably omitted the theophanies which accompany or precede the recognition scenes: the appearance of Diana in *Pericles*, the masque of Jupiter in *Cymbeline*, the betrothal masque in *The Tempest* (in sum, those very features which unify the romances as a group and distinguish them from Shakespeare's earlier work). Neoclassical critical theory, though predisposed to see individual works as totalities of structure and effect, to see their parts in terms of what they contribute to the whole, must do just the opposite when faced with Shakespearean romance. It breaks down a given play into local and isolated proprieties existing within the vast impropriety of the whole. Of course the neoclassical perception of artistic unity arises from the study of works whose unity is of a very different order from that of Shakespeare's romances or of romance in general. In breaking down the work in order to discuss it, neoclassical theory actually reveals its own breakdown before a certain kind of work. Johnson can discuss the romances only by ignoring their romantic character.

In the latter part of the eighteenth century a new poetics was establishing itself, one which would be better adapted to the appreciation of Shakespearean romance. This change of outlook involves a shift away from the Aristotelian and Horatian view of the work as an imitation of life and toward the Longinian view of the work as an imaginative world unto itself. It can already be seen in embryo in Nicholas Rowe's early *Life of Shakespeare*: "The greatness of this author's genius does no where so much appear, as where he gives his imagination an entire loose, and raises his fancy to a flight above mankind and the limits of the visible world." In such a view *The Tempest* figures importantly. Though pleased with Shakespeare's observance of the unities in that play, Rowe is fully aware that its "excellencies were all of another kind"; though "sensible that he does . . . depart too much from that likeness to truth which ought to be observed," Rowe shrewdly remarks that "he does it so very finely, that one is easily drawn in to have more faith for his sake, than reason does well allow of."[16] Joseph Warton characteristically goes even further. After paying tribute, in early eighteenth-century fashion to the propriety of Shakespeare's art as an imitation of life, he launches into an appreciation of *The Tempest* as the "most striking instance of his creative power," the play in which he has "carried the romantic, the wonderful, and the wild, to the most pleasing extravagance." And in a final burst of enthusiasm Warton stresses the principle of the audience's voluntary poetic faith as much as the neoclassical doctrine of the author's deliberate delusion of the audience: "The poet is a more powerful magician than his own Prospero: we are transported into

[16] *Some Account of the Life &c. of Mr. William Shakespear* (1709), in *Eighteenth Century Essays on Shakespeare*, ed. D. Nichol Smith (Glasgow, 1903), pp. 13-14.

fairy land; we are wrapt in a delicious dream, from which it is misery to be disturbed; all around is enchantment!"[17]

Although Warton is writing twelve years before Dr. Johnson published his *Preface*, his remarks on *The Tempest* directly prefigure the romantic poetics of Coleridge, whose notes on *The Tempest* bear so directly on the issues that concern us here they are worth quoting at length:

> We commence with *The Tempest* as a specimen of the romantic drama. But . . . there is one preliminary point to be first settled. . . . This point is contained in the words, probable, natural. We are all in the habit of praising Shakespeare or of hearing him extolled for his fidelity to nature. Now what are we to understand by these words in their application to the drama? Assuredly not the ordinary meaning of them. . . . But a moment's reflection suffices to make every man conscious of what every man must have before felt, that the drama is an *imitation* of reality, not a *copy*—and that imitation is contradistinguished from a copy by this: that a certain quantum of difference is essential to the former, and an indispensable condition and cause of the pleasure we derive from it. . . .
>
> Still, however, there is a sort of improbability with which we are shocked in dramatic representation. . . . Consequently . . . we must first ascertain what the immediate end or object of the drama is. Here I find two extremes in critical decision: the French, which evidently presupposes that a perfect delusion is to be aimed at . . .

[17] *The Adventurer*, Nos. 93, 97. Quoted in Herbert Spencer Robinson, *English Shakespearian Criticism in the Eighteenth Century* (New York, 1932), pp. 84-85.

the opposite, supported by Dr. Johnson, supposes the auditors throughout as in the full and positive reflective knowledge of the contrary. In evincing the impossibility of delusion, he makes no sufficient allowance for an intermediate state, which we distinguish by the term illusion.

In what this consists I cannot better explain than by referring you to the highest degree of it; namely, dreaming. It is laxly said that during sleep we take our dreams for realities, but this is irreconcilable with the nature of sleep, which consists in a suspension of the voluntary and, therefore, of the comparative power . . . in an interesting play—we are brought up to this point, as far as it is requisite or desirable, gradually, by the art of the poet and the actors; and with the consent and positive aidance of our own will. We *choose* to be deceived. The rule, therefore, may be easily inferred. Whatever tends to prevent the mind from placing it [self] or from being gradually placed in this state in which the images have a negative reality must be a defect, and consequently anything that must force itself on the auditors' mind as improbable, not because it *is* improbable (for that the whole play is foreknown to be) but because it cannot but *appear* as such.[18]

Coleridge has, in effect, rationalized Joseph Warton's response to *The Tempest*. The analogy with dreams to which both have recourse works in several ways to undermine the edifices of neoclassical theory. For one thing, it

[18] *Shakespearean Criticism*, ed. Thomas Middleton Raysor (Everyman's Library, London, 1960), I, 114-16.

broadens and deepens the meaning of "nature" beyond that of neoclassical theory. There is more in heaven and earth, Coleridge suggests, than is taken account of by French neoclassicists. We participate both in a nightime as well as a daytime reality, the one no more "real" than the other. For another, it establishes as the touchstone of a successful play, not its consistency with external "nature," however widely defined, but its consistency with itself.

The play must not violate its own poetic premises—only in such a case does the word "improbable" or "unnatural" apply. What enables Coleridge to make this leap is his insistence on the autonomy of the imaginative principle itself:

> *The Tempest* . . . has been selected as a specimen of the romantic drama; i.e., of a drama the interests of which are independent of all historical facts and associations, and arise from their fitness to that faculty of our nature, the imagination I mean, which owns no allegiance to time and place,—a species of drama, therefore, in which errors in chronology and geography, no mortal sins in any species, are venial, or count for nothing.[19]

[19] *Ibid.*, I, 117-18. The principle of romantic or imaginative unity enunciated here by Coleridge had been partially anticipated (chiefly with respect to Spenser and the Italian epic) by Richard Hurd, and termed "unity of design": "A poet, they say, must follow *nature*; and by nature we are to suppose can only be meant the known and experienced course of affairs in this world. Whereas the poet has a world of his own, where experience has less to do, than consistent imagination." *Letters on Chivalry and Romance* (1762), X, *The Works of Richard Hurd* (London, 1811), IV, 324. Hurd does, however, deny the applicability of this principle to the drama.

Even Johnson had sensed, however disapprovingly, that this was the kind of play he was dealing with when, in annotating Cleomenes' often-emended speech on the "isle" of Delphos in *The Winter's Tale*, he wrote: "Shakespeare is little careful of geography. There is no need of this emendation in a play in which the whole plot depends upon a geographical error, by which Bohemia is supposed to be maritime country."[20] Impossibilities in the parts of a work are tolerable in so far as they are not inconsistent with the prior impossibility of the whole.

The Romantic comparison of romance to dreams, however, is an essentially ambivalent and potentially invidious one. Dreams in virtually every age and culture have been regarded as either vehicles of a higher truth or as products of a diseased mind or distempered body. The imaginative mode that approaches so closely to the conditions of dreaming may therefore be either profound or frivolous, depending on how we view dreaming itself. In an essay which takes off directly from *The Tempest*, entitled the *Sanity of True Genius*, Lamb addresses himself to this problem:

> It is impossible for the mind to conceive of a mad Shakespeare . . . the true poet dreams being awake. He is not possessed by his subject, but has dominion over it . . . . From beyond the scope of Nature if he summon possible existences, he subjugates them to the law of her consistency. He is beautifully loyal to that sovereign directress, even when he appears most to betray and

[20] *Samuel Johnson on Shakespeare*, pp. 79-80.

desert her . . . . Caliban, the Witches, are as true to the laws of their own nature (ours with a difference), as Othello, Hamlet, and Macbeth. Herein the great and the little wits are differenced; that if the latter wander ever so little from nature or actual existence, they lose themselves, and their readers. Their phantoms are lawless; their visions nightmares. They do not create, which implies shaping and consistency. Their imaginations are not active—for to be active is to call something into act and form—but passive, as men in sick dreams. For the super-natural, or something super-added to what we know of nature, they give you the plainly non-natural.[21]

It is only a short step from Lamb's to Ruskin's endorsement of *The Tempest*, written in 1872 with all the momentum of Romantic bardolatry behind it:

For all these dreams of Shakespeare, as those of true and strong men must be, are . . . divine phantoms, and shadows of things that are. We hardly tell our children, willingly, a fable with no purport in it; yet we think God sends his best messengers only to sing fairytales to us, fond and empty.[22]

Whereas Coleridge had invoked dreams in order to describe the audience's experience of the last plays in the theater and to defend them as imitations of life, in Lamb and Ruskin it is Shakespeare who is doing the dreaming

[21] *The Complete Correspondence and Works of Charles Lamb*, ed. Thomas Purnell (London, 1870), II, 451-53.

[22] *The Works of John Ruskin*, edd. E. T. Cook and A. Wedderburn (London, 1905), XVII, 258.

and the plays which are his dreams. It is now an open question whether they are also ours. This shift of focus from the dreamlike effect of the last romances to their dreamlike nature is understandable in an age which comes increasingly to view poetry as an expression of the state of mind of the poet rather than, or more than, the representation of "the real state of sublunary nature."[23] But the new emphasis is also a source of new uneasiness about the dangers of poetic escapism at worst and of sublime egotism at best. Hence the need to establish the moral centrality and social involvement of the dreaming poet becomes very strong. Perhaps this is one reason why characterology, the celebration of Shakespeare's ability to "dart himself forth" into his fellow creatures, becomes the dominant approach to his work in the Romantic period. The breakdown of neoclassical poetic theory had created a vacuum which Romantic criticism could not satisfactorily fill. In Romantic accounts of Shakespeare generally, and of the last romances in particular, the side-by-side insistence on the imaginative autonomy of his plays and on the verisimilitude of his characterization, though not mutually exclusive, are not mutually sustaining either. In the effort to defend the seriousness of the romances, Coleridge inadvertently exposes them to new charges of truancy.

Given the post-Romantic stress on the poem as a reflection or revelation of the poet's state of mind, the most direct way of anchoring Shakespeare's last plays in reality is to view them as biographical allegory. Prospero's repudiation of his art and return to Milan becomes, from 1838 onward, Shakespeare's own retirement from the stage

---

[23] *Samuel Johnson on Shakespeare*, p. 29.

and return to Stratford.[24] (Other allegories were of course rampant, each linking the dream world with the real world in its own way, but this one was fundamental.) The state of mind that produced and is reflected in *The Tempest* could then be read easily enough out of or in to the preceding romances, and this is precisely what happened. *The Tempest*, in fact, becomes an allegorical summing-up of Shakespeare's entire career, which takes the shape of a romance. Keats's remark that "Shakespeare led a life of allegory; his works are the comments on it" might serve as epigraph to Edward Dowden's *Shakspere: His Mind and Art*, whose view of the playwright's career as a succession of periods, each conditioned by and reflecting a dominant personal mood ("In the World," "Out of the Depths," "On the Heights") exerted a potent spell over most late Victorian and Edwardian critics of the last plays.[25] His image of a middle-aged, somewhat fatigued but newly serene, Shakespeare reappears with only minor readjustments in the biographical readings of F. J. Furnivall, Morton Luce, Walter Raleigh, and many others.

My personal favorite is that of H. H. Furness:

Indeed, it is not difficult to fancy that at this period there may have crept into Shakespeare's study of imagination a certain weariness of soul in contemplating in

[24] For a useful account of allegorizations of *The Tempest*, see A. D. Nuttall, *Two Concepts of Allegory* (London, 1967), pp. 1-14.

[25] These phases of spiritual development, though not labeled until his *Shakspere Primer* of 1877, are already implicit in the earlier and fuller work. T.J.B. Spencer, "The Tyranny of Shakespeare," *Proceedings of the British Academy*, XLV (1959), p. 169, suggests that Dowden was reacting against the image of Shakespeare as a soulless businessman

review the vast throng of his dream-children. What possible joy can thrill the human breast that he has not experienced and revealed? What pain or anguish, remorse or guilt that can rack the soul has he not vicariously borne? And now a sufficing harvest of fame is his, and honest wealth, accompanied by honour, love, obedience, and troops of friends. Thus at last, safe moored within a waveless bay, what more has life to offer?

But inaction is not rest, and I can most reverently fancy that he is once more allured by the joy of creation when by chance there falls in his way the old, old story. . . .[26]

In the characteristic way this school of criticism adapts lines and situations from the late plays to Shakespeare's own life, we see a symptom of the circular logic, pointed out by Phillip Edwards, by which Shakespeare's mood and motives are first inferred from the romances and then read back into the romances to account for their existence and "illuminate" their nature. It is also a concomitant of this approach to have aided and abetted the work of the disintegrators. By insisting on a certain conception of the mellow old Shakespeare, anything in the last plays that struck the critic as insufficiently mellow, for example, the brothel scenes in *Pericles*, could be ascribed to someone else. And the working assumption that *The Tempest* "figures forth" Shakespeare's retirement from the stage

---

created by such Victorians as Samuel Smiles. Whatever his immediate motivation, Dowden represents the logical fulfillment of romantic criticism of Shakespeare.

[26] Preface to *The Tragedie of Cymbeline* (New Variorum Edn., Philadelphia, 1913), pp. v-vi.

lends added plausibility to the contention on stylistic grounds that he could not have returned to the theater to write *Henry VIII* by himself. The authorship of *Henry VIII* was never questioned before 1850. It apparently did not occur to Victorian critics that the decision to abjure magic expressed in *The Tempest* bears more directly on the protagonist and pattern of the play than on the career of its author.

But the Victorian idealization of the last plays, rooted as it is in Romantic principles, was vulnerable from the start and capable at any point of being turned back on itself. This is what Lytton Strachey, writing at the height of this Dowden-dominated epoch, does in a perverse and brilliant essay entitled "Shakespeare's Final Period." For the Victorians' serene Shakespeare, Strachey gives us a Shakespeare "Bored with people, bored with real life, bored with drama, bored, in fact, with everything except poetry and poetical dreams." For their ideal plays, Strachey gives us "unreal" plays:

> There can be no doubt that the peculiar characteristics which distinguish *Cymbeline* and *The Winter's Tale* from the dramas of Shakespeare's prime, are present here [in *The Tempest*] in a still greater degree. In *The Tempest*, unreality has reached its apotheosis. Two of the principal characters are frankly not human beings at all; and the whole action passes through a series of impossible occurrences, in a place which can only by courtesy be said to exist.[27]

[27] *Books and Characters* (New York, 1922), pp. 64-65. Originally published in the *Independent Review*, III (1904).

His essay gains much of its point and force by engaging the post-Romantic view of late Shakespeare at its supposed strengths: the revelation of the playwright's state of mind and the imaginative autonomy of his dream world. Although Strachey accepts the premises of Dowden's approach and looks at the same phenomena in the plays, he has no trouble coming to opposite conclusions. All he need do is play down the serenity and play up the fatigue already implicit in the received image of the ageing playwright. The robust dreamer of Lamb and Ruskin and the world weary dreamer of Strachey are the two faces of a single Romantic creation.

For all its perversity, Strachey's attack on them raises the historical problem of the romances in a very pure form: namely, what have these plays to do with life?—not Shakespeare's working life or his and our dream life, but life as we know it in everyday experience. His answer had been "little or nothing," at least when compared to Shakespeare's earlier work. In a sumptuous and suggestive appreciation of *The Tempest*, Henry James addresses himself to much the same problem, but his essay is almost a rebuttal of Strachey's and of the view of late Shakespeare that Strachey obliquely reflects. For one thing, *The Tempest* does not illuminate Shakespeare's later years, but wraps them deeper in "mystery." For another, the play does not illustrate anything like "declining powers":

> Were it a question of a flame spent or burning thin, we might feel a little more possessed of matter for comprehension [of *The Tempest* as Shakespeare's "farewell to the stage"]; the fact being, on the contrary, one can

only repeat, that the value of *The Tempest* is, exquisitely, in its refinement of power, its renewed artistic freshness and roundness, its mark as of a distinction unequalled, on the whole . . . in any predecessor.

Strachey had called attention to the presence of malignity and nastiness in the romances as evidence of Shakespeare's revulsion from life. James also notes this element in *The Tempest*; he speaks of "the instant sense of some copious equivalent of thought for every grain of the grossness of reality," but he does so to affirm the play's mimetic fidelity to life: "It [Shakespeare's power of "constitutive speech" in *The Tempest*] renders the poverties and obscurities of our world, as I say, in the dazzling terms of a richer and better."

Far from seeing *The Tempest* (and by implication the earlier romances) as an abdication on Shakespeare's part of the dramatist's function of holding the mirror up to nature, James insists in a revealing passage, on the truth as well as the beauty of this romance:

> Such a masterpiece puts before me the very act of the momentous conjunction taking place for the poet . . . between his charged inspiration and his clarified experience: or, as I should perhaps better express it, between his human curiosity and his aesthetic passion. Then, if he happens to have been, all his career, with his equipment for it, more or less the victim and the slave of the former, he yields, by way of a change, to the impulse of allowing the latter, for a magnificent moment, the upper hand. The human curiosity, as I call it, is always there—with no more need of making provision for it

than use in taking precautions against it; the surrender
to the luxury of expertness may therefore go forward
on its own conditions. I can offer no better description
of *The Tempest* as fresh re-perusal lights it for me than
as such a surrender, sublimely enjoyed.[28]

The tension James discerns in the mind of the artist between "human curiosity" and "aesthetic passion" corresponds to the tension in the finished play between *mimesis*
and *poesis*, the equal and opposite impulses to represent
life as it is and to give life a form it does not have, which
in successful fiction are resolved to the satisfaction of the
audience. James's account of *The Tempest* strongly suggests that romance, the form in which the shaping imagination has its freest expression, need not renounce all
claim to faithfully representing human experience. It
would be many years before the critics arrive at this point.

The first attempt since Coleridge to examine the romances systematically occurs a few years later in J. W.
Mackail's essay, "The Note of Shakespeare's Romances."
Like James, Mackail realizes that the difficulties of Shakespeare's romances have a great deal to do with the fact that
they are romances, and he proceeds to examine them as
such, distinguishing their presentation of life from the
"tense, concentrated life of tragedy or comedy." It is this
homogenizing tendency of the latter modes, "involving
as it does the rejection of accident and the subordination
of incident . . . which is the fundamental idea of high

[28] Introduction to *The Tempest, The Complete Works of William
Shakespeare,* ed. Sidney Lee (Boston, 1907), VIII, xxiv, xiii, xix, xvi-
xvii. I am indebted to George Fayen for bringing this essay to my attention.

dramatic art" and which is "at the basis of the so-called doctrine of the unities." Romance, according to Mackail, represents "the tendency to transcend or ignore these limits." The romances follow "not so much the chain of causality as the stream of circumstance." In his closing paragraph he summarizes his argument and prescribes a course for future criticism:

> Romance has a constructional or artistic quality of its own differing from that of tragedy and comedy, and . . . it is this quality, and not the serene temper of the group of the three late romantic plays, nor their happy ending, on which criticism may most profitably lay stress when it distinguishes them as a group standing by themselves.[29]

One could quarrel with several points in his formulation of the problem and with the blunt critical vocabulary in which he formulates it, but he is among the first and the few to recognize the existence and nature of the problem.

Over the past half-century criticism of the last plays has often repeated and refined this prescription while rarely attempting to fill it. We have, it is true, become more tolerant of romantic forms and more sensitive to the infinite variety of Shakespearean art. So much so, that a verisimilitude man like F. R. Leavis is able to find *The Winter's Tale* "not romantically licentious, or loose in organization, or indulgent in a fairy-tale way to human fondness. What looked like romantic fairy-tale characteristics turn out to be the conditions of a profundity and generality of theme." Leavis's regard for the romantic gravity of that

[29] *Lectures on Poetry* (London, 1911), pp. 212-15, 227.

play leads him to rate it even above the classical economy of *The Tempest*—a judgment, for whatever it is worth, which I suspect a growing number of Shakespeareans would share, and which would have been unthinkable among earlier critics.[30] Yet the degree to which our understanding of the poetics of romance remains inadequate to the task at hand is brought home, when Leavis, after praising "Shakespeare's ability to transmute for serious ends what might have seemed irremediably romantic effects" (mark well that persistent opposition of "serious" and "romantic"), goes on to maintain of *Cymbeline* that "the romantic theme remains merely romantic. The reunions, resurrections, and reconciliations of the close belong to the order of imagination in which they all lived happily ever after."[31] Why? How? It is not the negative verdict that bothers me but its unabashed intuitiveness, the fact that the grounds on which it is based do not begin to appear. Leavis, like most critics of the romances, fails to show why it might be that motifs common to both plays should prove serious and moving in the one and not in the other. Unless the attempt to establish the seriousness of romance, or of some romances as opposed to others, is grounded in a systematic examination of the poetics of romance, our judgments can be no more than impressionistic, arbitrary, and rhetorical.

G. Wilson Knight is another case in point. In a spirit of Nietzschean transvaluation, he asserts that Shakespeare's

[30] See, for example, Clifford Leech, "The Structure of the Last Play," *Shakespeare Survey 11*, p. 30.

[31] "The Criticism of Shakepeare's Late Plays," *The Common Pursuit* (London, 1952), p. 175.

romances are not "to be read as pleasant fancies: rather as parables of a profound and glorious truth." "Shakespeare has passed beyond interest in imitation" to "the mythic representation of a mystic vision," to "plays whose plots explicate the quality of immortality." In this vein and this vocabulary it is difficult to tell the truth. For Knight romance is not a literary mode and the romances literary works but religious experience. That there are internal contradictions in his polemic, sometimes, for example, he regards the romances as Christian, sometimes (as he might say) as meta-Christian, would not bother Knight, for he grants himself the broadest critical license. "We should center our attention always," he writes, "not on the poetic forms alone, which are things of time and history, but on the spirit which burns through them and is eternal in its rhythm of pain, endurance, and joy."[32] Yet his work on the romances is very much a thing of time and history, a reaction against the explicit or implicit condescension to romantic modes of Strachey on the one hand and of Eliot and the New Humanists on the other, an attempt to champion the cause of romance when it was down. Knight is the Don Quixote among modern students of romance, and like that worthy, his devotion to its cause has not been without its solid victories. Among them I would count, not his transcendental readings of the last plays, but his humbler demonstrations of poetic coherence in *Pericles* and *Henry VIII*, undertaken in the effort to restore them to Shakespeare. After the heroic frenzies of Knight, however, the

[32] *The Crown of Life* (London, 1947), pp. 30, 23, 31. The chapter from which I have been quoting originally appeared separately as *Myth and Miracle* in 1929.

work of demystifying the romances without debunking them needed more than ever to be done.

If G. Wilson Knight is the Don Quixote among modern students of romance, Northrop Frye is the Prospero. The foremost theorist of the romantic imagination since Coleridge, his accounts of "The Mythos of Summer: Romance" and of Shakespeare's contributions to it aspire to a godlike detachment and clairvoyance. Romance, for Frye, represents the great rising rhythms of life—birth, marriage, dawn, fertility—and because it is the closest of all literary modes to myth, it is also the most "primitive, popular, and conventional." His study of Shakespearean comedy and romance offers little in the way of "readings" of the plays themselves, largely because Frye is interested in the particularities of actual texts only as reflections or suggestions of that recurrent and universal myth which he claims organizes all literature, or that phase of it which organizes romance. Such questions as "What distinguishes Shakespearean romance from all other romance?" or even "What distinguishes *The Tempest* from *Pericles?*" do not trouble Frye, for his study "retreats from commentary into a middle distance, considering the comedies as a single group unified by recurring images and structural devices."[33] His grouping of the comedies and romances is fair enough, given his purpose, as is his grouping of the histories and tragedies for a later study. What distinguishes Shakespearean comedy from romance for Frye is its degree of "displacement" from myth, which means that the comedies are less primitive and more naturalistic, further from

[33] *A Natural Perspective* (New York, 1965), p. viii. See also *Anatomy of Criticism* (Princeton, 1957), pp. 186-206.

the bare and pure myth of romance that is his main focus and interest. The notion of "displacement" takes over the function held by "development" in conventional literary studies of dealing with the fact of change in the arts, though it spares him much of the sweaty labor of dealing with the facts of change. For Frye's "retreat from commentary" is also a retreat from history, from working out the relations Shakespeare's romances bear to other actual works, Shakespearean and non-Shakespearean, rather than to an abstracted and atemporal myth, and from working through the tangle of problems and controversies that have grown up around them over the centuries, rather flying over them.

To avoid the problem of history, however, is to doom oneself to repeating it, and the enlightenment Frye brings to romance is very much of the Enlightenment. His view of Shakespearean romance, deriving as it does from the study of Blake, has a regressive and primitivist cast, which expresses itself in his permissive attitude (hardly that implied by the plays themselves) toward their uninhibited or "natural" characters, notably Autolycus and Caliban. His refusal on critical principle to make value judgments, however well argued and earned they might be, leads Frye to see literature as a democracy in which all texts are created equal, in which *Pericles* is as good as *The Tempest* and Autolycus's ballads as good as *The Winter's Tale*. They all embody, after all, the same romantic myth. But do they? Shakespeare is not Blake, and his romances do not reduce to the same myth of human freedom. If *Pericles* embodies Frye's myth, *The Tempest* criticizes while embodying it—a side of the play that his bias prevents him from seeing but that would correct that bias if he could see it. For Frye, the whole problem of romantic escapism or truancy or solipsism that has surrounded Shakespeare's romances from their first days is implicitly dismissed as irrelevant, as an oxymoron or a truism, even though the romances themselves, particularly *The Winter's Tale* and *The Tempest*, self-consciously raise that problem. Frye's retreat from commentary and history into an insulated and synchronic world of myth, like Prospero's, issues in serious distortion of vision and values. By neglecting the historical status of Shakespearean romance, he also neglects its worldly ends, the side of these fabulous plays given over to *mimesis* as well as *poesis*, to nature as well as art, to truth as well as beauty, without which, as they themselves constantly remind us, they would be insubstantial pageants indeed.